MISSIONARY
MAMA

TALES OF AFRICA AND WYCLIFFE
BIBLE TRANSLATORS, 2001-2015

Therefore, go and make disciples of all nations …
And surely, I am with you always, to the very end of the age.
(Matthew 28:19-20)

Kathleen L. Carriger

WESTBOW
PRESS®
A DIVISION OF THOMAS NELSON
& ZONDERVAN

WestBow Press books may be ordered through booksellers or by contacting:

WestBow Press
A Division of Thomas Nelson & Zondervan
1663 Liberty Drive
Bloomington, IN 47403
www.westbowpress.com
844-714-3454

Interior Image Credit: Niger, Kenya, JAARS, and Cameroon photos were taken by Kathleen L. Carriger. Tanzania photos were taken by a fellow missionary, Mark Woodward.

Scripture quotations taken from The Holy Bible, New International Version® NIV® Copyright © 1973 1978 1984 2011 by Biblica, Inc. TM. Used by permission. All rights reserved worldwide.

ISBN: 978-1-6642-5494-7 (sc)
ISBN: 978-1-6642-5496-1 (hc)
ISBN: 978-1-6642-5495-4 (e)

Library of Congress Control Number: 2022901847

Print information available on the last page.

WestBow Press rev. date: 02/14/2022

DEDICATION

These memories are dedicated to the Lord God Almighty,
and to the friends and family members who supported me in
prayers, encouragement, and finances for fifteen years.

Thank you, Lord.
And thank you, dear friends and family members.

To God be the glory!

Called to missions:
A job to do, a life to live, a sacrifice, and love to give.
A place to go, perhaps to stay; a loving God enfolds the day.
A willing heart that struggles, too, as all I am reflects from you.
I long to serve, to meet your call, to answer, "Lord, I give you all."
While things of earth pull at my heart, how can I best do my full part?
When family needs cry out to me, I hear your voice, "Come, follow Me."
So give me strength to follow you and trust your plan in all I do.
You are the Truth, The Light, the Way. Help me to follow your path today.
Praise be to God alone!

(Poem written by Kathleen Carriger while serving in Kenya)

CONTENTS

DEDICATION v

INTRODUCTION xv

CHAPTER ONE.. 1

The Beginning of the Story

Learning to Follow His Path 1946-2000 1

The First Step Toward Missions: Preparation..................... 4

His Ways, His Thoughts 6

Beginning the Journey: International Travel 8

CHAPTER TWO.. 13

Niger, West Africa (January 1-June 18, 2001)

A Strange New World... 13

Initial Adjustments.. 19

A Tuareg Traditional Gathering.. 22

Housemates... 24

The Joys of Teaching.. 26

An Odd Sight 29

A Well-Traveled Suitcase.. 29

Stepping into God's Word.. 30

Gifts from Above 31

Trouble on the Bridge 32

Back to the Classroom 35

Beginning the Day 36

Transformation 36

Sand Storms!... 39

Crisis at Home.. 40

Tabaski Celebration...... 41

Easter in Burkina Faso...... 45

Giraffes in the Wild 50

Creatures Outside My Door 51

Sharing the Love of Christ...... 53

Faith Comes from Hearing and Seeing...... 55

My Three Beggars 57

Time to Go Home...... 59

Prayer Niger Airlines...... 60

Culture Shock! 61

CHAPTER THREE...... 62

Next Step: Training (October 1, 2001-February 28, 2002)

Why Wycliffe Bible Translators?...... 62

Step by Step 64

CHAPTER FOUR...... 70

Kenya, East Africa (July 2002-December 2004)

Sometimes, Getting There is Half the Battle 70

Home Sweet Home 72

Contrast of Nations...... 76

Settling in to a Missionary School...... 79

Snakes! 81

Monkeys in Our Garden...... 83

School Days 83

Sometimes the Teacher, Sometimes the Student...... 89

Upcountry House Dedication 89

Breathing! 91

Dangerous Elections...... 92

Bomas of Kenya 94

Warthogs and Children: The Safari Walk 95

Lake Naivasha and Lake Nakuru 97

Kariobangi Slum: Somali Territory 98

Brackenhurst...... 101

Mombasa...... 102

Malaria! 105

Weddings 106
Summer Visits 107
The Mother Teresa House... 108
Scalding Water 111
The Elephant Orphanage... 112
Masai Mara.. 113
Nairobi Game Park 118
Tsavo Game Park... 118
Mama Mary and the Water Pump 121
Prayer and Fasting 126
Lamu: Bringing Light to Dark Places 127
Apartheid 133
Uganda?... 136
A Week at BTL 138
Farewell Ritual at the Giraffe Centre.................................. 139
Car Accident!... 141

CHAPTER FIVE.. 144
Tanzania, East Africa (January-May, 2005)
Another Beginning... 144
New Nation, New Challenges.. 149
Afzal the Lion-Hearted.. 152
Life Comes with Surprises 155
School Days in Tanzania.. 157
Weekends in Tanzania.. 159
Faces of Worship.. 160
Tough Choices 163
Pasaka Njema 165
Possibly Prophetic 166
Visit to Dar es Salaam.. 168
The Beginning of the End 169
Back to Nairobi.. 172

CHAPTER SIX.. 175
Discipleship Detour (May 2005-May 2007)
Homecoming.. 175
Return to American Worship.. 176

The Desert Years.. 178

God's Grace 180

His Loving Care.. 182

Serving in the Quiet Moments... 182

Flickers of Hope... 184

Tough News from Africa... 185

Ocean Baptism.. 186

Saying Goodbye to Africa 187

Season of Growth 188

Job Search 189

CHAPTER SEVEN... 192

JAARS, INC. (June 2007-September 2015)

What is JAARS?.. 192

Seasonal Splendor 194

Culture Shock Again? 195

JAARS Assignments... 196

Longing for Home... 200

My Third Job Assignment 202

CHAPTER EIGHT.. 207

Cameroon, West Africa (May 11-June 20, 2011)

Holy Spirit Message... 207

Preparations and Concerns 209

Brave Young Girl Steps Out into the World 212

Welcome and Unwelcome.. 214

Teaching in Cameroon 216

Life Comes with Challenges... 219

Cameroonian Worship 221

Spring Concert.. 222

Drama Evangelism 226

Every Day a Miracle... 229

Banso 231

Sweet and Sour Moments.. 234

Trial by Fire 235

CHAPTER NINE 237
BACK TO JAARS (June 2011-September 2015)
    Spider Bites 237
    Bloom Where You are Planted 238
    Welcome Back, Mom!.. 240

CONCLUSION 241
    Counting the Cost... 241

AFTERWORD 243
    Unexpected Treasure.. 243

INTRODUCTION

Once upon a time, in a small California town, there was a middle-aged woman who announced to her family that she was leaving for Africa in a few months to serve as a missionary in Niger.

"What??" They replied. "You're a homebody—a soccer mom! You haven't left the country in over thirty years. Why would you go to Africa??"

When she reminded them that she had been talking about becoming a missionary for the past five years, her mother replied, "I didn't think you were serious." But one of her sons added, "Mom, if that's what will make you happy, then do it," and the other son agreed.

So began her adventure of a lifetime, learning to live as a full-time servant of the Lord, going wherever He led her, and trusting her family to His care.

Does that story sound like a fantasy? How could a person who was a confirmed homebody become a missionary in Africa?

In my case, the transition took five decades of God's gentle molding, and the end result was as much a surprise to me as it was to those around me. The spiritual changes occurred so gradually that I was not consciously aware of the dramatic shift in my life-goals. However, I was aware that the Lord my God was the sole motivation behind that shift. As I look back now, I realize that throughout my life, He had proved to me repeatedly that nothing is impossible for Him (Jeremiah 32:27). He alone had carried me every step of the way to bring about His purpose in my life.

CHAPTER ONE

THE BEGINNING OF THE STORY

||||||||||||||||

Learning to Follow His Path 1946-2000

*All the days ordained for me were written in your book
before one of them came to be.*

—Psalm 139:16b

I was blessed to be born into a family that valued regular church attendance. I grew up hearing about Jesus' words and actions, but in my limited understanding I thought that Jesus came to Earth, taught, died, rose again, and then went back to heaven to remain there forever. I had no idea that I could have a personal relationship with Him, or that He would return for His own at a later date.

When I was baptized at age four, the pastor explained to me that God is my loving Father and that baptism was His way of claiming me as His child, a concept I readily received, and one that has shaped my life. When I was thirteen, I was confirmed in my home church along with several of my classmates. As I participated in the beautiful candlelit ceremony, I experienced a deep sense of connection and of God's pleasure in my claiming Him as my Father, just as in baptism He had claimed me as His child.

A year later, I attended a Young Life camp where I heard, or understood, the full gospel message for the first time ever. It was then and there that I publicly proclaimed my desire to give my life to Christ. For the next eighteen years, I sought to grow in my Christian faith, with mixed results along the way.

I married at age twenty, and my husband attended church with me for a while. We lived in Germany as a military couple where I helped out with the youth group and worked in a military library while he worked elsewhere on the base. On weekends and vacations, we had the opportunity to see much of Europe and a taste of London. After eighteen months, my husband received orders to serve in Vietnam. When he returned to the States a year later, he ended his church participation for good. Nonetheless, we loved each other and remained committed to our marriage for twenty-nine years.

At age thirty, I began my first formal Bible study class, and finally, for the first time in my life, God's Word became a very personal message. At last, I began to understand what it truly means to follow Christ. I became an avid Bible student, and I rejoiced in the lessons I was learning.

Like every couple, my husband and I had our share of marital struggles along the way. In 1978, we hit an especially rough season, causing me to spend one night at my sister's apartment to think things through. As I lay on her couch crying, I prayed, "God, there is no human way to heal this marriage." At that moment, I sensed the Lord's physical presence, not only around me but also within me. When I returned home the next day, I saw the pain in my husband's eyes and realized I was not the only one hurting. The Holy Spirit had awakened in me a new sense of God's presence and guidance, and He had given me the ability to see beyond my own pain.

The next day, in God's perfect timing, a woman I had met at church called to invite me to a prayer meeting the following night. I had never been to a prayer meeting before, and when my husband and I discussed the possibility, we were both curious enough to think that I should go to check it out. Little did I know that when I attended that meeting, I would find like-minded believers, a place to grow in my faith, and the immeasurable gifts of group prayer and loving fellowship.

I became an active member of that prayer group. I quickly fell in love more deeply with God Almighty, and with my husband as well. The Lord had answered my prayer—He had given us a new beginning. Over the next years, my faith grew and matured as I actively sought to love and honor my husband and to be the Christian woman I had always wanted to be. I even began writing a weekly Christian column for the local newspaper, sharing and exploring the lessons I was learning.

In 1983, my life was full; I loved being a wife and mother! That winter, our family traveled to the mountains surrounding Lake Tahoe, California, for a family vacation. My husband and our two sons planned to spend their time skiing, but I was looking forward to the luxury of curling up by a fireplace with a cup of hot chocolate and a good book. Looking forward to that treat, I had packed a few paperback books that I had found in a sales bin at the local grocery store.

Among those books was one about Mother Teresa. As I began to read about this amazing woman, I was deeply inspired by her devotion to the Lord and her deep love for the poor of India. One comment she made has forever changed my life: she said she started each day on her knees, praying to Jesus, and she then looked for Him in the faces of those she met.

I remember praying at the time, "Lord, someday I want to have that kind of love and commitment to serve." In fact, I prayed and dreamed about that possibility for years. In my mind, I saw myself as a much older woman, widowed and encouraged by my grown children to go forth in the name of Jesus. At the time, our sons were only nine and three years old and my husband was deeply involved with a job that consumed his time and energies. Consequently, my focus was on family, school, and church responsibilities, along with working part-time as a teacher. I knew my prayer was only a distant dream, and that was enough for me.

But the Lord had heard my prayer, and He alone would orchestrate the circumstances to bring that dream to fruition. Twelve years later, when I was grieving the sudden and unexpected loss of my marriage, the Lord reminded me of the desire in my heart. He also reminded me that He promises to turn all things to good for those who love Him and are called according to His purpose (Romans 8:28). He was about to prove that promise to me once again.

I had known God's goodness throughout my life: He had rescued me from a brush with polio when I was six, a date rape situation when I was in college, and viral meningitis when I was twenty. He had given me

3

a miracle birth when the medical world had declared that I would never get pregnant. He had brought me through two winters of pneumonia and He had saved me and our children from a head-on collision with a drunk driver. I knew I could trust His guidance.

I received God's reminder and tucked it away in my mind as I entered a season of accepting that my heart and family were broken, and that once again I was a single woman. Our sons were twenty-one and fifteen years old, the older one away at college and the younger one living with his dad. Over the next several months, I began to deal with all the transition issues in my life: where to live, where to work, how to be financially independent, and how to survive the shock of losing everything that had defined me for the past twenty-nine years.

Around that time, a dear friend invited me to come visit her and her family in Davis, California. I drove from Half Moon Bay to Davis to spend the weekend with her family and to prayerfully seek the Lord's healing. While I was standing in their backyard crying out to the Lord, I experienced a strong sense that He was urging me to move to that town.

Several months later, after extensive thought and prayer, I moved to Davis to begin actively seeking God's reason for planting me there.

The First Step Toward Missions: Preparation

For I know the plans I have for you, plans to prosper you and
not to harm you, plans to give you hope and a future.
—JEREMIAH 29:11

When I moved to Davis, I had planned to visit each church in town over a few months' time to determine which one God had chosen for me. But during the first worship service I attended, I was deeply touched to witness the pastor and congregants commission a young couple to go forth as missionaries to an unnamed nation. In that moment, I knew the Lord had directed me to that particular church for His particular purpose. I was home! After the service, I visited with a few members and completed a small visitors' card indicating my interest in learning about the church.

A few days later, an older couple from the church came to visit me, and during our conversation I happened to mention my interest in missions. To my amazement, within days they had plugged me in to various mission-minded programs within the church. The Lord was on the move!

Shortly thereafter, when I attended my first women's luncheon at the church, I met a woman who knew of a job opening that exactly matched my skills and passion. She gave me her business card as an introduction to the woman who would soon become my boss.

I quickly became good friends with the church secretary, who helped me forgive and heal from the shock of divorce. I also became friends with the older couple who had originally connected me with the church mission programs. And by the grace of God, all three of them invited me to join their Bible study, a group of mature believers fifteen to twenty years older than I was. Welcomed and embraced by their hospitality, I felt loved and greatly encouraged to grow in my faith.

For the next five years, the Lord trained me for missionary work through my serving on the church Mission Board, joining the Bible study, attending college missiology classes, teaching Spanish-speaking children in an English immersion program, teaching international students how to speak English at the local university, and serving as a short-term International Homestay Mom for international students attending the university.

In the span of those five years, I housed thirty-five different young women from Asia, Europe, and South America while I also taught ESL (English as a Second Language) to co-ed students from those countries and the Middle East. I daresay I learned as much from my students as they learned from me. My worldview and understanding of vastly differing cultures expanded far beyond my greatest expectations.

During those years, I also assisted with the church youth group and accompanied them to Mexico during four or five short-term mission trips. I was commonly known as the team mom! In Mexico, I quickly discovered that I not only survived but thrived in Third World conditions.

I began personally supporting several church-sponsored missionaries through regular prayer and financial support. With each newsletter or prayer update I received, I rejoiced at the knowledge that God was using me in some small way to further the work of His kingdom.

After my first two years in Davis, I began the three-year application process to become a church-sponsored missionary. I asked the couple who had first introduced me to the church to mentor me for mission work. Then, in the summer of 2000, I researched various mission organizations and eventually chose one where I applied for a short-term assignment. Because I had had a minor foot disability since 1988, I felt it would be wise to try serving short-term first before committing to a long-term assignment.

His Ways, His Thoughts

Many are the plans in a person's heart,
but it is the Lord's purpose that prevails.
—PROVERBS 19:21

I was soon accepted to serve on a three-month mission trip to Bangkok, Thailand. I would be serving as a member of an evangelism team in an all-Muslim area outside of the city limits. Two other new recruits and I would fly to Bangkok together to meet the rest of our team and begin active ministry. I was excited about the possibility, though evangelizing was not my particular strength. But to my surprise, the Lord's plans for me were quite different than my own.

Shortly after accepting the Bangkok assignment, I was contacted by a woman named Jan who was serving with Wycliffe Bible Translators in Niger, West Africa. Her family had been sent out by the same church I was attending, and while she was home on furlough, she had heard of my interest in a short-term mission assignment.

She called to introduce herself and to ask me to go to Niger, where elementary school teachers were desperately needed. The assignment would be for six months. I was highly amused to be invited by a total stranger to go to a school in Africa! I quickly declined, informing her that I had already accepted an assignment in Thailand. But Jan persisted, "Would you at least pray with me about the possibility, and commit to praying about it for the next six weeks? Then I'll call you again." I agreed, we prayed together, she gave me her contact information, and the seed was planted.

I honestly expected that phone call to be the end of any conversation regarding Niger. However, the Lord had a better plan. Over the next six weeks, my first assignment began to fall apart. A person from the organization called to inform me that the other two recruits had withdrawn from the program. I would be flying to Bangkok alone where one of the team members would help me find a place to live in the city; he informed me that the rest of the team lived elsewhere. Then I would need to ride a public bus for an hour to reach a remote area that was known for hostility toward Christians. He warned me that I must be very careful in my interactions on the bus and at my destination. He told me one of the team members would meet the bus and connect me with the team.

Though I said nothing to him, I was stunned by the change in plans. I wondered to myself how they could seriously expect a middle-aged woman with a foot disability and no familiarity with the language or culture to be successful at such an assignment. I needed time to think this through. That night as I lay awake, I prayed, "Lord, I know You have called me to missions; what's wrong?" Lying there in the dark, I heard a single word in my heart: "Niger."

In the morning, I called the first mission agency to withdraw my commitment, and then I called Jan to learn more about Niger and Wycliffe Bible Translators. Soon thereafter, I began the long application process to become a Guest Helper in a city in Niger, West Africa.

The application process was challenging, to say the least, but eventually I was accepted. Then I began the next step: I spoke to small groups of interested individuals to share about my assignment and the need to raise prayer and financial support. Raising full support was one of Wycliffe's mandatory requirements. Following Jesus' and Paul's examples (Luke 10:1-9 and 1 Corinthians 9:11-14), Wycliffe founders firmly believed that from the president to the newest member, every missionary should be fully dependent on the Lord's provision through fellow believers who send them out.

I was amazed at how quickly the Lord raised the team of those He had chosen to back me up in prayer and finances. God had planted an amazing dream in my heart in 1983, and eighteen years later, I began to see that dream come true.

As a part of my commitment to Wycliffe, I promised to send monthly email updates to my prayer team, beginning the first week I arrived. Through that practice, I personally experienced the blessing of being actively supported by the body of Christ. I was the only one who physically left the United States, but there were about forty families who began the journey with me through their faithful prayers, finances, and encouraging email notes. In Davis, I had loved supporting several missionaries, and now it was my turn to be the one who was sent out and supported.

Beginning the Journey: International Travel

Then I heard the voice of the Lord saying, "Whom shall I send? And who will go for us?" And I said, "Here am I. Send me!"

—Isaiah 6:8

My father's favorite expression was "Life is what happens when you've made other plans." His words proved true as I carefully prepared for my departure to Niger in late December, 2000. Once again, I would learn the lesson that the Lord's ways were often different than mine (Isaiah 55:8).

Because I had a history of reacting to vaccinations, I had carefully spread out the dates for receiving them individually over a period of several months. About ten days before my departure date, I had received the last vaccination, the one for yellow fever. Then a day or two later, I became seriously ill. The doctor suspected I had been exposed to a respiratory flu beforehand, but taking the vaccination had amplified my body's response. She ordered me to bed for a week!

I promptly called the airline to change my ticket, and was informed I would have to mail the original ticket to their New Jersey headquarters. They reserved a new date for me, but would not issue the new ticket until they had physically received the previous one. I mailed the ticket immediately with all the extra postal precautions possible to make sure it would be delivered in a timely manner.

Several days later, a representative from the airline called to say that they had not received my previous ticket. They also told me that their area was experiencing an extreme snow storm, so all mail was temporarily suspended and they did not know when postal services would resume. If I wanted to fly to Niger before the New Year, I would need to buy a new ticket. They promised to refund the full price once the original ticket was received in hand. I took a deep breath, paid the fees, and again prepared to leave the country.

I finally left San Francisco on December 30, 2000, at 6:20 p.m. Because of the last-minute changes to my trip itinerary, I was given a revised copy as I checked in for the flight. I glanced at it briefly and put it away for later.

We arrived in Paris at 5 a.m. California time, 2 p.m. Paris time. Since my flight to Niger would not occur until the following morning, the travel agent had booked a room for me at a nearby hotel. After a close-to-sleepless night on the plane, I was eager to reach the hotel where I could climb into a warm bed and sleep.

I pulled out my revised itinerary to find the name of the hotel. I was shocked to discover that the travel agent had forgotten to include the hotel reservation details. When the plane steward asked me which hotel shuttle I planned to catch, I showed him my itinerary and explained my dilemma. He disappeared with my itinerary for quite a while, and when he returned, he had the name of my hotel! While we were in flight, he had called all the hotels near the airport and he had successfully located the one that had my reservation. Thank you, Lord!

Air France delivered me to the hotel, and off I went to bed, to sleep soundly for several hours and then go in and out of sleeping, reading, eating, and watching French TV for the next twelve hours. On New Year's Eve, I had expected the hotel to be alive with celebration, but, to my surprise, the place was almost deserted. I had perfect conditions for sleeping, but my body did not cooperate. With a nine-hour time difference, my inner clock was quite confused.

The next morning when I checked out of the hotel, I learned that though Air France had delivered me to the hotel I was on my own to get back to the airport. The desk clerk directed me to the "taxi turnabout" directly outside the entrance, where she said I would find a line of taxis waiting for clients. When I stepped outside, there was not even one taxi in sight; I guessed that on New Year's Day, most of the taxi drivers may have been home sleeping off their celebration.

I walked to the nearby underground metro, but with a foot disability, I could not safely maneuver the steep stairs while carrying a heavy nightcase. Consequently, I returned to the taxi roundabout with high hopes. Still there were no taxis. I walked quite a distance in the cold and rain searching for a taxi anywhere in sight. But the hotel was out in the middle of nowhere; I saw no cars whatsoever. By now, I was close to tears and was frantically praying for the Lord's help. I returned to the taxi roundabout one more time and just stood there in desperate hope.

To my delight, one taxi finally showed up—thank you, Lord! I climbed in and asked the driver to take me to "Terminal 2, Air France." He replied, "A, B, C, D, E, ou F?" I answered, "Je ne sais pas!" (I don't know!). I had no idea that Air France had multiple departure points, and the ticket gave me no clue in identifying the correct one to pursue.

Thankfully, the taxi driver was undeterred. He drove me to the airport and leaped out to go find the right location, returning quickly with the information I needed. When he dropped me off at the correct terminal, I thanked him profusely as I paid him. I was greatly relieved to be exactly where I needed to be.

Entering the airport was a major shock. I was confronted with a sea of people so crowded that they were elbow to elbow and moving rapidly. There was barely room for me to walk, especially while dragging my nightcase behind me. Every sign I saw said only, "Air France." I just stood there in a daze, staring at the crowd and the signs, not knowing what to do next.

In God's perfect timing, I spotted an airport official making his way through the crowd. I stopped him to ask in my limited French where I should be. He said I needed to register at Line 7. He pointed me in the right direction and quickly disappeared into the crowd.

Unfortunately, I was standing by Line 1; reaching Line 7 was a long, difficult walk, requiring me to squeeze past the mass of people around me headed in multiple directions. By the time I approached Line 7, I was thoroughly scared. I was surrounded by beautiful dark-skinned individuals in magnificent African clothing, a sight causing me to feel both lost and conspicuous. The area was so packed with people that I could not even determine where the line began or ended. In fact, as I watched, I realized there was no line—it seemed that people just pushed through until they reached the counter.

Soon, a French woman, her husband and son pushed past me, but I caught enough of their conversation to know they were going to the same city where I was headed. I tried to ask them for directions, but they totally ignored me. However, an African man standing nearby overheard me and responded to my question through gestures indicating where I should go. He also motioned that I must be bold. By then, it was almost 9 a.m. and my plane was leaving at 11 a.m. A sign warned (in French), "Closing time 10:15." I wondered if I would even reach registration in time. By the grace of God, my new friend assisted me, and together we eventually made it to the counter.

When the officials saw that I had no visa in hand but only a letter stating my visa would be issued when I arrived in Niger, they pulled me out of line and told me to wait in a chair nearby. They said (in French), "There's a problem with the visa." As I sat there, I listened to one of the officials discussing my situation on the phone, but when he hung up, he and the others seemed to forget all about me as they continued processing a steady flow of other passengers.

It was close to 9:30 a.m. when I began to pray, "Lord, only You can make the way clear." Another fifteen or twenty minutes passed while I watched more and more passengers pass me by. Finally, one of the officials approached me and asked if I had a return ticket. When I produced the ticket and he read it, I was immediately whisked off in a wheelchair, being pushed through the crowd at record speed.

To my surprise, I was delivered to a door which led outside and I was told to walk down a long flight of stairs into the rain! As I stepped out the door, the attendant locked the door behind me. I thought for sure that I had been dumped, but I had no choice other than to cautiously carry my night-case down the stairs in the rain. To my great relief, an attendant appeared at the bottom of the stairs and escorted me to an airport shuttle that drove me out to the plane.

We had made it just in time, or so I thought. It was a little before 11 a.m., yet I was the first passenger to board! Little did I know that various situations would hold up the flight until 12:30 p.m. Then finally, finally, we left cold, wet Paris behind. I was in for a long, uncomfortable flight, but the attendants were kind and the French cuisine was superb.

Niger
January 1-June 18, 2001

CHAPTER TWO

NIGER, WEST AFRICA
(JANUARY 1-JUNE 18, 2001)

||||||||||||||||||

A Strange New World

From heaven the Lord looks down
and sees all mankind;
from his dwelling place he watches
all who live on earth—
he who forms the hearts of all,
who considers everything they do.

—PSALM 33:13–15

I arrived in Niger at 5:30 p.m. on January 1, 2001, beginning a new year, new decade, and new century on a new continent. When I had left both California and Paris, the weather had been cold and rainy, so I was suitably bundled in wool pants and a heavy wool jacket, but when I arrived in Niger, the air was suffocatingly hot and dry. Needless to say, my wool clothing was no longer needed. After I made it through customs, I was met by the school principal, one teacher, and the personnel director, who all had a good laugh when they saw how warmly I was dressed.

But I was in for a much more serious challenge than just being overdressed for the weather. Though I had arrived safely, one of my two suitcases, the one with all my clothing in it, had not. It had been accidentally sent to Brazil! My first vital lesson regarding missionary life was that one should always carry extra clothing in carry-on luggage and disperse the bulk of clothing evenly among other suitcases, just in case something is lost. Nevertheless, I was far too exhausted to be upset by this development. The baggage clerk assured me the airline would find the suitcase and deliver it to me in the near future.

As we stepped out of the airport, I was first struck by the sight of military men everywhere carrying large machine guns. I was thankful to be in the presence of four expatriates who exhibited no distress at this scene. In fact, they assured me the sight was normal; armed military men were simply a part of the daily landscape in Niger. My companions packed me and my luggage into a nearby car, and we headed out to the main road.

As we drove through the busy streets, I had my first look at an African city. Taking in the sights around me, I felt like I had stepped into a storybook, a magical world of unbelievable beauty and intrigue. Niger is a Muslim nation where many people combine Islam with centuries-old tribal beliefs. Consequently, witchcraft and the fear of evil spirits is common. In 2001, the city where I lived was populated by approximately 130,000 people. Historically, Niger was a French colony from 1922 to 1946, then an overseas territory until 1958 when the nation won its independence. The French language and the incredible French bakery goods still reigned as evidence of the past connections with France.

While French remained the dominant trade language, the primary local languages were Zarma and Hausa. Though the city was in a desert region, the French colonists had planted rich green foliage and beautiful bougainvillea bushes displaying vibrant reds and pinks along the main roads. When I lived there, Niger was considered the poorest nation in the world, and yet the Nigeriens had somehow maintained the magnificence of the décor.

Everywhere I looked, there was a striking contrast of traditional African-style homes next to European-style buildings of three to five stories high. Some of the huts were made of straw, some of sand-colored adobe-like bricks, and some were only make-shift lean-tos of every possible description. There were also small stalls made of sticks and straw for sales display.

The roadways were crowded with bumper-to-bumper traffic and a mass of pedestrians dressed in colorful traditional attire. Some of the roads were paved while most of them were not. It appeared that drivers took the freedom to create their own road rules at the slightest impulse. I witnessed a few drivers make left-hand turns into the traffic from the far right, drive off the road onto the dirt to pass the cars in front of them, or even create their own lane when they felt so inclined.

Most of the cars were spitting out barrels of pollution. The heavy smell of car exhaust was overpowering while the thickness of the air made it difficult for me to breathe. I saw frequent piles of garbage along the edge of the roadways, and many of those piles were smoldering.

There were beggars of all ages along the main streets, many of them crippled, blinded, or missing limbs. Whenever the car came to a stop, children rushed to the car windows to thrust their hands out for a possible donation. I learned from my companions that the local mosque sent the children out each day to beg, and if they did not return with a certain amount of money by evening, they did not get dinner that night.

We dropped off the teacher and the principal on our way to the personnel director's house where we had dinner with her husband and their two school-aged sons. After dinner, her husband drove me to the "teacher cottage" within the walls of an SIL compound (SIL is Wycliffe's affiliate organization for those serving overseas). We arrived in the dark at 9 p.m., so I could not see what my new home looked like. However, the entrance was definitely impressive.

The compound had thick, six-foot high rock walls and a locked entryway. An armed guard came out to the car window and checked my papers before we were allowed to enter. Within the compound were a few other guards who were local tribesmen dressed in all black (including their turbans and face coverings) and carrying small saber-shaped knives in their belts. Though they looked quite intimidating, they greeted me with kindness and respect. I was escorted to the teacher cottage where they warned me to keep the front door tightly secured at all times so that no nearby cobra could slither into the cottage.

With their parting words, I was fully aware that I had entered a world that was entirely foreign to me, but God's presence sustained me and gave me peace. My soon-to-be housemate was on her Christmas break and would return in a few days, so the first few nights I would be alone in my strange new home—alone, yet not alone, for the Lord had always blessed me with a keen sense of His constant presence.

I took a quick look around; the 'cottage' was much larger than I had expected. There was a living room/kitchen space in the middle area with a separate bedroom/bathroom combination at each end, so I was blessed with my own private space. The floors were concrete and the windows were screened. The windows contained no glass panes, so there was a fine layer of sand everywhere and no separation from the sounds and temperature of the night.

Though it had seemed unbearably hot when I first arrived in heavy clothing, as I adjusted to the heat, I realized it was only about ninety degrees Fahrenheit. And, as the evening wore on, the temperature had dropped a bit. I was told to enjoy the cool evenings while I could, for the temperatures would be steadily rising in the next few months.

I climbed into bed, thanked God for an amazing trip, and said goodnight to the gecko on the ceiling. I thought he was my only companion, but the following day I discovered there were a host of geckos on the walls and window screens. They were cute, unobtrusive, and harmless, and when I learned that they ate mosquitoes, I enthusiastically welcomed them as regular companions.

I had been traveling for over thirty hours, so I slept soundly from 9:30 p.m. to 2:45 a.m., then lay there peacefully listening to the sounds of the country for some hours: crickets, occasional birds, the guards walking by the windows or speaking softly as they stayed warm by their small campfire, and the melodic Muslim call to early morning prayer sung from the loudspeakers somewhere nearby.

Eventually, I must have fallen asleep again, for at 10 a.m. I was awakened by the personnel director's insistent knocking on the door. After providing a quick breakfast, she escorted me to the main office where I was officially welcomed by the site director. He immediately informed me that a third of the team was down with malaria (including him), a third had a nasty stomach flu, and most of the remaining members were battling typhoid. Welcome to Niger!

After my meeting with the director, and in spite of the fact I was in the throes of jet-lag, I was given a quick tour of the compound.

Our compound consisted of a small business office, a three-story administration building used for local SIL gatherings and regional conferences, a linguistics resource library, a guesthouse which included four apartments for traveling missionaries, a maintenance shop, and our little teacher cottage. I was told that a high percentage of Nigeriens lived inside similar compounds, though the walls might not be made of stone. In Islam, theft was considered a serious sin, so all precautions were taken to prevent its occurrence.

After my tour of the compound, I was sent to an orientation meeting, along with four young college students (three girls and a boy) who had come to help with a translation team for six months. The purpose of the orientation was to teach us about the local culture and our roles as expatriates in this country. We were emphatically warned that women must never go anywhere alone, and that we women must always wear head-coverings in public. We were also informed that any time we drove past the king's palace, we must never stop or slow down because we could be immediately shot as a perceived threat to the king.

That news definitely increased my prayer life! My housemate and I would drive past the palace every day on our way to school. It became a habit for me to always pray silently as we passed the palace, for our car was very old and not entirely trustworthy. I praise God for His faithful protection and no incident involving the palace.

During orientation, we were further warned that if we ever cut our hair while living in Niger, we must never place the cuttings in the trash, but rather we must always burn them. That directive seemed like an odd one to me, but the instructor explained that the local workers might collect the hair cuttings to use in their witchcraft practices. Human hair was often used to create charms or fetishes for spells or curses. He shared that when the large conference building had been built on our compound, the SIL members learned that one of the workers had buried a charm under one of the foundation corners. Some of the missionaries had literally dug up the charm and destroyed it to make clear to the workers that our hope was in Jesus, not charms.

After the orientation meeting, the remainder of the day was spent in making preparations for my stay. The personnel director went with me to set up my finances, phone line, and email account, to buy a few basics at a local store, and to meet various key people among the SIL members and the African workers.

While driving around, she pointed out that our compound was on the same street as the American Embassy, the American Marines, and an American recreation club where we could go swimming now and then and buy a 'hamburger' of sorts (I would learn later that the pool water was hot and murky, not exactly inviting, but at least it was wet).

When we delivered my visa to the Embassy office, the clerk saw that I was a teacher and offered me a job on the spot! He handed me his business card, asking me to contact him later when I was settled. When we returned to the car, the personnel director made it abundantly clear to me that I would not be dividing my time between SIL and the embassy.

A day or two later, several of the women missionaries invited me and the college girls to join them to go shopping at a nearby open market. Though I had always hated shopping in the States, I found the experience in the Nigerien city to be a most enjoyable adventure. With small stalls displaying everything imaginable, including beautiful cloth, flip flops made from old tires, local foods and produce, and a variety of souvenirs, I was drawn in by the colorful enticements.

With our companions' urging, the college girls and I each bought some beautiful cloth to be made into dresses. We were told that traditionally, the Nigeriens would buy their cloth at the market and then take it to their favorite tailor to have it made into a customized dress or kaftan.

Next, we left the open market and drove through tiny back roads to reach a little hut some distance away. When we entered the hut, we were greeted by a Nigerien man who showed us a number of magazine-type photos of African dresses. Then each of us were measured and we chose the design for our garments. All of the transactions were completed in French, so I was relieved that there were others present who were fluent in the language. With their help, I was confident that the two dresses I ordered would be what I was expecting. We were told to return in a few days, and off we went.

Let me share a few of my initial reactions, as recorded in my journal:

January 2, 2001: A long day, beginning of a new life—a day filled with multiple responses.

January 3, 2001: Hmm, another night of strange sleep patterns—wide awake from 2 to 4 a.m.! Awake again at 8 a.m., but feeling less than great. The personnel director took me to a prayer meeting. What a gift to enter in to a body of serious prayer warriors! The songs were familiar (thank you, Lord) & the long list of prayers deeply humbling & informative—so many translation teams working in the area, & such obvious dependence & trust in you. Thank you, Lord, for this time to learn about another part of your family!

January 4, 2001: Well, I slept more & woke at 7 a.m. for a teachers' conference. My whole body feels drugged & draggy.

January 6, 2001: Lord, you are mighty. Lord, you are king! Thank you for this overwhelming experience in this place. I am experiencing a lot of unsureness as I discover how very different this culture is. But I'm learning, little by little. Help me not to panic.

I slept last night! I feel much better today. Various people keep saying, "Please stay for many years," and yet I don't think they recognize what a confronting time this is for me.

Initial Adjustments

Keep me safe, my God,
for in you I take refuge.
—PSALM 16:1

The first few evenings in Niger, I was invited to have dinner with various teachers and translators and, by the grace of God, several of the women lent me some of their beautiful African dresses to wear until my own clothing arrived. What a gift it was to be treated so kindly; from the moment I was met at the airport, I had been made to feel like one of the family.

Yet in spite of the sense of welcome, the days ahead were rough. I often experienced feelings of anxiety when I realized how little I knew about daily life in this culture. The language, food, customs, lifestyle, and landscape were all foreign to me. I did not know even the simplest of survival skills.

I had to learn how to enter and exit a mosquito net without letting the bugs in, how to prepare safe drinking water, how to wash dishes with boiled filtered water, and how to wash, bleach, and rinse fresh fruits and vegetables. Taking bucket baths and rinsing off in a cold shower was no problem, for I had developed that skill in Mexico, but learning social skills in Niger was drastically different than what was expected in Mexico. I had to learn the proper greetings and responses as well as appropriate behavioral interactions for a single woman in this culture.

I was not used to interacting with new individuals and new situations nonstop, so at times, I grew weary with trying to adapt and fit in. I felt very much the foreigner. Overall, I found these challenges both exciting and confronting at the same time, but my heavenly Father used my discomfort to teach me to depend more fully on Him. His presence and His Word faithfully sustained me.

As I settled in to my new home, I found there were plenty of fire ants building their little mud huts along the walls in our teacher cottage. I had never been exposed to fire ants before, so I was not in the least concerned. There were also small harmless-looking spiders along the ceilings, and the biggest cockroaches I had ever seen in my life—their bodies were about two inches long and one inch wide. The cockroaches had beautiful designs on their backs and were quite docile as housemates. When a friend was visiting me one day, she saw one by the door and insisted I should step on it, but there was no way I was going to step on a bug that large. Instead, much to her disappointment, I picked him up with a tissue and moved him outside. She said I had missed my chance to rid the world of one more cockroach.

I had never been particularly bothered by ants or spiders—until I moved to Niger. Within weeks, I would learn that being bitten by fire ants was extremely painful and that the innocent-looking spiders carried a dangerous toxin that could make a person seriously ill. But those lessons would come a while later.

The dust was another daily challenge, especially at night. That was when most people would travel while the temperature was a bit cooler, and that was when the locals would cook their food over open fires. The combination of dust and smoke was horrific in the evenings, causing me to develop a nasty night cough that led to a few minor asthma scares.

Intestinal parasites were a common challenge for all the missionaries, whether they were new to the field or seasoned veterans. We could not always control the cleanliness of produce or the source of the ingredients used by a hostess, so the possibility of digestive issues became a constant reality.

There were a number of diseases which were prominent in the area. Most expats were protected against polio, which was rampant among the poor in that region, and most of us were taking daily prophylactics to lessen the possibility of getting malaria. We could still come down with the disease, but at least the probability was lowered to only a possibility.

Of course, insomnia was another common malady for most of us. I had always loved warm weather, but I was accustomed to cool nights. When the evening temperatures steadily increased, sleep became progressively more difficult. A few seasoned missionaries shared their common coping skills with me: 1) take a cold shower and go to bed with wet hair, 2) wear wet socks to bed and keep a small electric fan blowing on your feet, or 3) spray the upper sheet with water (to cool it off) and then try to fall asleep before it dried. I found the first and third suggestions were helpful, but I never tried wet socks—I had always hated cold feet!

In spite of the tough moments, I was acutely aware that the bonuses to my new lifestyle largely outweighed the challenges: incredible scenery, a slower pace of life, a sense of being exactly where the Lord wanted me to be, new friendships, the joy of using my creative skills in the classroom, and the peace of listening to the African children singing beautiful songs in French at the Christian school next door to our compound.

Outside of the city, the scenery was a vast contrast to places I had lived in the past: sandy orange flatland speckled with hardy bushes and trees of varying greens and browns, savannahs visited by wildlife and herdsmen with their animals, small villages of a few huts each, and tiny roadside wooden shacks with metal roofs.

Another bonus was my exposure to the amazing birds who delighted both my eyes and my ears. I often saw a big royal blue parrot with long black tailfeathers who had a loud, screeching squawk. There was a light brown bird who sounded like a guinea hen, there were many black and white birds of various sizes, and there was another bird who kept himself well-hidden, but I could clearly hear his shrill, exotic sounds.

Our house-girl, Afousa, was a major blessing for me. In Niger, the African government required every expat (a polite name for foreigner) to hire at least one native worker to help support the local economy. Most of the missionaries had hired house-girls, cooks, or gardeners. Families usually had house-girls who helped out daily, but single ladies usually preferred to hire a house-girl only once a week. Consequently, Afousa served a number of different single ladies on a regular basis.

Before my housemate returned from her vacation, the personnel director brought Afousa to the cottage to meet me. She was a beautiful woman, a divorced Muslim who graciously served and who readily opened her home to many of the missionary families. At that time, in the Muslim culture, divorced women had no rights—a husband could simply send a woman away without her children or any material necessities. I did not know if Afousa had had any children, but she had returned to her loving birth family, and she was doing well.

I looked forward to her weekly visits. She not only cleaned the house but also made us a beautiful African meal before she left. Though she spoke only her own language and French, she and I were able to communicate a little through simple French, basic charades, smiling, and lots of laughter. She was one of several dear people who patiently encouraged my efforts to improve my communication skills in French.

A Tuareg Traditional Gathering

Share with the Lord's people who are in need. Practice hospitality.
—ROMANS 12:13

Only six days after my arrival, I was blessed to attend a traditional gathering of indigenous people. For some years, our SIL group had befriended a small tribe of Tuareg families who lived nearby, and they had been invited to come share an afternoon with us.

Several days in advance, a few of the women and a handful of children arrived to set up a traditional Tuareg tent—set-up was considered women's work. They brought stripped tree branches to use as stakes and a large tent covering that appeared to be made of many animal skins sewn together. Inside, they created a large bed raised about a foot above ground, to "keep the snakes out." Part of the tented area was a bedroom and the remainder was a large shaded area for socializing.

A few days later, the visitors brought not only their families and an amazing lunch for us to share but also a camel for the expats to ride. At the handler's instruction, the camel would kneel down to allow a rider to climb on to the saddle, and then the handler would instruct the camel to stand up. The camel first pushed up his back legs, and then the front legs, creating a challenging moment for the rider to maintain balance. Hang on, friend—camels are tall! The handler was extremely patient and considerate in leading the camel around the compound at a slow, steady pace. The experience was a lot of fun.

In preparation for the meal, the women spread large mats on the ground in one area while the men lined up chairs in another area. To my surprise, the men sat on the chairs while the women and children sat on the ground. The men wore long, solid-colored robes covering everything but their hands, and they wore black or white turbans and face coverings as well. The women wore colorfully designed long dresses and matching head coverings made of cloth, but they did not cover their faces. The girl children had elaborate hairdos which were spectacular. One thing I noticed that seemed odd was that the flies buzzing about would land all around the youngest African children's eyes, but not on anyone else.

Everyone was served food on communal plates that were twelve to fourteen inches in diameter. Each plate had seven or eight large spoons placed around the outer edge. Each person ate only the food that was closest to his or her spoon. The first course was rice and pasta with a meat and vegetable sauce, then we had salad and bread, and then dessert.

I had been strategically seated to share a communal plate with several children around me. Their hands were quite dirty. They kept pushing the meat bits from their sections to mine. When I asked one of the expats why they were doing that, she said they were showing me honor by offering me the meat. She said it would be an insult for me to refuse their offering. With a gulp and a prayer, I smiled and ate some of the meat.

After the meal, the dancing began! Four women sang while two men played drums. One drum was an animal skin stretched over a mortar and weighted to create the desired sound. The other drum was a very large gourd floating in a basin of water. The first drum was beaten with hands, whereas the second one was beaten with a rubber flip flop (flip flops were the most commonly worn shoes since the weather was warm and the people were quite poor).

Four men took turns dancing, sometimes one, two, or three at a time. They performed wild gyrations, swinging their flowing scarves and robes as they danced. They demonstrated fancy footwork with various levels of difficulty while they sometimes leaned on a stick for balance or used it to swing in the air.

When the dancing stopped, we were all offered tea prepared by the men—again, the invitation was meant to show us honor, for in most circumstances, it was only the men who drank tea. Because I was still experiencing plenty of nausea from jetlag, I was seriously reluctant to try it since I had been told how the tea was prepared. Thankfully, the focus was on the familiar missionaries who readily participated in the honor, so my reticence went unnoticed.

The gathering lasted from 3 p.m. to 7 p.m., and then the SIL hosts gave gifts to all the African families and drove them home. It had been quite a day!

Housemates

Make every effort to live in peace with everyone and to be holy; without holiness no one will see the Lord.

—HEBREWS 12:14

I was delighted when my housemate, Opal, returned from her Christmas vacation. I had been looking forward to having a partner, both in daily life and at the school. But I was in for a few major surprises. The two of us were about as opposite as any two people could be: I was an extrovert; she was an introvert. I was fifty-four, she was thirty-one. I was used to interacting with people of all ages, she preferred to spend time only with her peers. I was from California; she was from a southern state. I was new to the field, but she was completing her second and last assignment.

When I first met her, she promptly told me that she had not wanted a housemate, for she preferred to live alone. However, SIL had assigned my housing not knowing of her preference. The first night, she complained, "You are invading my space, and you are a year older than my mother!"

Oh dear; my expectations were dashed, but I knew we needed to find ways to live together in harmony. After living with thirty-five different young women as an International Homestay Mom in California, I felt certain we could figure it out. But after a few unsuccessful attempts, I asked the personnel director to help us.

The personnel director gave both of us written personality tests and then discussed the results with us, emphasizing that we were at opposite ends of the spectrum; we would each need to learn how to recognize and accept the other's natural personality traits. We did—it took effort.

Opal preferred to fix her meals alone in the kitchen and then eat in her room, so I would wait until she was done preparing her meal before I would come into the kitchen area to prepare mine. She preferred no conversation in the morning, so I learned to be silent as we prepared for the day and drove to school (it was a great time to pray silently for the day ahead).

She was an avid TV-watcher, and I was not. But her TV was on a stand in our shared living room area. Occasionally, she would invite me to watch the news with her, a good opportunity for us to spend time together without conversation or friction.

Watching TV in a foreign country proved to be an interesting experience. The only English-speaking station was AFN, Armed Forces Network, broadcast from somewhere in Europe. When the newscaster showed scenes of pouring rain and snowstorms, I felt like we had entered another world—how could others be freezing cold when we were melting?

Opal and I lived together for about five months, and I am sure that she, too, had to consciously adjust some of her habits to accommodate my presence. I will not presume to list what her adjustments may have been since I honestly do not know which of my character traits were a challenge to her. In time, each of us developed our own schedules and friendships, thus learning to coexist quite nicely.

I knew that her family planned to come to Niger for the last few weeks of school, so I voluntarily moved to the guesthouse for that period of time. There, I shared an apartment with a seasoned missionary who was on vacation from her assignment in another African country. She was a devout lover of the Lord who enjoyed getting up early to exercise, and she would often sing wonderful "Holy Spirit songs" as she exercised, fixed meals, or folded her laundry. What a contrast to my previous living situation: I went from a household of silence to one filled with lively conversation and open rejoicing!

Personality clashes are common anywhere, and the mission field is no exception to that reality. I had known that fact long before coming to Niger, partly because the missionaries I had prayed for in the past had asked their prayer supporters to pray for peace and harmony among team members.

When I witnessed a rather heated disagreement between two individuals at an SIL dinner, the personnel director asked me if I was disappointed to see missionaries arguing with one another. I assured her that I was fully aware that missionaries were no different than any other human beings; we all have our short-comings.

She commented that most long-term missionaries naturally have strong personalities, perhaps a necessary ingredient for endurance and longevity on the field. Consequently, occasional disagreements seemed inevitable to her. The challenge was for the individuals involved to always turn back to the Lord, and to be slow to anger and quick to forgive. Her words would ring true in the days ahead.

The Joys of Teaching

Fix these words of mine in your hearts and minds ... Teach them to your children, talking about them when you sit at home and when you walk along the road.

—DEUTERONOMY 11:18–19

A few days after Opal returned from her vacation, she drove us to the school for the first teachers' meeting of the new year. To reach the school, we drove from the SIL compound past the king's palace, along the edge of town, and to the only bridge over the Niger River.

The scene at the river was breath-taking: we drove across a long, skinny bridge barely wide enough for one lane each way, yet packed with trucks of all sizes, camels laden with wares, donkeys and donkey-carts, herds of sheep and goats, herds of hump-backed cattle, indescribable wagons of every size and shape, mopeds, fast-moving cars, an occasional bicycle, and colorfully dressed Nigeriens carrying burdens on their heads or backs. At the end of the bridge, there were also naked little boys gleefully leaping into the cool water below.

The school was a short distance beyond the bridge. Several decades earlier, it had been created solely to meet the needs of missionary families by providing K-12 Christian education for their children. During the time I taught there, we had approximately sixty to seventy students attending, most of whom lived within commute distance. However, about fifteen students lived in the on-site boarding house with a missionary couple who served as their house parents.

The campus consisted of an administration building, library, dining room, and three separate buildings for elementary, intermediate, and high school students. The classrooms were amply sized. We had no air-conditioning, but the ceiling fans cooled the classrooms well enough to keep us focused on the lessons.

Outside, the yards were huge. There was plenty of room for the children to run and play, and play they did! Kids are kids, regardless of the temperature; they were just as energetic at the African setting as the children were in other schools where I had previously taught (their faces just got a little redder).

The elementary students had beautiful outdoor play equipment, including a jungle gym, slides, ladders, and swings. The older students had an extra-large paved basketball court with an amazing concrete wall at one end. The huge mural painted on the wall depicted an ocean scene, complete with a whale, dolphins, a scuba diver, and a surfer! Previous students had chosen the motif.

Most of the teachers were in their mid-twenties, so I was close to thirty years their senior. There were teachers from the United States, United Kingdom, New Zealand, and Australia. When I met the teacher I would replace, she told me she was actually a translator who had stepped in to help out for a few months while the school searched for a teacher. Though she had planned to teach for another week so that I would have time to get over jetlag, she, too, had malaria, so she asked if I could begin teaching full-time the following morning. Welcome to Niger, hello jetlag. Ready, set, go!

I was assigned to teach first and second grade with only eight children, one each from Korea, Norway, the United States, Canada, New Zealand, Ghana, Cameroon, and Nigeria. For five of the students, English was their second or third language. The Norwegian girl had never been exposed to any English whatsoever until she had recently moved to her new home, and the Korean boy had been exposed for only a short while longer. When the other children attended French class twice a week, I remained in the classroom with those two students to instruct them in ESL (English as a Second Language).

School started at 7:45 a.m. and ended at 2:30 p.m. After the children were gone, the teachers met for a weekly staff meeting. Local African schools were open 9 a.m.–12 p.m. and 3–6 p.m. to accommodate the students' lunchtime at home and to give them relief from the heat of the day. However, our school had chosen to remain on a more traditional Western schedule.

Though I had not been able to transition with the previous teacher, I had taught school in the States for many years, so jumping into a busy classroom schedule was not particularly difficult. The teacher's manuals and the last of her lesson plans gave me a place to start, and the students were eager to help me acclimate to the program.

I was surprised to learn that I would be teaching P.E. (Physical Education) to all the primary grades a few mornings each week, but my previous trips to Mexico had taught me to be flexible in meeting whatever need was presented. With only eight students, balancing two grades, ESL, and P.E. was still a bit tricky, but I reminded myself that my grandmother had taught K–8 in a one-room school house, so two grades should be a piece of cake, right?

The temperature and pollution were bearable in the mornings, allowing us all to enjoy being outside for P.E. However, when I was on recess duty in the afternoons, I soon began wearing a facemask because of the pollution. Occasionally, a student or teacher would tease me about looking like I "should be in an operating room," but I continued the practice since breathing was more important to me than my appearance. Nowadays, I doubt that most people would even notice my wearing a mask!

An Odd Sight

When he saw the crowds, he had compassion on them, because they
were harassed and helpless, like sheep without a shepherd.
—MATTHEW 9:36

That verse well describes the scene I witnessed and my reaction to it as
we drove home from school each day. We passed a large building with a
narrow frontage road along the side of the building. There were always
fifteen to twenty cars inching along that section of the road. After noticing
this consistent pattern of traffic at that particular location, I asked some
of the missionaries why there was always a backup at that same building.

They said the large building was the local hospital and that the side
road led to the morgue. In Nigerien cities, poor people usually went to
the hospital only to die, and because of their Muslim culture, the family
was expected to bury the deceased member the same day that he or she
had died. Consequently, the morgue released all the day's bodies every
afternoon in the heat of the day, and the families lined up to receive their
loved ones' remains.

Knowing the reason for the line-up brought me great sorrow for the
families waiting so patiently in their cars. Not only had they lost a loved
one, but they did not have the hope of eternal life or resurrection. Seeing
that same scene five days a week reminded me to pray for my Muslim
neighbors.

In contrast to the sad scene at the hospital, I think the funniest sight
I saw in Niger was that of a small white pickup truck driving along with
a full-grown camel sitting in the back!

A Well-Traveled Suitcase

On January 12, shortly after Opal and I had returned from school, we
heard a knock at our door. When I opened it, an airline representative
was standing there with my suitcase. Hallelujah! We brought it inside
and set it upright on the floor, but when I started to open the zipper,
the two halves of the zipper popped apart and spilled out the contents
all over the floor.

When we examined the suitcase, we found that the zipper was damaged beyond repair. Thank you, Lord, for the miracle of holding that suitcase together until it arrived! It had traveled from California to Brazil to Paris and then to Niger, and not one item had been lost. I was blessed with all my own clothes and the family photos I had so carefully packed. Now I was truly at home in my new surroundings.

And, wonder of wonders, shortly thereafter, I received an email from the airline administrator in New Jersey telling me that my first airline ticket had been found and they would be reimbursing me the full $1500 for the replacement ticket. That was a nice surprise!

Stepping into God's Word

All Scripture is God-breathed and is useful for teaching, rebuking, correcting and training in righteousness.
—2 Timothy 3:16

Living in Niger and teaching in the heat of the day brought new meaning to many of the Scriptures I had known all my life. For example, "as the deer pants for streams of water, so my soul pants for you, O God" (Psalm 42:1) well described my dependence on His constant presence. Like David, I experienced daily thirst for water AND for God. The harsh living conditions and cultural challenges naturally caused me to cling more closely to the Lord, and the desert heat created an intense thirst for water. Young and old alike, we often experienced tacky, dry mouths, alleviated only by the frequent replenishment of water.

Foot-washing (John 13) took on a whole new meaning when I was wearing sandals on sandy surfaces. My feet were often hot and sticky with the fine, gritty sand stuck to them like mud. Washing my feet was the only way to feel clean and comfortable. Now I understood why the tradition of foot-washing was so important, and why it was usually provided by the lowliest of servants.

The story of the woman at the well (John 4:4-42) became much richer for me after I personally experienced what it was like to hike out into the desert to collect water. The trek was long, hot, and difficult, and the company of others made it more bearable. I better understood how desperate Jesus' companion must have been to daily make the trip alone. For her, the pain of the women's harsh judgment or rejection must have been worse than the pain of loneliness. No wonder she was surprised and responsive to Jesus' kind words.

I was humbled by the example of Abraham and Sarah as they obediently followed the Lord into unfamiliar territory (Genesis 11-25); my move was only temporary, but their move had been forever. That kind of obedience takes tremendous courage.

Their son, Isaac, too, had been faced by endless challenges, including settling the arguments over Abraham's wells (Genesis 26). Now that I better understood the life-giving importance of water, I could see why the herdsmen may have quarreled over access to the wells.

But best of all, my eyes were opened to more fully understand Jesus' words about separating the sheep and the goats (Matthew 25:31-46). Until coming to Niger, I had not known that in desert countries sheep grow no wool. In Niger, sheep and goats were often herded together, and at first glance I found it almost impossible to determine which animals were sheep and which were goats.

I had always understood that Jesus was saying He would separate the believers from the unbelievers, but now I realized He was implying that some unbelievers may hide among believers, taking on the mannerisms of faith without personally committing to submission and obedience. He was saying that He truly knows each man's heart and motives, and that our actions will demonstrate the truth of our hearts.

Gifts from Above

Every good and perfect gift is from above, coming down from the Father of the heavenly lights, who does not change like shifting shadows.

—JAMES 1:17

Watching Bible stories come alive was exciting, the first of many unexpected blessings. Another was the intense love I developed for Africa within days. I felt oddly at home among a people group I had never expected to meet.

I fell in love with the country, the people, the slower pace of life, the climate, my beautiful students, and the joy of personally witnessing Bible translation in action. I also fell more deeply in love with God as I saw the magnificence and magnitude of His ministry and love.

As the days passed, I became acutely aware of one more blessing I never could have imagined: my mobility indoors was no different than in the United States, but when I was outdoors, I was walking on sand most of the time, allowing me to be more mobile than I had been in fifteen years. Within weeks, I formally committed to joining Wycliffe for long-term service.

Trouble on the Bridge

Trust in him at all times, you people;
pour out your hearts to him,
for God is our refuge.
—PSALM 62:8

February 9, 2001, was a scary day in our city. As I have mentioned, I lived on one side of the Niger River and the school was located on the other side. There had been four riots on the bridge in the five weeks I had been living in Niger. On two occasions, we had been unable to drive to school in the morning because the police had closed the bridge. Seasoned missionaries told us that university students occasionally protested when their needs were not being met, and their protesting usually occurred on or near the bridge.

University students were supposed to receive a monthly stipend from the government for food and housing, but sometimes the government was slow to follow through, leaving many students in dire straits. Then the students would protest and the university would close for a few weeks or months to allow both sides time to cool down. Consequently, it took most students seven or eight years to complete their four-year education.

Each year, when the money stopped or some other infringement occurred, the students protested on the bridge, and the police shut down the bridge. On some occasions, the students had been persistent, the police had thrown tear gas, the day had gotten hot, and the students had gone home by 3 p.m. The cycle was basically accepted as a regular occurrence in that city.

But February 9 was different; February 9 was the anniversary of the death of seven students who had been killed in a riot some years earlier. On February 8, the Embassy called SIL to warn our members that no one should try to drive over the bridge on the following day. For whatever reason, the students had publicly announced that they had every intention of protesting, and that they would be specifically targeting the cars of expatriates for destruction. Our cars were easily identified because of our expat license plates, so making that threat a reality would not have been difficult.

The Embassy's warning created a serious dilemma for some of us teachers, for our principal had announced that she expected every one of us to come to school, regardless of where we lived. Some of the teachers were in agreement with the Embassy's warning to stay home, but some were not, including my housemate. She had been there the previous February and the school had been unaffected by the riots, so she saw no reason to stay home.

On the other hand, I saw no reason to go. I had promised my mother that I would not knowingly put myself in harm's way, and it seemed to me that the Embassy's authority outranked that of the principal. I called our SIL site director to discuss my dilemma with him, resulting in his directly ordering the two of us to stay home the following day. I was greatly relieved, but when I told Opal, she was not happy with me, a fact which created considerable tension in our household.

The following day, we both stayed home. On the radio, we heard reports about hundreds of students marching through the city to the bridge. Atypical for years past, we could hear the tear gas guns as late as 5 p.m. We were far from the ruckus, but we seriously wondered what was going on at the bridge.

When we drove to school on February 10, we saw that the small village of huts next to the school had been burned to the ground. I grieved deeply for the beautiful people who had lived there; they had had so little, and now they would have to start all over again. But for them, beginning again was a way of life; their lives had always been difficult. The strength and resilience of the Nigerien people touched me deeply.

One of my students lived in the boarding house on campus. I was horrified when she excitedly told me and her classmates that she and a few others had sat on the compound wall to watch the rioting on the bridge and the burning of the neighbors' homes. Later that day, we learned that three people had been killed on the bridge—Africans, not expats.

The sight of the burned village and the news of three deaths had rocked me to the core. I seriously grappled with the reality of facing unforeseen dangers on the mission field. I prayed for God's strength and courage, and I prayed for the many Nigeriens who had been negatively impacted by the latest event.

A week later, parents and staff members came together to discuss the events of February 9 and to seek ways to better protect the students in the future. It was agreed that at the first sign of trouble, the children would be evacuated to a safe haven. But with only one seven-passenger vehicle kept on the campus during the day, I wondered how the staff expected to evacuate close to ninety people in a timely manner.

The principal had served at Sahel for many years, and she calmly informed me that if we needed to evacuate, the Lord would provide the time we needed to do so. Her faith seriously challenged my own heart, causing me to wrestle through my concerns with the Lord. Remaining at school daily was hard, but I was thankful that we never had to test her perspective.

An undercurrent of tension continued for some weeks. Protests were smaller, fewer, and less violent, and the police patrolled the bridge regularly. Things gradually calmed down and life returned to 'normal.' In fact, most people appeared to go on with their daily lives as if nothing had happened. I was puzzled by the nonchalance exhibited by those around me, but recognized, too, that we were all expected to shift our focus and get back to the business at hand—not an easy task, but a necessary one.

I was learning that a missionary's life includes the constant ebb and flow of the joys and challenges of ministry, and that survival depended solely on one's ability to stay focused on God. I was learning there was a certain rhythm to maintaining spiritual and emotional balance: pray, trust, listen, and proceed, in His power and strength.

Back to the Classroom

And whatever you do, whether in word or deed, do it all in the name of the Lord Jesus, giving thanks to God the Father through him.

—COLOSSIANS 3:17

January and February were pleasant weather (in the nineties or so), but in March, the temperature and humidity began to steadily rise. Plus which, the winds from the Sahara Desert carried sand into the classrooms every day. There was always a fine, gritty layer of dust on everything.

Bube (pronounced Boobay), the school janitor, cleaned all the classrooms both before and after school each day. Bube became a good friend to me, readily conversing each morning and afternoon as he cleaned the room. Thanks to him, my limited ability to speak French and my understanding of the language improved significantly over time.

I remember one morning that was especially amusing. The temperature outside was about 115 degrees Fahrenheit. With ceiling fans, the classroom temperature was usually ninety to ninety-five degrees, which felt cool when we came in from outside. It was the rainy season, which meant the humidity was high and our skin was always hot and damp. Bube told me we could be sure that (something) would not happen that day.

I did not understand what it was that would not happen. I began to ask him questions and he continued to try to describe what would not happen. Eventually, he told me I could find it in the top of a refrigerator. As I pictured the top of our fridge at the teacher cottage, I realized the freezer was at the top and it had a considerable buildup of frost in it—snow! He was telling me that at least it would not snow that day! Obviously, Bube had a great sense of humor, though I will admit I was surprised that he even knew what snow was. I reasoned that he must have seen pictures in a book sometime, though I had no idea whether or not he was literate.

Boniface, the dining room cook, became another treasured friend. He, too, always had time to greet me and share a sentence or two while I walked through the line to get a hot meal at noontime. He was a great cook, usually creating local African favorites, but sometimes surprising the students with something as familiar as a hotdog or hamburger, or even a plate of spaghetti.

On one occasion, he got the day off when the Korean mothers got together to cook and serve an amazing traditional Korean meal for everyone to enjoy.

African meals usually consisted of a stew-like mixture of very tough beef with carrots, potatoes, and a luscious gravy. A person could develop strong jaw muscles chewing on that beef! Chicken was never served; in fact, I saw a chicken dish only once at a friend's house, and the poor thing was so scrawny that there was barely enough meat for the two of us to share.

Fresh fruits were always a welcome addition to school lunches: sweet, juicy pineapples, mangoes, papayas, and bananas. There were mango trees all over the campus, but we were strictly instructed not to pick them, for the fruit belonged to the workers.

Beginning the Day

Every weekday, I arose at 5:30 a.m. to begin my day with God's Word and private prayer. When I arose, my ears were filled with the sounds of Muslim chanting broadcast over the loudspeakers near our compound. God used that sound to constantly remind me why I was serving in Africa: among other things, I was there to pray for these beautiful people who were spiritually lost. Sometimes, the sense of the Holy Spirit's grief for them came close to breaking my heart.

Overall, a sense of spiritual oppression was very strong in Niger, and the prayer covering of our supporters and fellow believers was a vital protection for me and the other workers as we dared to serve where God had planted us.

Transformation

Do not conform to the pattern of this world, but be transformed by the renewing of your mind. Then you will be able to test and approve what God's will is—his good, pleasing and perfect will.

—ROMANS 12:2

Each week, I had the amazing privilege of meeting and praying with Bible translators, some of whom had been on the field for twenty or more years.

I loved witnessing their gut-level dependence on the Lord and hearing their stories of the incredible life-changing conversions of local people. To my delight, I had the opportunity to personally attend one of the churches that had sprung up as a direct result of those conversions.

As mentioned earlier, our SIL unit had been effectively ministering to the Tuareg people for a number of years. Tuaregs were considered one of the fiercest tribes in the area. They had a scary reputation for aggression. And yet, in spite of their reputation, a small number of them had become Christians. Through SIL's open hospitality, they had been exposed to the Word of God and the promise of eternal life through Jesus, and a new church had been born.

One Sunday morning, the college boy and I drove to an African neighborhood of small and medium-sized huts surrounded by adobe-like mud brick walls. Ours was the only car. We went through the gate into the compound and entered a long, open-air hut. The walls were made of small staked tree trunks about three inches in diameter, spread several feet apart and covered with woven straw mats. The walls did not come all the way to the ground but left four to six inches open at the bottom. The roof, barely over our heads, was somewhat slanted, and was also covered with straw mats. The bare sand was covered with a few straw mats here and there. The only opening was the doorway, covered by a cloth, but the woven mats allowed plenty of light and air to pass through the walls of the hut.

The church was created by a group of Tuareg men who had renounced Islam for Christianity. The pastor spoke French while the interpreter repeated his words in Tamajeq, the language of the Tuaregs. Everyone sat on the mats barefoot, but all the men sat to the far left while all the women and children sat to the far right. There were about twenty to twenty-five people present.

As we entered, the college boy and I separated to the opposite sides. I sat a short distance behind the other women, not wanting to intrude. We greeted one another in French and they gestured that I should move closer to them. I put up my hand and smiled and nodded, trying to convey that I did not want to crowd them, but they urged me to move closer and pointed to a large number of fire ants near where I sat. Knowing that fire ant bites could be quite painful, I quickly moved closer to the women. Consequently, we were tightly squeezed together, allowing little movement among us. Oddly enough, it felt natural and inclusive to be so close.

I immediately felt a connection with the women around me, especially the three who were directly in front of me. One of them held a baby who readily interacted with me. The women smiled and nodded as the baby touched my hand and babbled and flirted. At various times, each of the three women held the child, but one held him most of the time. Then, to my surprise, that woman passed the baby to the third woman who had held him the least, and that woman began to nurse him. Afterwards, she took him outside for a while, and when she returned, the child was less clothed—he had no pants on his little bare bottom! No one seemed surprised or concerned in the least.

Once the service began, I did not even notice the passage of time because I was totally drawn in to the worship. There was a Scripture reading and a long sermon, and one song sung by a man who accompanied himself on a guitar. We also sang several songs together in Tamajeq, accompanied by the guitar. The women shared their songbooks with me. The songbooks contained text printed in Roman-style script, though some of the letters were upside down or had added marks on them that were unfamiliar to me. It was fun to try to sing along.

But what held my total attention was the obvious love and devotion of the pastor. Though I could not understand his words, his message was obvious—he was worshiping the one true God and inviting us to do the same. The sense of worship and unity was powerful, something that went far beyond words.

After the service, the women and I conversed for a short while as best we could, and then they politely exited. When they had left, two missionary families who were present approached the college boy and me for a short visit. The older children complained that the service had been too long while one of the men mentioned how hot the hut had become. It seemed the service had continued for two and a half hours, but the time had flown for me and I had not even noticed the temperature.

In contrast to the indigenous worship service we visited, I usually attended a service downtown that was primarily attended by missionaries sent out from eighteen different nations. I would guess there were usually about fifty to sixty of us worshiping together. Thankfully, the early service was in English, so I had no difficulty understanding. The church had a different pastor each week, a fact that had its positive and negative side: if the pastor was a great speaker, we were sorry to see him go, but if he was not particularly gifted in the pulpit, we could easily exercise sincere patience, knowing the discomfort was only temporary.

Communion was usually served in glasses holding two or three ounces of red liquid, and the liquid was usually hibiscus juice, a wonderful sweet nectar. However, on one occasion when I visited a different church, they used the same size glasses with what appeared to be hibiscus juice, but as I gulped down the full content of the glass, I almost choked! I made the startling discovery that the red liquid was an unexpectedly strong wine. After that little surprise, I was more careful to sip the communion liquid instead of emptying the glass in one swig.

Sand Storms!

The wind blows to the south
and turns to the north;
round and round it goes,
ever returning on its course.
—Ecclesiastes 1:6

By the time I had lived in Niger for a month, I had developed an annoying night cough. The dust in the air seemed to be endless. I was tired of eating, breathing, and wearing dust, and of rubbing it out of my eyes. But when I experienced my first mild harmattan (a seasonal sand storm), I recognized that the day-to-day dust was nothing in comparison.

Moments earlier, I had stepped out of a building on the compound and was headed toward the teacher cottage when the wind suddenly and forcibly increased, raising a cloud of dust all around me and beating against my body. I quickly covered my head with the long shawl around my neck and just stood there, waiting and praying that the wind would die down.

I did not dare move for fear of getting lost, for I could not see in any direction. Besides, the wind was so powerful I was not sure I could safely reach the building I had just exited, located somewhere behind me. The winds died down in a matter of minutes, but that short introduction to "The Harmattan" gave me new respect for the power of a sand storm and new tolerance for the constant dust.

Crisis at Home

*"Truly I tell you," Jesus replied, "no one who has left home
or brothers or sisters or mother or father or children or fields
for me and the gospel will fail to receive a hundred times as
much in this present age: homes, brothers, sisters, mothers,
children and fields—along with persecutions—and in the
age to come eternal life.*

—MARK 10:29-30

I am thankful to have served overseas at a time in history when the world had ready communications by internet. I was able to communicate with my mother and sons, as well as my extended family members and prayer partners, on a fairly regular basis. The email system was not particularly dependable, but usually communications were possible within a few days.

When I received an email message from my older son saying that there was a family crisis, I was understandably upset. New to the mission field, I did not know what was expected of me in such a case. I contacted the personnel director and tearfully told her of my family's situation. I told her that most likely the circumstances would take several months to unfold, but what should I do? Should I go home immediately to support my family members or complete my assignment first?

She advised me to remain until June, as planned, and to entrust my family to the Lord's care. She assured me that if I was seriously considering long-term service, I would need to recognize that there would be times in the future when I might be unable to return home for family situations. Was I willing to make that sacrifice? We prayed together and I told her I would remain in Niger until June. Then I returned to the cottage to pray some more.

I knew the Lord was calling me to long-term missions, yet the situation at home concerned me greatly. Had I begun to make long-term plans ahead of His timing? As I prayed, the Lord brought to mind that "even if I give my body to be burned but have not love, I gain nothing" (1 Corinthians 13:3). He also brought to mind the stories of Eli's and Samuel's failures as effective parents—they were so focused on serving the Lord that they had neglected their duties as fathers and had painfully reaped the consequences in rebellious sons (1 Samuel 2, 4, and 8).

My sons were grown; my primary parenting years were over, but the fact that they were grown did not mean they did not need my active involvement in their lives. How was I supposed to weigh my love for them against my desire to serve? After much prayer, I wrote an email to a few key prayer warriors, asking them to join me in seeking the Lord's perfect will for any long-term decisions to be made. Then I had the peace that the outcome was in God's hands, and once again I was able to focus on the commitment before me.

Tabaski Celebration

I swear by myself, declares the Lord, that because you have done this and have not withheld your son, your only son, I will surely bless you and make your descendants as numerous as the stars in the sky and as the sand on the seashore.

—GENESIS 22:16–17

In early March, our house-girl, Afousa, invited several of us expats to her house to participate in a traditional Tabaski feast. Tabaski is a two-day celebration, a Muslim ritual observed a certain number of days after Ramadan. The exact dates change each year, following the lunar calendar. The purpose of the feast is to demonstrate gratitude for God's faithful provision.

Both the Bible and the Koran tell the story of Abraham's test: the Lord had told Abraham to take his son to Mount Moriah to sacrifice him on the altar as an act of obedience. But at the last minute, the Lord had provided a replacement sacrifice, sparing the life of Abraham's son. Muslims believe Ishmael was the son who was spared, whereas the Bible clearly states that it was Isaac, the promised child, whose lineage would lead to Jesus Christ.

To celebrate Tabaski, the families took hundreds of sheep into the streets on the first day of the feast. The sheep were slaughtered and stripped bare, then staked around large fires to cook all day. The legs and tails were removed, and the heads were saved to cook separately for the family later.

Each year, while the meat was cooking outside, the families opened their homes to share their elaborately prepared feasts with honored guests. Guests might be invited to two, three, four, or even five different houses, so they would move from house to house, feasting all day long. Then the following day, the "mouton" (the sheep that had been cooked in the streets) would be distributed to their neighbors and the poor.

In 2001, the first day of Tabaski was oppressively hot. As we drove through the streets, we saw the open fires everywhere with meat appropriately staked around them. When we arrived at Afousa's compound, she came out to greet us with her sister-in-law. They ushered us into her small house through the cloth 'door' into a room where she had arranged her furniture in a circle around a low rectangular table. Her brother-in-law and two-year-old nephew were introduced to each of us. Our group consisted of three single women and one married woman with her three children.

Everyone was wearing their finest clothing, and the table was set for royalty: tablecloth, cloth napkins, beautiful dishes, ornate glassware, and simple flatware at each setting. I found the elegance of the table setting quite unexpected in such a tiny little hut-like house with a dirt floor and huge cockroaches climbing up the wall behind me.

Afousa immediately served us Coca Cola in glasses with ice. I wondered about the source of the ice, but did not ask; we had been trained never to order ice in a restaurant because it was usually made with contaminated water. But we had also been trained that we should always accept the food offered us in a private setting to avoid offending the hostess. With a quick prayer and a glance at the others who were already drinking their coke, I also began to take sips.

With the conversation underway, another expat family arrived, consisting of mother, father, and three young children. Afousa settled them at a second table next to us and served them drinks as well.

Afousa spoke fluent French, as did most of the visitors. However, Opal spoke none at all. I understood enough to follow the general flow of conversation part of the time, though occasionally they lost me altogether. We were both grateful that the others stopped talking periodically to graciously interpret key elements into English and to draw us into the topic being discussed.

After a few minutes of conversation, Afousa and her sister-in-law served us a delicious meal with multiple courses. Our plates were piled with food again and again, and we were expected to eat everything to show our pleasure with the food. We completed each course before the next one was served. Though the guests had been presented with utensils, I noticed that the Nigeriens ate with their hands. I did not know if there had been a shortage on utensils or if the hostess and her family simply preferred to eat in the manner that was more customary for them.

The first course was a green salad served with coke or water, then small meat tarts and a lemon/mint/ginger drink, then the first main course: a spicy pasta dish with beef and a sauce of tomatoes and onions, along with a strange mound of what looked like mashed potatoes. The white mound was actually manioc, a main staple in Africa. The manioc was made from a cassava root that had been boiled and energetically beaten, then formed into a mound. The manioc was topped with a delicious peanut sauce.

The second main course was an elegant spiced fish with vegetable sauce, along with more manioc, this time covered with a spicy sauce made of tomatoes, onions, and vegetables. I was told I would learn to love manioc, but I never did—the texture was too strange to my tongue (dry and glue-like) and the bitter taste seemed quite unpleasant to me. Yet because we had been trained to eat everything set before us, I managed to choke down my share of manioc on multiple occasions.

Then came dessert, or so I thought: a glorious fruit salad of fresh mangoes, pineapple, papaya, bananas, and something red and squishy (maybe hibiscus), served with the traditional tea made by the men. As I mentioned before, women were offered the tea only when they were being honored as guests.

In orientation, I had been educated about the traditional process for making tea. The men would start by placing very strong leaves in a teapot, adding unfiltered water, and cooking the content for a long time, pouring it repeatedly into tiny glasses and back into the pot, adding sugar each time. The tea was initially very bitter and would eventually be served in what looked like shot glasses.

The guests were expected to drink it down quickly with great praises to the tea-maker, then the glasses would be collected and the process would begin a second time with the same tea leaves and more sugar. The glasses would be passed again (not necessarily to the same people), the tea would be consumed, and the process would begin a third time. The same teapot and glasses would be used for all three rounds, but never washed; instead, the tea-maker would wipe the edge of each glass with his hand, which may or may not have been particularly clean.

I was not at all sure my stomach could handle the challenge of drinking the tea. I was thankful that Afousa knew I was still adjusting to the many digestive challenges in my new environment, so she was not offended by my politely passing on that part of the meal.

I learned there was a traditional saying which equated each round of tea to the ingredients of a good life: the first round (bitter) signified learning perseverance, the second (still very strong) signified the importance of daily strength, and the third (much sweeter) signified that love is the sweetness of life.

But back to the Tabaski feast! Next, our hostess brought us frozen yogurt with strawberries and trays of homemade cookies that looked delicious, but by then I was too full to even taste any of it. Perhaps my full stomach was God's grace, making my turning down the tea more acceptable to the men.

We had eaten the meal in a leisurely fashion, enjoying each other's company and the relaxed pace of conversation. The feast had continued for two and a half hours. To this day, what I remember most about the meal is Afousa's kind hospitality, generosity, and friendliness. For her, the whole day was devoted to developing relationships. Neighbors dropped in, were introduced, visited a while, ate some, and then left.

At the end of the meal, we were escorted outside and given a tour of the compound. When we came to one of the open fires with a sheep cooking over it, we noticed a sheep's head lying in the dirt. Afousa apologetically explained that we had not been served the sheep's head and feet because they were considered the choicest parts of the animal, to be consumed only by the men of the family. Needless to say, we were far from offended!

Afousa informed us that traditionally a family took pictures of their houseguests, so we cooperatively lined up for several group photos. Then our hosts escorted us back to our cars, and off we went in the blazing sun to wind our way among the narrow streets still lined with people and staked "mouton."

As I mentioned, on the second day the families would cut up their "mouton" and quietly distribute it to their neighbors and the poor. These people who had so little had shared all that they had to demonstrate their gratitude for God's continual provision—and this demonstration in what was considered the "poorest nation in the world," according to U.N. statistics at that time. Surely, all of us have something important to learn from the example of these precious people.

Easter in Burkina Faso

He is not here; he has risen, just as he said.
Come and see the place where he lay.
—MATTHEW 28:6

At the school, Easter vacation was normally observed for two weeks to allow the parents serving in other African nations time to come retrieve their children and go back home for a relaxed family vacation. When the school break approached, all the young teachers made plans to travel together to Benin. It was made very clear to me that I was not included in the plans. Consequently, I approached the French teacher, a married woman whose family was going to Burkina Faso, and asked if I could accompany their family as a nanny for the four children: a sixteen-year-old boy, fourteen-year-old girl, twelve-year-old girl, and a lively five-year-old boy. She and her husband liked the idea of having some time alone, so I was invited to go along.

The eight-hour trip to Burkina Faso was on the worst dirt "roads" I had ever seen in my life. The ruts were dangerously deep and jagged. Even though we were traveling in a four-wheel-drive vehicle, we were mercilessly thrown around like sacks of potatoes (in 2001, most of the overseas cars did not have seatbelts).

With a French father and American mother, the children were fluent in both languages. They frequently switched from one language to the other as they conversed with one another. The youngest was loudly unhappy about the miserable roads, and he let all of us know it repeatedly. Because I had taught primary grades for so many years, I had a large repertoire of silly songs, so I invited him to sit in my lap while I sang one after another. From the looks on the others' faces, I would guess that they, too, were amused by the entertainment, or perhaps they were grinning because Little Brother was no longer complaining.

By the time we reached the border, we were all aching from head to toe. We were relieved to get out of the car and stretch our legs for a bit, and then we got the reminder that nothing happens fast in Africa. We were detained for an extended period of time while the border officials examined and approved our visas and passports. As a novice to Africa, I was quite happy to have the added time to absorb more of the scene around us.

Near the immigration building, there was a large bus parked by the border. The bus was piled high with bundles tied on the roof of the vehicle, and there were at least fifty Africans sitting or standing under the trees. Some were chatting, some eating, and some napping; everyone appeared quite content to just wait. My friend explained that the bus would not leave the border until the driver considered it to have reached full capacity. I could not imagine how they could pile the bundles any higher. As people arrived and paid their fare, she said it was normal for them to wait two or three days for the bus to actually leave.

Most of the people were dressed similarly to what I had seen in Niger, though some of the local women wore no tops, only skirts and multiple strings of beads around their necks. We bought some soda pop to drink and, as usual, the drinks were quite warm. My friend said that Africans found it strange that expats preferred to drink cold soda.

The bathroom facilities were fairly typical: a small enclosed building with four walls, no ceiling, and a concrete floor with a small hole in the middle.

At last, our paperwork was approved, and we were on our way. We were headed for Ouagadougou, the capital city of Burkina Faso. Because Burkina was a little higher on the economic scale than Niger, we saw noticeable differences in the capital city. There were bigger, better maintained buildings, more established vendor booths, more stores and restaurants, hundreds of bicycles and mopeds, but no camels and very few donkey carts. There were even some people in business suits, though most were in traditional African attire, and there were not nearly as many beggars in evidence.

We saw no livestock wandering the streets, but we did encounter vultures everywhere we went. Shortly after we arrived, I was standing near the car when a vulture walked right up to me, a very strange feeling indeed. I was not sure if he saw me as food or was just curious to take a closer look, but whatever his purpose, he soon lost interest and walked away. The one day I did not have my camera with me, we saw ten vultures sitting on a phone wire and another ten in the tree next to it—amazing! Every day, we went past that same corner, which we had nicknamed Vulture Corner, but we never again saw that many of them at one time. I had missed my Kodak moment.

The weather in Burkina was even hotter (about 120 degrees) and more humid than it had been in the Nigerien city. We checked in to a guesthouse, with the family staying on the fourth floor and me on the second floor. My room reminded me of scenes in the movie "Casablanca," starring Humphrey Bogart and Lauren Bacall, a movie that had greatly impressed me as a teenager. Because of the heat, we found it even more difficult to sleep in our lush rooms than in Niger. But it was not just the heat that kept us awake; we had the added challenge of coping with no mosquito nets, and the mosquitoes were voracious. We sincerely prayed that our prophylactics would protect us from contracting malaria.

The family and I shared our meals together (and sometimes paid for enjoying the local fare). We toured, shopped, watched videos, and played games together. Each afternoon, we visited a local hotel where we could pay to lounge in the shade and swim in the large, refreshing pool. Occasionally, the parents would go off for some time alone and I would stay with the children. We all had a delightful, restful vacation.

On Easter morning, we sought out a local church to celebrate the resurrection of Jesus Christ. We drove to an exceptionally large concrete building in the middle of a flat, sandy field. There were many cars parked on the sand near the building and scores of people pouring out of the cars and also arriving on foot. The air was hot and dusty, but it was filled with the chatter of friendly voices.

The temperature was a bit cooler inside, though the building was far from air-tight. The ceiling was very high and there were lots of windows. I would guess the building could hold 400-500 people. We sat on wooden pews, the floor was concrete, and there was a large raised platform in the front of the building. Several people stood in matching African clothing on the raised platform, where there were a number of microphones set up.

The building was reaching full capacity as people continued to enter very quietly. The congregation was seated in small family groups, all wearing colorfully designed cotton traditional costumes, covering them from neck to ankle and also their upper arms; no bare-chested women were here. Almost all the women wore traditional head-coverings, and some of the men wore colorful caps. Most of the people present were African, though I did see a few pale faces in the crowd. I also noticed one little African girl who had a very fancy Western-looking dress and a matching hat that could be considered an Easter bonnet. Her appearance definitely surprised me.

The left front section of pews was entirely empty until right before the service began, at which point a few women led fifty to seventy children in to be seated together. Later, these children would go onstage to sing. In fact, there were five choirs! The first was the small group on the raised platform who sang lively contemporary songs, the second was an all-women's a cappella choir who sang and danced traditional African songs, the third was a popular African band (a small group of men and boys who sang while accompanied by various drums and percussion instruments), the fourth was a formal co-ed choir in long Western-looking robes who sang hymns with organ accompaniment, and the fifth was the children, who also sang a cappella with clapping, clicking, and movements. All of the songs were spectacular, but the two teens in my group were especially thrilled to see the popular African band in person.

The entire service was in French and a local language. The order of worship seemed similar to a service in the United States, but with much more music intermingled. There were one or two Scripture readings (we stood), a sermon (we sat), and later what I thought was a testimony turned out to be weekly announcements (oops—wrong cues from his body language and tones—he was so demonstrative!).

Since I knew only survival French and none of the local language, I was left to figure out what to do by observing others. When they stood, I stood; when they sat, I sat. When they took communion, I watched carefully for several rows of people so that I would know what to do when it was my turn. The bread was a flat bread and the 'wine' was the usual hibiscus juice, served in medium-sized glasses. I did pick up a few key phrases during the service—God, Christ, and Holy Spirit.

Oddly enough, no one looked at anyone else during the service, and though the music was lively and inspiring, facial expressions were nondescript. No one in the congregation raised their hands or swayed, though they did clap. The service was almost three hours long, and we had not even noticed; Africans seriously know how to worship.

At the end of the service, people filed out quietly with very little talking, but outside there was lively conversation as we were offered free drinks and snacks. I was introduced to a number of missionary families who had known my companions for some years.

When we finished visiting with those around us, we drove to the home of a German missionary family who were long-time friends with the French-American family I was accompanying. We had a sumptuous meal with conversation flowing in French, German, and English. The others were pleasantly surprised that I could speak a small bit of German as well as French, and though I could not understand most of the conversation, we all had a pleasant and restful Easter Sunday. The day had been piping hot, so when we returned to the guesthouse, we changed into swimwear and went swimming at the hotel in the early evening—what a relief!

The next morning, our little family unit packed up and headed back to our homes in Niger, traveling once again on those horrible dirt roads. Sadly, the older boy had contracted malaria, so the trip was especially miserable for him.

When we returned to our homes, we discovered that the heat and humidity had increased in our Nigerien city as well. I was informed that the "hot season" had officially begun. I wondered to myself, "Then what were the last three months??" Nonetheless, it felt good to sleep in my own bed once again, and to enjoy the luxury of a mosquito net. Thank you, Lord, for simple blessings!

Giraffes in the Wild

Now the Lord God had formed out of the ground
all the wild animals and all the birds in the sky.

—GENESIS 2:19A

As had often happened in the past, I again found myself playing the role of 'Mom' or mentor for two of the college girls far from home. Occasionally, one or the other would ask to meet with me privately to discuss her concerns and to pray together. I considered it an honor and privilege to be used by the Lord in this way, and the girls and I became close friends. Actually, I became good friends with all four of the college students, and sometimes the five of us would venture out together to explore our new world.

One day, they invited me to join them on a giraffe-seeking tour. They had hired a local guide who knew where to find the giraffes out in the wild. What an amazing experience! He drove us out 'into the bush' in a jeep-like vehicle, and when he saw a group of giraffes in the distance, he parked and we proceeded quietly on foot. There were seven giraffes, five full-grown and two younger ones.

To my amazement, the giraffes were not the least concerned about our presence. As we approached, they calmly continued grazing on the tree leaves above their heads. We got some amazing pictures and were actually able to stand eight to ten feet from the giraffes. After a while, the leader giraffe gave some kind of signal that caused all of the others to slowly begin to turn and follow him up a slight incline, and as they departed, they began to lope, looking almost like rocking horses. I had never before seen giraffes in their natural habitat, so I did not know that they could lope.

We watched them in the distance until they were out of sight, and then we slowly returned to the jeep for a peaceful ride home. There is something very mellow about seeing animals in their natural habitat. The experience created a sense of sweet peace and contentment within me.

Creatures Outside My Door

We had had to travel out to the bush to see the giraffes, but I could step out my front door to see amazing lizards every day. There were big, middle-sized, and little ones, blue and purple, yellow and orange, hints of green, and even some who were primarily brown. I loved watching them scamper about, and I took plenty of photos of them to share with my family later.

One day, I saw a large blue and purple one chasing a smaller brown one, and I assumed the chase was a mating dance. But when the big one finally caught up with the smaller one, he promptly ate it! That was definitely not a mating dance.

I had always loved lizards, but not snakes. When the guards had warned me that they had killed a cobra near the cottage door a few days before I arrived, my prayer became, "Lord, if there is ever a cobra near me, may I see him before he sees me!" I avoided going outside alone at night because of my concern about snakes; I knew that when the temperature dropped, the snakes were more likely to slither out of their hiding places into the open.

Meanwhile, we had a resident tortoise who lived on the SIL compound. He was about two feet in diameter and maybe six inches high. He was free to wander wherever he wanted. He seemed to travel fair distances on a regular basis. One day, I stopped to admire him on my way back to the cottage. I noticed he had a large wad of plastic wrap stuck in his throat. When I realized that he was trying to spit it out, I took hold of the plastic wrap and slowly, gently pulled it out of his mouth.

The plastic wrap was very long and it was not easy to remove, but when I had successfully removed it, I felt like such a hero. The tortoise slowly meandered away, apparently unperturbed by his recent trauma. I suspected a passerby had accidentally dropped the remains of some plastic-wrapped delicacy which the tortoise had found enticing. The compound grounds were usually immaculate, but thereafter, I kept my eyes open for any trash that might endanger my friend, the tortoise.

The few times that I went to an outdoor restaurant, there were dirty, scrawny cats wandering around who would come to the tables and beg. We had been warned not to touch the cats because they often carried diseases. There was no animal control in the city at that time and the overpopulation of cats was clearly evident. Their unhealthy condition was sad to see.

At one point, I had the opportunity to visit a small zoo in the city and immediately wished that I had not—the small cages with concrete floors and the sad-looking animals imprisoned within them were quite distressing to observe. I remember one large spotted cat, perhaps a leopard or cheetah, who looked miserably defeated. What a terrible outcome for an animal of such beauty and splendor.

In contrast, I was delighted to learn that the region near the school was an area where archeologists had unearthed an extensive number of dinosaur bones. First and second graders generally love to study dinosaurs, so I created a number of lessons focused on the most popular ones. Then I took a bunch of small, flat stones and used a black permanent marker to draw pictures of dinosaur bones on the stones. I hid the 'bones' in a large pile of light grey construction sand near our classroom, and I gave the students trowels and paintbrushes to go on a "dig" one morning.

The students had a ball digging in the sand to find the dinosaur bones. Then they carefully brushed them off to identify them and excitedly brought their treasures back to the classroom. Days after our class dig, the students could still be found at recess time digging in the sand pile in search of more dinosaur bones.

The following week, our class went on a field trip to visit the local dinosaur museum which displayed full-sized models of the actual bones pieced together to represent the dinosaurs that had lived in that area. Both the students and their teacher were fascinated by the experience of seeing real dinosaur bones in their natural habitat. How many school kids can honestly brag that they have lived where dinosaurs once roamed?

Sharing the Love of Christ

"Everyone who calls on the name of the Lord will be saved."
How, then, can they call on the one they have not believed in?
And how can they believe in the one of whom they have not
heard? And how can they hear without someone preaching
to them? … faith comes from hearing the message, and the
message is heard through the word about Christ.

—Romans 10:13–15, 17

When I agreed to go to Niger as a teacher, I never dreamed that I would have the opportunity to actually witness Bible translation teams in action. Through a host of unexpected invitations, my time in that nation had greatly extended my understanding of missionary work.

One weekend, I visited the specific tribe of Fulani people whom our mission board had been praying for in Davis. Jan, the woman who had originally asked me to come to Niger, had been a part of the translation team for several years. The Fulanis were a Muslim group who was generally resistant to the gospel message, but they welcomed the missionaries for their friendship and linguistic abilities. Though Jan was on furlough at the time, the SIL translator who had been teaching first and second grade before I arrived invited several of us teachers to go with her to visit the tribe for the weekend.

We drove out into the bush for a long time before reaching a village of small straw huts constructed with young tree limbs, straw, and mud. There was one hut large enough to house all of us teachers for the night. We were greeted by curious men, women, and children. The Fulani men and boys were shepherds. They traditionally dressed only in blue, whereas the women and girls wore only beautifully designed cloths of yellow and red.

When we arrived, many of the men gathered in a group to one side and kept pointing at me. I asked the translator why they were so interested specifically in me. She said they wanted to know why I had come with the others—was I the mother of one of the younger teachers? She told us that at that time, the life expectancy for Fulanis was generally around forty-three years of age, so they had never seen someone as 'old' as I was. When she told them that I was another teacher, they laughed, telling her in their language that, "If the wind blows, it will knock her over!"

We all laughed about their joke, but when the women invited us to join them in their daily activities, the men's meaning became much clearer. First, we accompanied the women on a long trek into the desert to draw water from a deep well. I would guess the temperature was around 115 to 120 degrees Fahrenheit. The women were carrying plastic or metal buckets, large clay jars, or huge hollowed-out gourds on their heads. There was no shade in sight. We walked for a long time.

When we finally reached the well, which was nothing more than a deep hole in the ground, the women took turns pulling up a long, thick rope attached to a sheep's skin sewn in the shape of a bag. After they poured multiple bags of water into their containers, they put the containers on the ground and waited patiently while each woman had her turn to draw water. They offered each of us teachers a turn to draw water, but when I gave it a try, I found I could not pull the heavy bag out of the well.

When all the Fulani women had filled their containers, we began the long trek back to the camp. I was astounded to see that women of all ages carried such heavy objects on their heads with no apparent difficulty.

When we returned to the village, the women prepared a delicious meal over the open campfire, and after we had all eaten, the women entertained us by singing several songs. One of the teachers had brought his portable tape recorder, so when they finished singing, he played the recording for them to hear. They were amazed and delighted to hear their voices coming from the small, strange device.

We visitors (five women and three men) said goodnight to our hosts and settled into the hut for the night, sleeping in sleeping bags in our clothes, elbow to elbow. We had no mosquito nets, but it was not the buzz of mosquitoes that kept us awake. Instead, it was the loud, startled whispers of one of the young teachers when a mouse ran over her sleeping bag! After the guys used their flashlights to search for the offender, we all went back to sleep, hoping the mouse had successfully escaped.

The next morning, the Fulani women invited us to help them crush the millet used to make flour. They used huge wooden poles about six or seven feet tall and maybe five inches in diameter. They placed the millet in a bowl-like indentation on the earth, then grabbed the pole with one hand and pounded it up and down until the millet was flour—one woman did it while carrying a baby with her other arm!

Several of us visitors took a turn, but when I tried, I could barely lift the pole using both arms. I began to understand why their tribe had such a short lifespan, and why they considered me to be weak. Their survival required massive strength and endurance. Surely, their bodies must have aged much faster than those of us blessed with modern amenities.

Faith Comes from Hearing and Seeing

How beautiful are the feet of those who bring good news!
—ROMANS 10:15B

On another occasion, several of us teachers were invited to spend an overnight in a Gourmantche village. One of the translators, the father of a few children who attended our school, drove his four-wheel drive vehicle to school to meet us and lead us to the village. We followed him in a very old rented car.

Sometime after we left the city limits, we were surprised to see the translator's vehicle leave the only road in sight and head out into open country at full speed. He knew every bush, tree, and rock, and though his vehicle was made to handle the dips and bumps, our car moaned and groaned as we slowly inched along. Nonetheless, he delivered us to the village without incident.

His wife met us as we arrived and gave us a walking tour of the area, where we found a number of small straw huts. The temperature was about 120 degrees Fahrenheit. When I asked the translator why one hut had a tall skinny tree trunk sticking up in the middle of the roof, she said the metal at the top of the limb drew enough power to facilitate a TV set in the hut. That was not the answer we had expected!

She filled us in a bit on the history of this particular village. The Gourmantches were another fierce tribe, but unlike most of the African tribes, they had never succumbed to Islam. In contrast, this entire village had accepted Jesus, and now these new believers were actively evangelizing their neighbors.

After dinner, we helped spread large colorful "pagnes" (squares of cloth) on the ground and then seated ourselves on one of them to silently watch the evening unfold. The sky had grown darker and the temperature had dropped a bit, but the evening was still plenty hot. We watched as many families began to arrive quietly and seat themselves on the pagnes. Eventually, about 150 neighbors had arrived. They had come to join the village residents in watching the Jesus film in their own language.

In some of the prayer letters I had received in recent years, I had read of various missionaries presenting the Jesus film to their adopted communities. The film had been translated into innumerable languages throughout the world to allow local people groups to fully understand the message of Jesus Christ in their own tongue. Though I had known of these events, I had never expected to witness one in person. I think I may have been as excited as the curious neighbors seated all around me.

When the film was over, the neighbors and local residents silently arose and dispersed into the dark. We were a little surprised that there was no conversation, but perhaps the silence was expected in their culture. Or, perhaps the message of the film would take a while to penetrate the minds of those who had never before heard of Jesus.

The translators led us to an area where we set up cots on the open ground. Though the temperature had cooled a little, it was still very hot, and the mosquitoes never stopped biting. Without mosquito nets, we were ready bait for the persistent insects. I doubt that any of us slept more than a little that night as we spent our time swatting mosquitoes, trying to hide under our coverings, and praying that we would not get malaria.

The next morning, we joined the Gourmantche people and their pastor for a Sunday morning worship service unlike any I had attended before. We were seated on backless wooden benches under a large tree while the pastor stood speaking from a small wooden podium in front of us. A cow, some pigs, and some chickens wandered about freely while we sang songs and listened to a sermon in a language we did not understand.

Then it was time for us to head back to our city. The man who guided us to the village again directed us through the open country. However, both teachers in the back seat were feeling quite ill. At first, we assumed they were carsick because of the rough ride, but as the day progressed, we realized one of them had malaria. When we reached the paved road, our guide turned his car to return to the village, waving goodbye and leaving us to continue home on our own.

Shortly thereafter, our car overheated and came to a jolting stop on the side of the road. Parked on blacktop in the heat of the day, it was later estimated that the temperature on the tarmac was probably about 125 degrees Fahrenheit. We covered the top of the car with several pagnes to make shade because the teacher with malaria was too sick to climb down the side of the road. I stayed with her while the others climbed down to the shade of a large tree. Then after a while, they decided to hike to a nearby village they could see in the distance. When they reached the village, some of the villagers returned with them, bringing grossly dirty water to pour into the car radiator.

We had all run out of safe drinking water some time ago, and we knew our situation was becoming dangerous. Sadly, the dirty water did not help us start the car, but the Lord had a better plan. While we were all standing with our heads together under the hood, a missionary couple had driven by and had recognized one of the teachers. The couple immediately turned their car back around to check on our welfare, and within minutes we had said farewell to the villagers and had all piled into the couple's car. As we rode back to the city, we guzzled the fresh, cool water offered by our rescuers. They assured us that someone from SIL would return the following day to get the car.

The next day, all of us were suffering from dehydration, but we were so thankful for the Lord's perfect timing in sending the couple to rescue us and to get the sick teacher to a doctor. Most of us taught that day with splitting headaches while we urgently prayed for the girl who had malaria. She was young and strong, and with the proper treatment, she recovered fully. Thank you, Lord, for Your love and healing touch.

My Three Beggars

Truly I tell you, whatever you did for one of the least of these brothers and sisters of mine, you did for me.
—MATTHEW 25:40

Driving to and from school every day, we were confronted by beggars at every stop. My heart was wrenched by the sight of so many in need. I knew

I could not help every beggar, but how could I best honor the Lord in my response to the daily evidence of need? After wrestling with this concern for a couple of weeks, I asked several long-term missionaries how they dealt with the poverty all around us.

One man's answer especially impressed me. He said that we cannot make a difference for everyone, but each of us can help one or two individuals. He said he and his wife had 'adopted' a few by occasionally offering them small portions of food when they encountered them. He suggested that I could buy tiny bags of peanuts or figs at a roadside stand, and then keep them in my purse, ready to share when I saw my particular beggars.

I liked his idea and expanded on it a bit. I 'adopted' three beggars, or maybe they adopted me. The first was a man missing one arm, the second was a woman missing one leg; she walked with a homemade crutch made from a tree limb wrapped with old rags. The third was a man who was unable to walk at all. He sat on the ground at the same stop sign each day, lifting his hand toward the people who passed him by in the cars. The two mobile individuals regularly looked for me at certain stops along the route to school, and I always knew where to find the other man.

I never spoke to either of the men, though we communicated some with our eyes and simple hand gestures. I learned how to greet the woman in Zarma, and we, too, primarily communicated with our eyes and facial expressions. Though we never shared any conversations, I quickly developed a real sense of love for "my" beggars and looked forward to seeing them often. I developed the habit of picking up extra produce or snacks when I bought groceries so that I would be ready for our encounters. Knowing that I could make a difference for these three individuals helped me feel content that at least I was able to help someone.

My one regret was that when it was time for me to return to the United States, I had no way of telling them that I would no longer be coming by. I remember the sadness in my heart as I said goodbye to each of them, knowing they could not understand my words. I sincerely prayed that the Lord would bring new people into their lives to help provide for their daily needs.

Time to Go Home

*In all the travels of the Israelites, whenever the cloud
lifted from above the tabernacle, they would set out.*
—Exodus 40:36a

God's cloud over me was about to lift. I had been in Niger for only
five and a half months, yet I was amazed at the intensity of lessons,
growth, adventure, and challenge the Lord had packed into that short-term
assignment. My life had been changed forever.

In some ways, I felt like I had lived in Niger for years, and in other ways
I felt like I had barely begun to settle into a new culture and lifestyle. My
emotions of gratitude, anticipation, and sorrow were closely intermingled
as I approached the time to leave. I was understandably anxious to see
family and friends, but desperately sad to leave the new friends I had come
to love and appreciate.

I had had the awesome privilege of becoming personally acquainted
with many of the language teams that were working in the area, and I had
been blessed to observe the width and breadth of their ministries. I saw
the process of evangelism and Bible translation up close, and I had begun
to recognize the level of sacrifice the translators accepted as a normal
part of life. Most of the translators I met had been active members of the
communities they served for ten to twenty years. They had left their loved
ones in their home countries and raised their children in African nations
for the sake of the gospel. I was humbled by their dedication.

I knew I would miss the students and the school when I left, and the
camels and the lizards, the friendly Nigeriens and the incredible scenes of
daily life in Niger. But I knew, too, that I would not miss the oppressive heat
and the mosquitoes, nor the daily proximity to cobras. In His graciousness,
the Lord had answered my early prayer: I had never seen a single snake
while living in Niger. Thank you, Lord!

I am serious when I say that those few months had changed my life
forever. Not only had the Lord clearly confirmed He was calling me to
missions, but He had also given me a specific passion to support the work
of Bible translation. He had transformed me from an American focused on
her own ethnocentric perspective to an individual with a Christ-centered

view of the world. I did not know where or when I would serve in the future, but I was ready to begin the process of becoming a long-term member of Wycliffe Bible Translators.

Shortly after returning home, I would attend my first WBT training camp to learn about available teaching positions throughout the world. But before that event occurred, I looked forward to spending quality time with my own loved ones. I was returning to a family of unbelievers who probably would not understand my decision to join Wycliffe, but I had the confidence that the Lord would help smooth the path for the days ahead.

I wrote another email letter to all my prayer supporters informing them of my decision and concerns, and asking them to join me in seeking the Lord's will. Then I relaxed and trusted that the Lord would reveal His plan in His time and way. I turned my focus back to enjoying every minute of those last few days in Niger before climbing on a plane to begin another long, arduous international journey, with the sincere prayer that my luggage would successfully follow me home!

Prayer Niger Airlines

Rejoice always, pray continually, give thanks in all circumstances; for this is God's will for you in Christ Jesus.
—1 THESSALONIANS 5:16-18

A few days later, I arrived at the airport to begin the first leg of my journey, but it was not my luggage that proved to be a problem; it was the airplane. Air Niger Airlines was commonly nicknamed Prayer Niger, and I was about to learn why.

The passengers had all been boarded, but long past the time to depart we were still sitting on the tarmac. Eventually, the pilot announced that a bird had flown into the engine as the plane was landing and it would take the mechanics a while to repair the damage. The airline hostesses plied us with snacks and started a full-length movie. Because we were still on the ground, the air-conditioning was limited, but at least the air was circulating.

After four or five hours and two complete movies, the pilot announced that while the mechanics were fixing the engine, one of them had dropped a wrench into the enclosure. Now they would have to take the engine apart to remove the wrench. We were all instructed to get off the plane, reclaim our luggage, and go through customs to reenter the airport. We were told to return at 7 p.m. that night to reboard the plane and depart for our destinations.

I called SIL and they sent a driver to retrieve me, returning me to the compound to rest in the guesthouse for the day. In the early evening, an SIL driver drove me back to the airport and I repeated all the steps to successfully board the plane once again. This time, we waited only an hour or so before takeoff. Looking out the window, I said an emotional goodbye to Niger, and I flew to Padua, Italy, to spend a week with one of the international students who had previously lived with me in Davis.

Culture Shock!

Going directly from Africa to Italy proved to be a major psychological adjustment. My friend and her family spent the week showing me the local sights, including taking me to a concert one night in a huge marble cathedral. While sitting there in a plush velvet chair surrounded by centuries-old architecture, I listened to the orchestra playing Bach, and I thought back to the Tuareg gathering I had so recently attended. Only a few months earlier, I had been sitting in the sand with people who lived in tents and danced with sticks, and now I was surrounded by ancient luxury and magnificent music.

As we toured Padua and Venice, my hosts shared the history of ancient buildings and towns while I struggled to digest the fact that these two cultures, located only hours apart by plane, had drastically differed in the ways their societies had developed. Yet in spite of their vast differences, I found endless beauty in the people and the land of both countries.

In late June, I returned to the United States, and to a family that was more than a bit surprised by my decision to begin a new career as a missionary. Yet God honored my desire by giving my family time to adjust to my news, and the steps for long-term commitment began.

CHAPTER THREE

NEXT STEP: TRAINING
(OCTOBER 1, 2001-FEBRUARY 28, 2002)

|||||||||||||||||

Before I left for WBT training camp, the Lord gave me three full months to spend every possible minute with my sons, my mother, and extended family members. He gave me time to make it abundantly clear that I loved them with all my heart. Then it was time to begin intense training for the new call upon my life.

Why Wycliffe Bible Translators?

As the rain and the snow come down from heaven,
and do not return to it without watering the earth
and making it bud and flourish,
so that it yields seed for the sower and bread for the eater,
so is my word that goes out from my mouth:
It will not return to me empty,
but will accomplish what I desire
and achieve the purpose for which I sent it.

—ISAIAH 55:10–11

Why did I choose Wycliffe Bible Translators? Actually, I did not make the choice—the Lord did. I had researched a number of possible organizations to join, and Wycliffe was not even on the list. Before going to Niger, I had never dreamed of going to Africa, but I had dreamed of going somewhere that I could minister to the poor like Mother Teresa had done. When asked to go to Niger, I had reasoned that my time there would be a good testing ground for the lifestyle, but not necessarily a permanent destination.

Yet while I was in Niger, I had discovered there is more than one way to minister to the poor. Mother Teresa had demonstrated the love of Christ to the sick and dying primarily by ministering to their physical needs, whereas Wycliffe missionaries demonstrated that same love by primarily ministering to their spiritual needs. Both methods are valuable in the eyes of the King; only He knows which choice best fits a specific missionary and a specific culture.

After experiencing worship in Niger and Burkina Faso, I felt like I had had a glimpse of heavenly worship before the King with people from every tribe and nation (Revelation 7:9). I saw firsthand the awesome power of the Word of God.

Previously, I had had a taste of that power in my own life. I had come to know Jesus because a committed Christian had told a roomful of squirmy, self-conscious teens about God's love, and he had challenged us to dare to believe. Reading the written Word was what had later allowed my faith to grow, and I wanted to offer that same opportunity to others.

Having struggled to communicate in French during my stay in Niger, I better understood the vital need for Bible translation. Basically, as Americans, we are accustomed to reading the Bible in English, and we even have a variety of versions from which to choose. But suppose there were no Bible in English and we had to read it in Spanish or French, or in Latin! A small percentage of us might be fluent enough to understand the basic message, but most of us would grasp only a few simple words in each sentence, entirely missing the big picture.

For just a moment, try stepping into the shoes of those who need Bible translation. Write down a favorite Scripture verse and then cross out some of the less common words to see if you can still clearly understand the passage. For example, suppose we start with John 3:16:

> *For God so loved the world that he gave his one and only*
> *Son, that whoever believes in him shall not perish but have*
> *eternal life.*

Now remove the less common words:

> *For God ____ the world that he ____ his ____ that ____ in*
> *him shall not ____ but have ____ life.*

I think you get my point: Bible translation is vital to fully understanding the message of salvation. Every person needs to hear and/or read the Bible in his or her own language, the 'mother tongue,' to truly absorb the good news and make an informed choice.

When I saw the translators in action and the amazing results the Lord was producing through them, I knew I wanted to be a part of the process. If I could support linguistically trained teams by teaching their children, then they could stay focused on translation and I could contribute to the process of bringing the Word of God to new ears and hearts. That possibility was exciting!

Step by Step

In you, Lord my God, I put my trust.
—PSALM 25:1

In October, 2001, I attended Wycliffe's week-long Training Camp in the scenic mountains above Temecula, California. It was a week of listening to missionaries who had served all over the world as they presented topics that were meant to inform and challenge those of us who were seriously considering Wycliffe membership.

Topics included how to maintain one's health, family and peer relationships, spiritual warfare, loneliness, professional readiness, Bible knowledge, healthy spiritual life habits, emotional strength, and spiritual gifting. Of course, we spent a lot of our time worshiping, singing praise songs, and praying together as well. We were also given access to a binder with extensive descriptions of available positions all over the world so that we could begin praying for the Lord's direction on our specific assignments. I found the week exhilarating and confirming in my decision to become a member.

On the last day, we candidates and our instructors gathered together in a circle to sing the chorus of Rich Mullins' song, *Step by Step*, thus committing together that each of us would trust every step of our future to our loving Father in heaven. Then we were each given a blank notecard on which we were instructed to write a short note to God, place it in an envelope, and mail it to ourselves. I had written the following words, which I later received and pasted into my Wycliffe binder to keep forever:

> I am yours, Lord—broken, incomplete, humbled, and deeply loved. Take me and use me where you will. I give my family and all worldly concerns to you. For you are mighty, King of Kings and Lord of Lords. I relinquish my will to yours.

Then I returned home to complete the application processes for Wycliffe Bible Translators and for my home church. The Wycliffe application required months of gathering and mailing all my educational and professional records; references from previous employers, pastors, and friends; an essay describing my faith walk and another describing why I felt called to missions. I was also required to complete extensive Bible knowledge testing in a controlled testing environment. The church application had been underway for almost three years with many similar components.

Both the church and Wycliffe required that I go forth to speak to many small groups to present my interest in missions and my need for prayer and financial support. Though the church would supply one-fourth of the monthly 'salary,' I would have to raise the remainder by sharing my news with friends, family, and church members. Putting my heart and soul out there was not an easy task, especially when the audience's response was occasionally minimal. But bit by bit, dollar by dollar, and prayer by prayer, the Lord began to build my team of supporters.

In January, 2002, I flew to JAARS (Wycliffe's training base) in Waxhaw, North Carolina. There, I joined a missionary community of six hundred individuals, three hundred of whom were retired missionaries or missionaries on furlough and three hundred of whom were volunteers fully committed to supporting the goal of Bible translation throughout the world.

I had enrolled in an intense seven-week course commonly known as ICC, or Intercultural Communications Course. The goal of the course was to train new missionaries to be "spiritually fit, relationally mature, and culturally sensitive." The topics were similar to Training Camp, but were covered in more depth. The purpose of the course was to give us a realistic view of life on a mission field and to provide us with the tools we would need to succeed in a new culture. The staff members intentionally presented us with a host of unexpected difficulties to observe how we responded under pressure.

We listened to lectures, participated in small group discussions, spent hours and hours at night reading massive homework assignments that would be discussed the following day, were given linguistic lessons on how to "negotiate language" when we did not understand, and attended assigned 'foreign' churches every Sunday to learn how to cope with unfamiliar language and customs.

Assigned to a Korean church along with three other candidates, I had a slight advantage because of my recent experience overseas and my having housed Korean students in the past. However, I found the majority of the overall training far more difficult than my six months in Niger. When I mentioned that observation to one of the trainers, she said my perspective was accurate. One of the purposes of ICC was to open the eyes of every participant and to weed out the individuals who would not meet with success on the field.

During the course, we also learned some of the history of Wycliffe Bible Translators. In 1917, William Cameron Townsend had left his college studies for a year to sell Spanish Bibles in Guatemala. When he began his travels through the country, he was shocked to discover that the majority of Guatemalans he met did not speak Spanish well enough to read and understand a Spanish Bible. They spoke only Cakchiquel, their "mother tongue." He continued to evangelize, but he was not content that new believers had no Bible they could understand.

He decided to personally take on the task of learning Cakchiquel so that a Bible could be written in that language. With the help of a Guatemalan friend and believer, he began a linguistics school to teach others his methods, and what started out as a one-year commitment became a lifetime passion.

With time, his school grew and his trained students began Bible translations throughout most of North, Central, and South America. In 1942, what had begun as the Summer Institute of Linguistics became known as SIL. The rest is history—Wycliffe Bible Translators and SIL became involved in translation projects throughout the world.

We further learned that since 1999, Wycliffe and SIL had been actively involved in Vision 2025, the vision of starting a Bible translation project in every language that needs it by the year 2025. Wycliffe leaders had always recognized the importance of partnering with other like-minded organizations to meet that goal, and as the number of partnerships and indigenous believers grew, they began to turn many of the translation projects over to the indigenous believers themselves.

Yet as more and more language groups were discovered by sending out language survey teams, it was clearly evident that Wycliffe's goal of reaching "the least, the last, and the lost" would require a steadily growing number of missionaries specifically called to the work of translation.

Many of the younger candidates in my ICC class had chosen to begin years of training in linguistics to become effective translators, but because I was already in my fifties and was a fully trained teacher, I felt the Lord could better use me in a support role. Wycliffe was seeking teachers, nurses, pilots, plane mechanics, IT experts, business administrators, and a host of other qualified individuals who were already fully trained to perform necessary roles to keep the translators and their families on the field.

Another major topic for study was "friend-raising," otherwise known as seeking out those individuals whom the Lord had touched to become our prayer and financial supporters. We took classes on public speaking, effective email communications, and letter-writing for our monthly updates and quarterly newsletters. We were provided with a plethora of helpful resources, and we were urged to promise that when we reached the field, we would faithfully communicate with those at home at least once a month.

Our instructors emphasized that keeping our supporters well-informed was vital in motivating them to pray and/or to send their monthly pledges to our personal Wycliffe accounts. The importance of prayer backing was constantly emphasized, and our instructors pointed out that if our supporters lost interest, prayer support and receipt of our monthly donations might drop as a result, causing havoc with our effectiveness on the field and our financial well-being.

Because it was all too common for lay people to think the only "real" missionaries were those who were actually translating the Bible or openly evangelizing in foreign lands, our instructors also taught us to share an important analogy that Wycliffe had created.

Wycliffe explained the connection between translators and the support personnel by comparing Bible translation to the parts of a tree—the fruit is new lives changed by the living Word, the leaves are the translators who bring them that Word, the branches and trunk are the support workers like me who perform the jobs necessary to keep the translators on the field, and the roots of the tree are all the individuals at home who provide vital strength to the tree through their prayers, encouragement, and finances. Of course, the successful growth of any tree (or translation project) also depends on God's provision of the sun and rain (Holy Spirit's guidance) to nurture healthy growth.

At the end of the course, the teaching staff met individually with each candidate to share their evaluation of that person's readiness for the field. When it was my turn for the interview, they asked me if I was still seriously considering overseas ministry in spite of my medical history, which indicated I had had multiple health challenges since childhood.

My answer was simple: "I know the Lord is calling me to this ministry, so I trust that He will sustain me." I was excited to hear that since I was willing, they felt confident I was ready to go forth as an ambassador for Christ. Praise God!

After much thought and prayer, I had chosen and was assigned to a school in Kenya, East Africa. I returned to California to continue building my prayer and financial support team, and to spend every minute I could with my precious family members. Like the first time, the Lord again blessed me by raising my support team in a timely manner. After four more months of making presentations in churches and living rooms, I met Wycliffe's full budget quota and was released to fly to Kenya in time to begin the school year with all the other teachers. Thank you, Lord!

Kenya
July 2002-December 2004

CHAPTER FOUR

KENYA, EAST AFRICA
(JULY 2002-DECEMBER 2004)

|||||||||||||||||||

Sometimes, Getting There is Half the Battle

Consider it pure joy, my brothers and sisters, whenever you face trials of many kinds, because you know that the testing of your faith produces perseverance. Let perseverance finish its work so that you may be mature and complete, not lacking anything.

—JAMES 1:2–4

Missionaries do not have a charmed life just because they are following the Lord's lead to a location He has chosen—look at the life stories of the twelve disciples, the apostle Paul, Hudson Taylor, David Livingston, or even Mother Teresa, who stood against major opposition when she dared to follow the Lord's lead out into the streets of India.

Spiritual warfare can look different in every situation. For me, the first obstacle was again my health. A week before I left for Kenya, I met with a woman who would be renting my house for the year. Unfortunately, when she arrived to discuss details and pick up the key, she was very ill with a respiratory flu. The day before I left for the first leg of my trip, I came down with that flu, but hoping it would be short-lived, I flew to Waxhaw, North Carolina, to spend two and a half days at the JAARS Center before leaving for Kenya.

After two good nights of sleep, I was transported to the airport, where I connected with Lena, a young woman I had met at ICC who would also be teaching at West Nairobi School. We knew there was a third teacher, Penelope, who was traveling on the same date, but she was coming from Minnesota. Neither of us had met her in advance, but we had been informed that the three of us would be living together near the school.

Lena and I departed from Charlotte to begin our journey. Between the two of us, we had a pile of luggage to check in (560 pounds!), but we had no difficulties with the process and were soon on our way. The first oddity was that the pilot announced our non-stop flight to London would be stopping in Baltimore "to pick up passengers." Then when we reached Baltimore, we were told to disembark because the plane needed some maintenance. It seems a bird had flown into the engine while the plane was landing. Again? That had happened when I was departing Niger!

We disembarked, learned our luggage was temporarily missing, boarded a bus with all the other passengers, and traveled to Dulles Airport to catch a new flight. However, when we arrived at Dulles, we learned there was no flight available until the following day, so the entire busload was driven to a nearby hotel to sleep for a while (1:30–5:15 a.m.). Then we were awakened to hurriedly return to the airport, check in again, reclaim and check in our newly-found luggage, and continue our journey to London.

Because our flight had been extensively delayed the previous night, instead of a thirteen-hour layover, we barely made our connection at Heathrow Airport with only fifteen minutes to spare. We rushed to the boarding gate and were admitted on the plane just in the nick of time. We had bought our tickets separately, so we were not sitting together. Consequently, we headed opposite directions when we entered the plane. We noticed that most of the other passengers were Africans, probably returning home from a visit to the States.

As I was searching for my seat, a blond woman began to pass by me. Without thinking, I asked her, "Are you Penelope?" I am not sure which of us was more surprised—me for asking her if she happened to be the third teacher traveling to Kenya, or Penelope that a total stranger seemed to know who she was. We introduced ourselves quickly, found our seats, and then settled in for the long flight to Nairobi, Kenya. Lena and Penelope would meet mid-flight several hours later.

Since I was not feeling well, I slept most of the way. Upon arrival at 9 a.m., I was placed in a wheelchair because of my foot disability and we three were whisked off to meet up with the principal and Makena, one of the returning teachers. I was definitely embarrassed to be in a wheelchair the first time I met my boss and fellow teacher. The principal was noticeably concerned, but I assured him I would be fully mobile once we reached our home.

Then we learned that we would not be driven to our new home. Instead, the principal had made arrangements to place each of us in a separate homestay family for a few days to help us acclimate to our new country. His plan was well meant, but in my case, it was a huge disappointment. I had been looking forward to sleeping off the flu and jetlag in the privacy of my own bedroom. Instead, I was placed in a home with a large family who had a curious five-year-old who kept sneaking into my bedroom to dig through my suitcase and ask me an endless number of questions.

In contrast to my losing much-needed sleep because of the child's curiosity, her mother took excellent care of me, plying me with homemade soup, Tylenol, and plenty of filtered water. After four days, I was feeling much better, and I asked the principal for permission to move into my new home. The principal granted my request since he knew I was already well-versed in basic house-keeping skills for Africa.

Home Sweet Home

My people will live in peaceful dwelling places,
in secure homes,
in undisturbed places of rest.
—ISAIAH 32:18

When the principal picked me up at the homestay, I expressed my sincere gratitude to the family for their kind hospitality, and we engaged in multiple hugs all around. Then the principal drove me to the 'teacher house,' which was located in a suburb on the outskirts of Nairobi.

Unlike in Niger, most houses in that region were surrounded by their own private walls. The teacher house had a tall, thick white wall with broken glass embedded in the top of the wall to make it even more secure from intruders. There was a high metal double gate that had a small padlocked door on one side of the gate. The principal got out of the car, unlocked the small door, went through it and opened the gates wide to drive his car inside the compound. Then he immediately closed and locked the double gates and returned to his car to help me carry my suitcases into the house.

The appearance of our compound was spectacular. There was a roundabout driveway with colorful flowers and greenery in the middle and a cleared area at the far end which was large enough for several cars to park. The brick walls of the house were covered with plush vines, there was a large lawn in the front and a vegetable garden on the side. There was a huge avocado tree in the middle of the lawn and a banana tree on the side. The entire yard was surrounded by colorful flower beds and other smaller trees and bushes.

Compared to my Nigerien home, this place was a mansion! The house was huge—a two-story, five-bedroom house with four bathrooms, a gigantic living/dining room, and an ample kitchen. At the top of the stairs, there was a metal grated security gate which could be locked at night to prevent any intrusion by thieves. There was also a smaller apartment behind the house which was meant for the house-girl, and a small patio in between the two structures which was used for hanging wet laundry.

I learned from the principal that the property had previously been used as a dormitory for ten to twelve students plus house parents, thus accounting for its size. The house came fully furnished with a house-girl, a gardener, a large German shepherd trained as a guard dog, and from 8 p.m. to 8 a.m., we also had a night guard who walked the premises and sat (or slept) in the guardhouse by the entrance.

The principal gave me a quick walk-through of the house, showed me the food that had been stocked for us and where the water filter was, and then said his farewells. I was excited to settle in! I took a closer look at the rooms upstairs and down, finding personal notes on the pillows of the three rooms chosen and prepared for us. One of the missionary wives had kindly prepared the rooms in advance to make the house seem warm and welcoming, and she had done a great job. My bedroom was the only one downstairs (because they were unnecessarily concerned that I could not climb stairs).

As I began to unpack, I was caught off guard by the sudden occurrence of a gushing nosebleed. I had never had one before in my life, nor did I ever again thereafter. I was told by seasoned missionaries that my body was adjusting to the elevation (about 6000 feet above sea level), but it seemed odd to me that I had been in Nairobi for several days before it occurred. Nonetheless, the problem was quickly resolved, I finished unpacking, and I peacefully slept in my new home, knowing that the dog and the guard were outside to protect me.

A day or two later, my two housemates, Lena and Penelope, arrived, both in their mid-twenties. For them, Kenya was their first assignment, Lena having committed to a two-year Guest Helper position, and Penelope having become a new Wycliffe member, like me. Though there was a thirty-year difference in our ages, we got along great, and they were wonderful about including me in all the adventures of living in a new culture.

The three of us had bought a car together in advance, at SIL's recommendation, so we were ready to begin acclimating to our new home right away. Of course, we did have to become comfortable with driving on the other side of the road, but that adjustment happened fairly naturally. When cars seem to be approaching directly in front of you, it is easy to figure out you need to move!

During one of our first conversations as housemates, I asked Lena and Penelope to please always leave the grated security gate at the top of the stairs open at night so that in the event of a break-in I would be able to flee upstairs before they closed and locked the gate. I was relieved that they readily agreed to my request.

Within days, we had discovered that in Kenya, electricity, plumbing, and phone lines were not particularly dependable. With almost daily outages, we quickly adjusted to making the best of the situation. There was no hot water in the kitchen or bathrooms, but boiling water was not difficult for washing dishes. We did have hot water in the showers, via an electrical unit installed directly above the showerhead, a unit commonly referred to as 'the widow-maker' because the source of electricity was so close to the flowing water. Thankfully, none of us were ever shocked or electrocuted, so evidently our units had been properly installed.

The three of us took turns preparing meals and washing dishes. Lena was a great cook who enjoyed trying new recipes and Penelope not only cooked but loved baking fresh goodies. When it was my turn, I usually cooked vegetarian meals for all of us. With our multiple skills and favorites, our meals were always appealing. We enjoyed buying local watermelon year-round and eating bananas right off our own tree—the first year, we were amazed to discover our tree held eighty-two bananas on one long stem!

We often invited several other young teachers to join us: Charlotte was in her late thirties while Makena and Trudy were in their mid-twenties. Because our house was so large, it naturally became the expected location for any staff gatherings or parties that came along, a fact that suited us just fine. I thoroughly enjoyed my new home situation and the lively friendships that developed.

When it came to weekend meals, we also enjoyed sampling the local fare, which was similar to what I had eaten in Niger: tough beef stew with carrots, potatoes, and a tasty gravy. We were introduced to super-sweet chai, chapati (similar to a tortilla), and mandazi (African donuts) which were super popular with the Kenyans. They stopped at 10 a.m. every morning to enjoy that particular treat with their chai.

There was one other traditional food that became a favorite of mine. Upon occasion, our house-girl, Jackline, invited me to join her for Sukuma wiki and Ugali, which proved to be cooked greens (similar to collard greens or kale) served with a white mound of cold cornmeal porridge. I loved it! She taught me how to cook it, and also how to eat it the traditional way, using my fingers to pick up a small bit of Ugali and scooping up a portion of Sukuma wiki, then popping it all into my mouth at once. Jackline could eat it without making a mess, but I never developed the technique very well. Nonetheless, I had fun trying and she had fun laughing at my efforts!

A few nights after the other two had moved in, we heard what sounded like five gunshots nearby. We would learn the next day that several thieves had been caught breaking in to a nearby compound, and the police had shot them dead on the spot. Sadly, local thieves knew they could be killed if they were caught, but many men were desperate enough to risk it to feed their families.

In orientation, we were warned that break-ins were all too common, so we needed to be diligent about locking up each night. Our house had an emergency system in both the main house and the servant's quarters with an alarm button to push in the event of a break-in. A loud, shrieking siren would erupt and the police would automatically be notified.

We were also told that when we went downtown, we should never wear any gold jewelry because it might be ripped right off of us, even if it were pierced earrings. We were informed that, generally speaking, one out of three missionaries was accosted in some form, be it robbery, beating, molesting, or hijacking. We were further instructed to keep our car windows up when driving downtown to avoid meeting the 'crap boys,' teen-aged boys who would push human feces into the face of the driver and then rob the passengers in the confusion created. Ugh!

Knowing one is living in a dangerous city can definitely build one's prayer life, and one's dependence on the Lord. We were aware of the dangers, but felt relatively safe within our own compound and at school. I thank God that we were never victims of any crime, though we were aware of multiple incidents within our immediate community.

During our third year in Kenya, there was a local street thug known as John Wayne, who would stand on a deserted road with two pistols in his hands. When he spotted a car with a lone woman driving, he would jump in front of the car and point the guns at her, she would instinctively slam on the brakes, and he would pull her out of the car and beat, rob, or rape her. I am guessing he was nicknamed John Wayne because of the two pistols, but I found the name inappropriate and offensive, considering that the real John Wayne was a favorite American actor who always played the good guy.

Hearing the recurring reports of frightening incidents reminded us to be alert, cautious, and intentional in our comings and goings. I was (and am) forever grateful for our heavenly Father's precious protection over us.

Contrast of Nations

I will praise you, Lord, among the nations;
I will sing of you among the peoples.
—PSALM 108:3

Knowing of the diversity among American regions, I should have expected that all African nations were not the same either, but I had not given that fact much thought until after I arrived in Kenya. Nairobi was markedly different than the city I had previously experienced. Initially, I was a bit disappointed because the overall appearance of the city was considerably westernized compared to what I had seen the previous year.

I would discover later, though, that Kenya's countryside had much of the same charm as Niger. Unlike the sandy colors of the desert, our immediate neighborhood exhibited plush green foliage everywhere, lush green lawns, and elaborate gardens. However, other areas of the city were marked by an almost total absence of plant-life and bare, dusty roads. 'Upcountry' more closely resembled Niger with expanses of dried yellow grasses punctuated by occasional hearty bushes and trees and native huts or villages. In contrast to Niger, Kenya also had heavily forested areas.

Two obvious differences in the nations were their religions and their crime levels. Whereas Nigerien religion was primarily Islam over a layer of ancient tribal beliefs, Kenya had not yet been overcome by Islam. The people of Kenya exhibited a wide diversity of ancient religions as well as a growing population of Christians. In fact, Kenya was a central base for many Christian organizations that were ministering to nations throughout Africa.

Theft was not a major issue in Niger, but in Nairobi, theft and violence were common, perhaps partly because there were almost fifteen times as many people. Poverty in Niger was subtle, but in Nairobi, poverty was blatant. There was a huge contrast between the haves and have nots.

In 2002, the population in Nairobi was close to three million people. Downtown resembled any other large city throughout the world, packed with tall buildings, heavy traffic spewing out nasty fumes, and streets crowded with people. There was no evidence of native huts or shacks within the city limits, but there were blocks and blocks of stores and businesses. To my amazement, there was even a three-story mall with a wide variety of stores, a food court, a movie theater, and a glass elevator.

On the outskirts of the city, there was also an abundance of street-side businesses where all the wares were displayed in the open air: furniture, kitchenware, dry goods, souvenirs, and secondhand clothing from huge barrels of Good Will clothes that had been sent from the U.S. Most of these businesses had small covered stands behind them where the salespeople could stay out of the sun and collect the customer's money.

The traffic was heavily congested, but unlike the scenes in Niger, there were only cars, trucks, and bikes in the city—no camels or donkeys; no herds of goats, sheep, and cattle. The air quality was even more unbreathable than Niger because of the greater volume of car exhaust and burning rubbish.

Downtown, the main streets were paved, but in the outskirts and suburbs, most of the streets were dirt, so a passing car would raise a cloud of dust. Many of the missionary children had allergy and asthma problems because of the constant exposure to dust and pollution. I was grateful that our home and school were in a suburb with much cleaner air than downtown, and we had the blessing of paved streets in our immediate neighborhood.

I found a much smaller percentage of the population wore traditional African attire in Kenya where readymade clothing was popular and where fewer people sought out tailors except for special occasions. Though most women still wore the traditional wrap-around skirts (pagnes), many of them wore western-style T-shirts or blouses instead of the highly designed matching tops seen in Niger. Some women wore the head-coverings, but many did not. Likewise, the majority of men typically wore clothing that showed a western influence: they still sported colorfully printed shirts, but they often wore plain dark-toned pants. Some of the men wore colorful caps, but few of them wore turbans and none of them wore face-coverings.

Because Kenya had been an English colony in the past, English was the primary trade language in Nairobi. There were twelve dominant tribes in the area, with each one having its own distinct language spoken at home. Because of the diversity of tribal backgrounds and the proximity to one another, most Kenyans spoke several regional languages.

Regarding the frequency of multilingualism, my friend and fellow missionary shared a funny story with me. When a Kenyan man asked her what languages were spoken in the United States, she answered, "English." He asked what other languages were common and she replied, "None; just English," to which he responded, "Are Americans of normal intelligence?" She laughed at his assumption that all people groups throughout the world were multilingual unless they were intellectually challenged. As far as I know, we Americans are "of normal intelligence," but most of us have not had the need or the opportunity to learn multiple languages.

Similar to the daily scenes in Niger, within a few miles of our home we occasionally saw Maasai men herding their sheep along the roads' edges. Because the government had forbidden the tribe to continue their centuries-old tradition of hunting and killing lions, the government had given the Maasai men permission to herd their animals wherever they could find food for grazing.

Near our home, there was a small one-block shopping area, but it, too, was far more developed than anything I had seen in Niger. We housemates usually shopped there together for our groceries each weekend, and we often stopped for a "fast food" meal African-style, which meant placing an order and waiting while they cooked and packaged it at a noticeably leisurely pace. Our favorite fast foods were the delicious samosas and the fish and chips.

Occasionally, we joined a large group of friends to enjoy a night out at a local or downtown restaurant. Nairobi was a relatively international city, so various ethnic dishes were available, including pizza, which was popular. We especially loved a downtown restaurant called The Carnivore, where we could taste a variety of popular game meats like ostrich, eland, zebra, and crocodile. I remember the zebra was especially delicious, and the crocodile meat was quite flavorful, though gristly, so each bite took a long time to chew.

Settling in to a Missionary School

The Lord will keep you from all harm—
he will watch over your life.
—PSALM 121:7

Teaching in Kenya was a delight, once we worked out a few bugs. A day or two after Lena and Penelope arrived, we attended a tour of the campus. I was in for a major surprise. Though SIL and the school had known of my foot disability in advance, no one had mentioned that the campus was built on the side of an unusually steep hill. When I saw the campus layout, I wondered why they had been concerned about my climbing stairs to the second floor at the house when the school buildings were actually built on seven different levels!

The tarmac parking lot was at the top of the school grounds and the playground was at the bottom. In between, on various levels, were the administration building, intermediate building, student bathrooms, 'bandas' (lunch pavilion), and primary building, all of which were accessed by steep concrete walkways or concrete stairs with no railings.

When I saw the school layout, I was silently horrified, but evidently the look on my face was enough to give me away to Charlotte. She quietly asked me what was wrong and I whispered to her that I could not physically walk up and down such steep surfaces, and that climbing the stairs would be very dangerous for me without a hand rail.

Because she was a returning teacher, she was not shy about speaking up. She immediately shared my concerns with the principal, and to my great relief he had two hand rails installed before school started. He also decided to move my classroom to the intermediate side of campus to limit my difficulties in walking, and instead of sharing recess duty with the other teachers, I was assigned to serve on lunch duty—the bandas were not nearly as difficult for me to access as the recess yard at the bottom of the campus. I was very grateful for his kind response and quick action, and for my fellow teachers' understanding.

The next day, those of us who were new returned to the campus to begin preparing our classroom materials. The teachers' workroom was located in the administration building. As part of our orientation, we had been shown how to turn off the alarm system when we entered the building. However, the first time I tried, I had difficulty getting the alarm system to respond and the loud shrieking sirens began to shriek. To my horror, I looked out the front door and saw three angry-looking security guards headed toward the door with Billy clubs in their hands. I stepped out, threw my hands in the air and yelled, "I'm sorry! I'm sorry! I'm a new teacher! I didn't mean to set off the alarm!"

To my great relief, they lowered their weapons and started back toward their security van. I would later learn that throwing my hands in the air was the safest move I could have made. Several other new teachers were on campus at the time, so they had come running when they heard the alarm. It took me a while to live down their amused teasing about my initial introduction to Kenyan security.

Though the nights were cold, the daytime temperature in Kenya was generally seventy to eighty degrees Fahrenheit, so eating outside at the bandas was quite pleasant. The children enjoyed sitting wherever they wanted at lunchtime, allowing them the opportunity to expand friendships or to connect with their siblings. They brought their lunches from home most of the time. However, a few Ethiopian mothers treated us to a magnificent (spicy!) meal biweekly, for a minimum price.

Every day at the end of the day, all the classes lined up together near the administration building to sing songs, listen to a brief biblical encouragement from one of the teachers, and pray together before they headed home.

The school campus was next to a forested area, so the general temperature in our region was slightly lower than in other areas of the city. I would guess the night temperatures dropped to fifty to sixty degrees, making warm blankets a must. The school buildings were constructed of concrete floors and walls, accounting for chilly classrooms in the mornings.

I was teased by the other teachers for always carrying or wearing a sweater, but my body had become acclimated to much hotter weather. After living in Niger, Nairobi seemed cold to me, especially in the mornings and evenings. Some days were cold, too; on particularly cold days, I actually wore long-johns under my long dresses. Long johns in Africa?? Yes! To my total surprise, Africa was not all arid desert! In fact, one winter, we not only experienced drenching rains but also an incident of pounding hail, which built up on the ground, a sight I never expected to see in Africa.

Snakes!

You will keep in perfect peace
those whose minds are steadfast,
because they trust in you.
—ISAIAH 26:3

A few days after we arrived, our gardener knocked on the front door, and when Lena answered it, she called to Penelope and me to join her. The gardener wanted to show us the medium-sized black snake he had just killed, which was headed for our front door. The door had a one-inch gap at the bottom, and the snake was small enough in diameter to have fit through the opening.

When the gardener poked the snake to show us that it was dead, the snake raised up its head to bite him! He struck the snake once more, and this time it was definitely dead. He told us the snake could be a black mamba, a very aggressive and deadly snake that can grow to be quite large. We had been told in orientation that black mambas and green mambas were common, and that they were deadly. We had understood that the mambas were primarily seen 'upcountry,' so we were not happy with the possibility that there had been one in our yard. It seemed that in moving from Niger to Kenya, I had traded one deadly snake for another.

On further discussion, we learned from the gardener that most Africans kill all snakes on sight because of their fear of mambas. He told us that he had noticed we sometimes opened the upstairs windows to let in the fresh air, but he warned us that the snakes could get into our house by climbing the vines that covered the front of the building and slithering through the grates on the windows.

After killing the snake, the gardener had shown us a large hole in the middle of the roundabout garden area which he was convinced was a snake hole. In the three years we lived there, we never knew if the hole was a snake hole or not, but the gardener killed three black snakes. We also never knew if they were dangerous or not, but we were thankful for the gardener's quick actions each time he spotted one.

The next time we went shopping after the first snake was killed, I bought a pair of garden clippers and cut the vines away from the windows, praying the whole time as I clipped that the Lord would protect me if there were any snake presently hidden in the foliage. When I began to cut away the vines I could reach from the window, the weight of the vines pulled more of them away from the house, and I was able to resolve the problem of access to the windows.

On one occasion when we were driving upcountry, we saw a green mamba that had been flattened on the road; it was an almost translucent green, about three inches in diameter, and approximately seven to eight feet long. Even though it was dead and harmless, the very sight of that thing made our skin crawl. We had heard of two men who were riding motorbikes upcountry when one of them drove past a black mamba who rose up and bit him on the neck. He did not live long enough to reach assistance, but died there on the road. Stories like that definitely kept us on the lookout for snakes!

Monkeys in Our Garden

We soon learned that snakes were not the only nearby danger. I do not think I ever got used to seeing baboons strolling along the side of some of the roadways. In orientation, we had been warned that baboons and most monkeys were very dangerous because they could be quite aggressive and they had sharp teeth. We were told that we should never approach either species.

Sometimes when I was up on the second-floor balcony of our home, I would see a small black-faced monkey exploring our yard, stealing vegetables from our garden, or even occasionally sitting on the balcony wall to stare at me. But when I woke up one morning to see a monkey staring in my bedroom window, I was especially amused. In the United States, we go to the zoo to see the monkeys in the cages, but here was a monkey outside staring at me inside! I doubt that he appreciated the irony of the situation.

School Days

Come, my children, listen to me;
I will teach you the fear of the Lord.
—PSALM 34:11

I taught at the school for approximately two and a half years. There were 120 students, about sixty in intermediate grades and sixty in elementary grades. Though it may have been unusual to put a classroom full of first-graders next to "the big kids," the plan was relatively successful that first year. In fact, the sixth-graders loved having us next door. They came to read with the first-graders once a week, an event both age-groups thoroughly enjoyed, and an activity that resulted in the older students becoming like big brothers and sisters to the younger ones.

The school was within walking distance of our house, so most mornings the three of us walked to school. We often saw a few Kenyan women with large packs of sticks tied to their backs. They walked through the neighborhood every morning collecting fallen tree branches. Later in the day, they would sell their collected firewood at the market so they could buy milk for their children. We would greet one another or nod our heads and then proceed to our individual destinations.

I loved teaching in Kenya! My students were all MKs (missionary kids). Because of their parents' ministries, many of them often traveled with their families, so the number of children in my classroom on any given day fluctuated regularly. When the children would travel, I would create lesson plans for them to complete while they were gone, and then when they returned to Kenya, they would rejoin our classroom and I would grade their homework.

The first year, my students' home countries included Canada, Australia, Germany, Korea, South Africa, the United States, and Kenya. However, most of the children had been born in Kenya. The twin girls were the only ones born of Kenyan parents, but they had been adopted by an American missionary couple. They were the two youngest of four siblings born to a Kenyan prostitute who had died.

Their five-year-old sister had kept all four of them alive while living on the streets of Nairobi. Thankfully, someone had found them and taken all four girls to a local orphanage. The twins were only eighteen months old when they were found, and no one knew how long they had survived on the streets.

The orphanage was sponsored by a local church and directed by an American missionary wife. When she and her husband met the girls, they adopted the twins, but not the two older siblings. However, they continued to have regular contact with the other two girls, and when I last heard, they were in the process of adopting one of them. I lost contact with the family after that first school year, but I would guess they eventually adopted the fourth girl as well.

During my first and second years, I team-taught with Makena, the kindergarten teacher, a few hours each week to share various hands-on activities. In the process of sharing our students, the kindergarten teacher and I developed a friendship that has lasted for decades. The students loved combining classes and looked forward to our frequent projects.

I remember one amusing incident after we had had an all-school emergency drill. Because our classes were together when the siren blared, we lined them up together and quietly exited the building to meet at the appointed location. When the principal explained that we were practicing for emergencies, one little kindergartener piped up with, "That wasn't an emergency. No one was screaming or running!"

Halfway through the first year, we added another little girl to first grade. Her parents were missionaries from South Africa, serving in Sudan in an area where there were no other children. The family of four often returned to Kenya for several weeks at a time. Both siblings desperately needed social interaction with other children, so her four-year-old brother often joined his sister in our classroom for the day.

On one such occasion, all the students were walking to lunch with me when a small airplane flew over our heads. The four-year-old dropped to the ground and began frantically speaking to his sister in Afrikaans. His big sister tried to soothe his fear by gently replying in their native tongue. She turned to me and explained that their village had been bombed several times in Sudan, so he was afraid of small planes. How sad for a child that young to have such a fear, and a plausible reason for it.

The second year, I got brave and moved to the primary side of campus. The principal had promised to put up railings or create some gradual inclines for my benefit, but that never happened. Each year when school began, I would pull off my shoe and sock the first day to show the first-graders the scars on my foot. I would explain that without a metatarsal muscle in that foot, I had no "brakes' walking downhill. I explained to them that I sometimes pitched to the right unexpectedly, but they did not need to be alarmed; I knew how to fall safely.

The kids were amazing—they always watched out for me, holding my hands when we were on the walkways. In fact, during the third year, one little boy insisted on walking behind me with his hands on my back to make sure that I did not fall. Partly thanks to him, I never did. I continued to love my job, but the pain of walking on concrete at an angle eventually caught up with me, contributing to my later decision to request a transfer to another school.

The second year of school, I started out with only six students: five boys and one little girl who had no trouble holding her own with the boys (she had two brothers). She and one boy were of American descent, one boy's parents were from India and the U.S., one was born in Russia but adopted into an American family, and two were Korean-born.

One of the Korean boys had been at the school for a while, but the other had just arrived from his home country and spoke not one word of English. Both boys received regular tutoring from our ESL (English as a Second Language) tutor, and because I had been fully trained to teach ESL, I could readily present most of the classroom lessons with an ESL flavor.

All the students enjoyed watching and mimicking my ESL charades! They also enjoyed helping their classmates learn English, so both Korean boys were soon able to communicate quite well with their peers. For three months, we also added a Korean sixth-grade girl to our classroom in the afternoons. The purpose for her presence was to help her improve her English in a nonthreatening environment and to allow her the much-needed opportunity to be an assistant to younger children, thus building her self-esteem.

One of my challenges that year was maintaining classroom peace. The Russian child had developed unusually aggressive behavior while he lived in a Russian orphanage for the first five years of his life. Aggression may have been necessary for basic survival in his previous environment, but his negative behavior was not acceptable in a first-grade classroom. Now that he was living in a safer environment, curbing his quick temper and tendency to bully was a job that required frequent cooperative efforts on the part of his parents and me.

To the sole girl's delight, halfway through the year we gained three more girls, a Brazilian girl who had lived all over the world and spoke four languages, an American girl whose parents were on their first assignment overseas, and an enthusiastic Kenyan girl who talked nonstop. The four of them became a happy little club of their own, and then the original girl went home on furlough. We also gained another boy from Australia. Teaching overseas is definitely a mini-United Nations experience, and a constantly changing scenario.

The third year, I had fourteen students of multiple nationalities, including two with special needs—one was a girl with Downs Syndrome, and the other was a boy born four months prematurely. The little boy had major physical and educational disabilities, but was a sweet and cooperative child. The little girl was another story. Though my past experience had been that Downs children were generally loving and docile, this little girl was the exception. Before school started, her parents had met with me and the principal privately to inform us that she was used to getting her way by throwing tantrums and they were depending on my Special Education training to break her of the habit.

The principal had told me the previous Spring that I would be receiving two Special Education students for the following school year, so their arrival did not catch me by surprise. I was pleased that the Lord could use my extra training for His purposes on the field; He never wastes a thing! Before school started, the principal met with me and a Teacher Aide to create a classroom situation that would work for everyone involved. We figured out effective ways to incorporate the two children into the majority of mainstream activities while also providing for the extra time and tutoring needed to meet their individual needs.

Each school week included Friday morning Chapel Day for elementary students. At the beginning of Chapel, the students and teachers recited two pledges that I had never heard before:

> I pledge allegiance to the Christian flag and to the Savior for whose kingdom it stands. One Savior, crucified, risen and coming again with life and liberty for all who believe.
> I pledge allegiance to the Bible, God's holy Word. I will make it a lamp unto my feet and a light unto my path. I will hide its words in my heart that I might not sin against God.

The teachers rotated responsibility for creating a morning of worship, songs, and a brief play about that week's theme. Each theme was centered around a positive character trait and a Bible story with a related Bible verse. Quite frankly, I am not sure which activity the students enjoyed more— the weeks that they were an audience or the weeks that they performed. Everyone looked forward to Chapel Day!

Personally, I found the students' requirement to memorize a weekly Bible verse a perfect motivation for me to do the same. Each day, we would practice our verse with hand movements to help the children remember the words. Thankfully, they loved the activity, and the hand movements helped me to memorize as well.

Spiritual vitality was a constant goal for the students and the staff. Besides Chapel Day, the staff members came together twice a week for early morning prayer and devotions. We also had the option of meeting in small groups once a week for more personal prayer times. Generally speaking, there was a positive sense of camaraderie among children, parents, and teachers. We were all one big happy family! Chapel Days, daily lunch breaks and recesses, and the occasional theme days contributed to a positive sense of family and community.

Teachers and students alike annually celebrated several all-school theme days, including Pajama Day, the One Hundredth Day of school, Sports Day, the annual Soccer Competition, and Book Characters Day. On the hundredth day of school, every primary student brought a collection of one hundred items he or she had collected (stickers, coins, pebbles, drawings, buttons, etc.). Then the primary grades spent the day doing group activities together to count to one hundred in a variety of ways.

On Sports Day, the children were divided into multi-age color teams to participate in several hours of competitive relay races involving activities such as three-legged races, carrying raw eggs on spoons, running, hopping, and throwing bean bags for distance.

For the Soccer Competition, all grades went down to the recess field to sit on the bank and watch the Kenyan workers play a soccer game against the male teachers and staff. The Kenyan men played soccer barefoot on the rough, stickery field while the staff members played in sports shoes, but nonetheless the Kenyans were always the victors.

Book Day was celebrated after a week of focusing on the Dr. Seuss challenge for every child to read daily. Each child kept a log of pages read and a brief description of each book completed. Then on the last day, the children and teachers dressed up as their favorite book characters and had a parade class-by-class from room to room.

Out of all the school activities, I think my absolute favorite was teaching the weekly Bible story lessons and helping the children memorize their Bible verses. After teaching in American public schools for many years, I greatly valued the freedom to speak of Jesus in the classroom. I could often feel the presence and pleasure of the Lord when I was teaching His stories. I was deeply honored to be contributing to the students' knowledge about the faith that had brought their parents to Kenya.

But I was not the only one instilling the Word of God into these children. The first year I taught, I had a child in my class who was already an accomplished preacher. His father was an indigenous church-planter who took his six-year-old son with him to visit and encourage distant new churches. During the Sunday morning worship, he would place his son on a chair to give a brief sermonette to the Kenyans. Lord, how great Thou art!

Sometimes the Teacher, Sometimes the Student

When we were not educating children, five of us teachers became the students at Hekima Language School. During each class session, we were challenged to increase our Swahili language skills by actively listening and answering our teacher's constant questions and conversations, and by studying the conversations as homework.

One of the first words we learned was the word 'Kiswahili,' which is the Swahili word meaning "language of Swahili." A few other key words included Karibu (welcome), Asante (thank you), Habari (hello/how are you), Mzuri (very well), Rafiki (friend), Matatu (taxi), Nyumbani (home), Pole (sorry), and Pole pole (slowly).

Learning to speak a new language was not an easy task for any of us, and we each found that when we were unsure of how to answer a question, we often unconsciously switched to another foreign language we had previously learned, usually Spanish, French, or German. We would not even realize we had done it until our teacher or classmates would laugh and our teacher would repeat the question, asking us to answer in Kiswahili.

Upcountry House Dedication

Put your outdoor work in order
and get your fields ready;
after that, build your house.
—PROVERBS 24:27

One weekend, Joel, one of the school workers, invited school administrators and teachers to join him and his family for a traditional celebration 'upcountry.' Joel had been engaged for some time, and in their tribe's tradition, he was required to build his bride a new home upcountry before he could marry her. Even though they would be living at the school most of the time, the requirement still stood. He had successfully completed building their home (with the help of many family members), and now he was ready to host the traditional celebration for the house dedication.

That Saturday morning, we all piled into a couple of school vans and drove out into beautiful, untouched grasslands far from the city. We began to see occasional trees and bushes and little gatherings of huts. Eventually, we stopped at a small cluster of simple-looking houses and huts. When we emerged from the van, a Kenyan child stepped forward to present each of us visiting women with a large armload of flowers and a few shy words of greeting.

Then three Kenyan men offered to give the visitors (mostly women) a walking tour of the area. The ground was uneven, so I was noticeably choosing my steps carefully. One of the men noticed my hesitancy. He found a large fallen branch, quickly carved off the leaves, and gave it to me with a big grin on his face. I readily accepted his gift of a walking stick, expressed my thanks in smiles, and continued the walking tour with him at my side.

When we returned to the larger group, one of the other missionaries asked me where I had found the stick. When I answered that one of the men had presented it to me, she laughed and explained that by accepting his gift, I had indicated my interest in spending time with him. Oh dear, my mistake. I immediately thanked him, set the walking stick down and did not pick it up again. Thank you, Lord, for safety in numbers and the close proximity of well-informed, protective friends.

Then our host invited all of us to gather together to begin the dedication ceremony. Joel and his bride-to-be stood in front of their new house, made of cinder blocks with a tin roof. The newness of the home stood out in the midst of more traditional mud and straw huts.

A prayer was said, a song was sung, one of our administrators was asked to say a few words, and then he cut the large ribbon tied around the new house's front door. When the ribbon was cut, there was great cheering, everyone toured the new house, and a beautiful meal was served to all the guests. After an enjoyable afternoon, we returned to Nairobi fully content with the day's adventure, and I am happy to report that I never saw my new admirer again.

Breathing!

The Spirit of God has made me;
the breath of the Almighty gives me life.
—Job 33:4

One weekend, the three of us housemates decided to drive into the city to visit a larger grocery store with a greater selection of foods. We were walking up and down the aisles when I began to experience pronounced chest pain. At first, I ignored it, but after walking a few more aisles, the pain had become excruciating. I realized I was having difficulty breathing. I knew it was my lungs and suggested to the girls that we should finish up shopping and go home. But they were worried that I was having a heart attack, in spite of my protesting that the pain was from my lungs.

We finished our shopping, left the grocery store, and headed for a hospital. One of the girls called the principal, who met us at the hospital a short time later. We remained in the waiting room for a long time, what felt like hours, but eventually I was seen and the doctor confirmed that I was having an asthma attack; my heart was fine. He prescribed an inhaler which proved to be a mixed blessing—though it helped me breathe a bit better, it also caused me to act very silly and to giggle uncontrollably. Needless to say, I was suitably embarrassed by the unwanted side effect, so I used the inhaler as little as physically possible.

On a later date, a similar event occurred, but this time the emergency doctor immediately applied an oxygen mask to my face. The mask was attached to a breathing machine that misted medication into my lungs. After that incident, my housemates and I agreed that when they went downtown, I would remain at home. Avoiding the heavy pollution of the city did help me breathe better for a while, but the inhaler proved to be only a temporary fix.

Dangerous Elections

But you, God, see the trouble of the afflicted;
you consider their grief and take it in hand.
The victims commit themselves to you;
you are the helper of the fatherless.
Break the arm of the wicked man;
call the evildoer to account for his wickedness
that would not otherwise be found out.

—Psalm 10:14–15

Elections in Kenya were not at all similar to the elections I had experienced in the United States. But then, the history of Kenyan politics was nothing like the history of American politics. Though Kenya theoretically had a democratic system, the presidency and power had been controlled by one party ever since winning independence from England in 1963. That power had been maintained primarily through violence. But 2002 was different—that year, the people had seen the first free general election in the history of the country.

The KANU (Kenya African National Union) party had successfully dominated the government for decades until 2002 when they found themselves confronted by a new coalition formed from fourteen opposing groups and a portion of KANU. The incumbent president was retiring, but he had personally chosen his replacement candidate, and his choice was not favored by all of KANU's members.

The disagreement led to a split in the party and the reshuffling of alliances. By joining together, the opposing groups had created a new party called NARC, the National Rainbow Coalition, which offered the voters an enticing opportunity to defeat KANU and to end the stranglehold the party had had on the country for decades.

Starting in September, 2002 (only two months after we had arrived), the two opposing sides began to riot on the streets of the city. Various embassies warned SIL to have their people ready to evacuate on a moment's notice if things got uglier. SIL advised us all to keep a small suitcase packed with a few clothes and key paperwork inside it, just in case we had to evacuate in a hurry. One morning, I had written in my journal,

September 19, 2002: "*This is My Father's World*" comes to mind as the day begins and I hear the birds singing outside in these Paradise-like surroundings. I have so many emotions mixed together—peace at being where you want me, delight at teaching here in Kenya, frustration about congestion, concern about physical safety as the rioting continues downtown, sadness about my mom's loneliness, and thanksgiving for such great people to work with! I lay all on your altar and praise you, Father. You are the great I AM! Like Habakkuk, I recognize and rejoice that you are sovereign. Praise be to God. Alleluia!

Then after a weekend away, I had written,

October 13, 2002: And now we're back—to a city of political unrest and high crime rate, a city of friendly nationals and desperate nationals who have no jobs or food—a city where we daily have to think about security issues whether in our house or car. I'm not used to having to think this way.

In early and mid-December, the newspapers reported that, as usual, KANU was waging a campaign of intimidation, murder, and corruption, but because NARC had become so popular, the new party was still expected to win the election. It was further noted that during past election seasons, key opponents had either been killed or had mysteriously disappeared. In fact, the previous December when the NARC party was formed and Mwai Kibaki had been chosen as the sole presidential candidate, he had narrowly escaped death in a car accident, but the cause of that accident was never clearly determined. In spite of the fact that there was rioting again in 2002, the newspapers reported that there were noticeably fewer deaths than during previous election seasons.

When Election Day finally arrived on December 27, Mwai Kibaki successfully won the election. He was the first true people's choice president in thirty-nine years! To everyone's relief, the rioting calmed down instead of getting worse, and we missionaries unpacked our suitcases.

But the losing party had not given up yet, or so it appeared. About a month later, the plane carrying the majority of the new president's cabinet members mysteriously crashed on the way to a cabinet meeting. At the time, the newspapers reported that the plane was sabotaged, but later the reports implied the plane may have accidentally brushed a tree before crashing. Regardless of the cause, many of the new leaders had been killed and others had been badly injured. The president's party replaced the newly emptied positions and held their control of the government, but from then on, the president mandated that no more than two cabinet members should ever travel together.

Shockingly, when the presidential palace changed hands, reports circulated that torture chambers and prison cells were found in the underground rooms below the administrative floor, and it was suspected that the mystery of what had happened to previous opponents may well have been uncovered.

The sad thing is that by the time I left Africa in 2005, though the new party in power had fulfilled many of its promises to improve the overall governmental system, there were definite signs of weakness and possible corruption which still needed addressing.

Bomas of Kenya

'Bomas of Kenya' was the name of a magnificent tourist village and cultural center on the edge of the city. The village was built to preserve the history of the dominant Kenyan tribes. 'Boma' means 'house' or 'homestead' in Kiswahili. Though there were more than forty tribal groups within Kenya's borders, the displays highlighted only a few of the dominant tribes. I do not remember the names of all the tribes that were reported to be in our immediate region, but I do remember my Kenyan friends speaking of the Kikuyu, Luo, Luhya, Kamba, Swahili, Maasai, and Samburu.

The city of Nairobi had set aside a large portion of land where a traditional hut of each major tribe had been built full-size, accompanied by a display of typical surroundings or structures that would be common in that tribal village. There were brief descriptions of tribal life posted on the structures. Visitors could wander from display to display or they could hire a guide to accompany them and share more details about the tribes and their lifestyles.

There was also an enormous indoor auditorium with stadium-type seating where visitors could sit to watch traditional dances on the floor below them. My housemates and I visited the park on several occasions, and at one point Makena and I took our combined kindergarten-first grade classes there for a tour. Each time we visited, we learned more about this country that had become our home. Watching the men and women perform in their magnificent traditional costumes and hearing their voices, their instruments, and their traditional songs was a lively treat. Watching the Maasai men jump straight up in the air during their dances was a sight to behold!

Warthogs and Children: The Safari Walk

You made (men) rulers over the works of your hands;
you put everything under their feet:
all flocks and herds,
and the animals of the wild,
the birds in the sky,
and the fish in the sea,
all that swim the paths of the seas.
—PSALM 8:6–8

A few months after we settled in to the school routine, my housemates and I began to branch out a bit to become more familiar with Nairobi. We invited our house-girl, Jackline, to join us for a visit to the Safari Walk near the entrance to the Nairobi Game Park. On weekdays, Jackline lived in our servant's quarters behind the main house, and on weekends she usually caught a matatu (taxi) upcountry to visit her children. On this occasion, we invited her to put aside the housework and come with us for the adventure.

Though she had lived in Nairobi all her life, we were surprised that she had never been to the Safari Walk, but then we were just beginning to understand how truly destitute most of our Kenyan workers were. She had three young children to support and no extra money to spend on such frivolities. We were excited to take her along for her first look at her wildlife neighbors.

We parked the car in the parking lot and started walking toward the front entry when we spotted a most amusing sign:

SPEED LIMIT
20 K.P.H.
WARTHOGS and CHILDREN
HAVE RIGHT OF WAY

I could not resist the Kodak moment, asking Penelope and Jackline to pose on opposite sides of the sign. I doubt that Jackline understood why I found the sign so amusing, for in her world, the sign may have made perfect sense. I knew the Kenyans deeply valued their children, and wondered if perhaps the sign simply implied that children and warthogs were equally impulsive about running into the street.

After paying the entrance fee, we began the adventure of following the protected pathways and raised wooden boardwalks to observe a multitude of animals in their natural habitats. The Safari Walk covered a number of acres of land which had been developed to represent the three natural eco-systems of the animals who lived in Kenya: wetlands, savannah, and forestland. Each habitat area was extensive in size, allowing the animals freedom of movement and giving the guests a better sense of their natural habitat.

We saw leopards, lions, cheetahs, eland, impala, gazelles, antelopes, pygmy hippos, ostriches, zebras, Cape buffalo, wildebeest, hyenas, baboons, various monkeys, and an unbelievable number of bird species. During the time that I lived in Nairobi, Kenya was believed to have more bird species than anywhere else in the world. The Safari Walk was also a rhino sanctuary, so we were blessed to get a close look at a full-grown rhino without risking any danger to our personal well-being.

It took us about two hours to walk the full circle. The experience was a great introduction to the wildlife living in Kenya, and watching Jackline's response was a treat for all of us. She was very quiet as we walked, but her eyes were the eyes of a child, filled with great wonderment. Jackline was finally getting a chance to observe the animals so common in her world, but not necessarily accessible for her viewing.

The longer we lived in Kenya, the more we understood why the world sees the United States as the land of wealth and opportunity—because it is! For Jackline to have lived nearby and never have seen most of the local animals seemed unthinkable to us. Our ethnocentric view of necessities and luxuries was being seriously shaken as we rubbed shoulders with the poor of the world.

Lake Naivasha and Lake Nakuru

Early in the school year, 2002, the entire school staff traveled to Lake Naivasha together to hike around the peninsula and observe the incredible wildlife. Have you ever had a picnic lunch sitting next to a herd of zebras in their natural habitat? I have! But I remember at the time feeling like I was in a dream, sitting there munching on a sandwich while the zebras were grazing right next to us.

When we were walking past a few African huts, a small child began to scream and cling to an old woman. The child continued screaming and sobbing in sheer terror as we approached. The old woman tried to comfort and appease her to no avail. I asked a Kenyan staff member why the child was so upset and she said that Kenyan parents often told their children that if they did not behave, the mazungus (white people) would come to eat them. No wonder she was crying! I would guess she was a model child for the next several days.

We also had occasion to meet up with a number of large bees near an outhouse. We were warned to keep our distance, for the sting of that particular type of bee was considered deadly. When several of them came dangerously close to me, I silently prayed for the Lord to keep me calm and safe, and He did. Nonetheless, I was relieved to continue our journey away from the bees.

About a month after the school trip, my housemates and I decided to return to the area for the weekend. We visited both Lake Nakuru and Lake Naivasha together. We saw zebras, giraffes, gazelles, hippos, rhinos, Cape buffalo, water bucks, dik-diks (small deer-like creatures), a variety of spectacular birds, and literally thousands of flamingos. The flamingos were spread out over a huge marshy area, and the smell was overpowering.

We held our breath to take a handful of photos before making a rapid retreat back to the landscape where the aroma was more pleasant.

We saw a mother giraffe and her five-day-old baby, who had already lost one eye to a hyena attack. Our guide told us that the mother's only defense was to kick at the hyenas and, evidently, she had been effective enough to scare them away before they could kill and eat her newborn.

We also saw a fifteen-foot python, an amazingly beautiful and mesmerizing creature. Our guide told us that the python was hunting for dik-diks, so he was not the least bit interested in us. I see why Satan is sometimes referred to as a serpent—we found the large snake's markings and subtle movements so fascinating that we just stood there for a long while, entranced by his quiet slithering and the beauty of his long, shiny body.

Kariobangi Slum: Somali Territory

God is our refuge and strength,
an ever-present help in trouble.
—Psalm 46:1

In late 2002, my two housemates and I experienced much more of an adventure than we had planned for a quiet Saturday afternoon. We had been living in Kenya for only a few months when a missionary couple invited us to visit their home on the other side of the city. We readily accepted, looking forward to exploring a bit more of the amazing world of people and scenery all around us.

As new residents in Kenya, we had been thoroughly instructed regarding acceptable procedures for survival in the local culture: assault and robbery were common, so we had been urged to always stay aware of our surroundings in public places, never walk anywhere alone, never use our cell phones in plain sight of strangers, do not make eye contact with men we did not know, never smile at a stranger, and when driving, keep our windows closed, stay on the main roads, and do not enter any slum area, especially the Kariobangi slum.

Kariobangi was where the Somali Muslims lived. We had been seriously warned, "The Somalis do not like strangers, Americans, whites, foreign women, or Christians. Any stranger who enters their territory after dark is not likely to be seen again."

Because of these warnings, our hosts had given us careful instructions on how best to reach their home safely, and we had followed those instructions to the letter. The roads were packed with heavy traffic. Though the cars were moving steadily, it took us almost an hour to travel from one side of the city to the other. We arrived safely without incident and had a wonderful afternoon of visiting with our friends. Then we started back home around 3 p.m., expecting the trip to take us about an hour once again, but such was not the case.

On a daily basis, the three of us took turns driving the car. On this occasion, Lena was at the wheel with Penelope next to her on the passenger side while I was comfortably situated in the back seat. We started to follow the directions our hosts had given us to return home, but soon found ourselves caught up in a terrible traffic jam with two or three "lanes" of cars as far as the eye could see.

Traffic in Africa had a flavor of its own because, generally speaking, the drivers were not particularly concerned about the rules of the road. When drivers grew impatient, they often created their own lanes or drove right off the side of the road to bypass the other cars. Such was the case on this occasion. The scene around us grew steadily more congested as drivers sought out shortcuts, cut off other cars, and grew steadily more agitated.

We continued inching along with very little progress for over an hour. We were boxed in on all sides, and there was only one traffic officer who was desperately trying to direct the cars to follow his lead. Many drivers were totally ignoring him, and the officer was getting frustrated.

After a while, we became aware of the hostile stares coming from the officer and from the people in cars near ours, and it was then that we noticed we were the only white people anywhere in sight. We remembered our training and were careful to avoid looking directly at anyone.

Suddenly, the driver of the car to our left abruptly drove right down a dirt embankment to find his own way, and to my shock, Lena followed him. She said she did not feel safe in that crowd and that she had a good sense of direction. She was sure she could easily get us home by another route. But moments later, we followed the car ahead of us right past a sign that read, "Kariobangi." There was a stream of cars immediately in front and behind us and the road was painfully narrow, so there was no turning around now. We all grew quiet as we realized where we were.

But our God is gracious—we were not traveling alone! After we prayed aloud together, we agreed to continue praying silently, and each time we reached a crossroad, we stated aloud the direction we heard from the Holy Spirit: right, left, or straight ahead. Repeatedly, we all three named the same direction.

The stream of cars was still moving very slowly, and occasionally a male pedestrian would walk over to our car and pound his fist against the side. We adhered to the practice of not looking directly at the individual but keeping our eyes straight ahead or down. Each time it happened, the man continued on his way, and in God's perfect grace, we all three remained calm and quiet as we continued to travel.

After a few incidents of the car-pounding, the thought crossed my mind that one of the men might break into our car and drag us out. I was aware I might die that night trying to protect the two younger ones from being raped or molested. Oddly enough, I could honestly tell the Lord I was willing to do exactly that, if need be. I prayed that He would protect us and the vehicle from any harm, but I was also confident that I was willing to go down fighting, if it came to that.

We continued our slow journey, and at each crossroad we again verbalized the direction the Holy Spirit was leading—until we got to one corner where the other two said they were not hearing any direction. But I was. I was hearing the words, "Follow the sun." By this time, we were approaching dusk, and as we proceeded, we followed the direction of the setting sun. The sky was getting darker, and we knew we could be in serious trouble if we did not find our way out soon. We discussed our options and decided to call a friend whose fiancé was a Kenyan; maybe he could direct us out.

I lay down on the back seat with my cell phone well-hidden underneath me and called our friend's fiancé. Sure enough, when I described the scene around us, he knew exactly where we were. Thankfully, we were very close to the edge of the slum, and he was able to successfully direct us the rest of the way out. We reached familiar territory just as the sun went down. Thank you, Jesus!

We drove home greatly relieved and acutely aware of the Lord's grace in rescuing us from a possible disaster. Though we all slept soundly that night, the next day we were a mess. The Lord had carried us in His peace and presence during the entire ordeal, but when we were back on safe ground, the reality of the danger we had escaped manifested itself in headaches, body aches, and extreme exhaustion. We had personally witnessed the magnificence of God's protection, and my guess would be that none of us will ever forget that day.

Brackenhurst

Then the Lord God formed a man from the dust of the ground and breathed into his nostrils the breath of life, and the man became a living being.

—GENESIS 2:7

God alone can give us life and breath. I was reminded of that truth in late December, 2002, when the entire staff attended a five-day conference at the Brackenhurst Conference grounds, high in the hills outside of Nairobi. The focus was on the book of Nehemiah, and the overall message was to persevere in all circumstances. Ironically, that theme was what I was personally living as I battled a migraine headache and extreme chest pain.

After several days of my growing discomfort, my roommate, a lovely British lady, became concerned. She fetched a doctor from the conference and brought him to our room. He examined me and determined the pain was not from my heart. However, he suspected the elevation at over 7000 feet was most likely contributing to my discomfort. Much to my disappointment, he sent me to bed. I missed the Scottish dancing and the evening's Watchnight service to greet the New Year.

When we returned to Nairobi a few days later, the pain in my chest got worse, not better. Once again, we headed for the Emergency Room where the doctor prescribed another misting treatment. He and the nurse assured us that the mist would take only fifteen to twenty minutes to clear my breathing, but this time I was on the misting machine for forty-five minutes.

On January 4, 2003, I had written in my journal:

> A trip to Nairobi Hospital revealed bronchitis, pollution, and elevation had caused bronchial asthma, and a treatment with an oxygen mask and medicated mist opened my lungs—thank you, Lord! I can breathe!

This third incident made it abundantly clear to everyone that I needed to find a long-term solution. I contacted SIL to request transfer to a less polluted area only to learn that most of the translation work being done was in seriously polluted parts of the world. Consequently, if I wanted to continue serving with Wycliffe, I would have to find a way to survive high levels of pollution.

When I returned to the U.S. that summer, I researched asthma and the suggested methods of treatment. I returned to Kenya armed with several industrial face masks, which were highly effective in protecting me from the worst of the pollution when I could not avoid heavy exposure. Thankfully, wearing a mask did not make me act silly! My housemates and I continued the practice of my remaining at home when they ventured out to Nairobi proper, and the issue of my asthma slowly became of little concern.

Mombasa

Come to me, all you who are weary and burdened, and I will give you rest.
—MATTHEW 11:28

In contrast to Kariobangi or Brackenhurst, our times in Mombasa were amazing! For starts, the fresh sea air gave my lungs a much-needed respite from the pollution of Nairobi. The first time we went, there were four of us: Penelope, Lena, Trudy, and I flew to Kenya's coastline for a week of vacation at a popular tourist hotel. We found ourselves surrounded by luxury far beyond our expectations: elaborately decorated rooms, a huge reception area, multiple swimming pools, and ready access to the private beach behind the hotel. For meals, we walked to the main dining room where there was a daily variety of delicious foods served buffet-style.

For entertainment and refreshment, we lounged around the pools or basked in the sun near the beach, and on one occasion we hired a local tour guide to take us boating and snorkeling. The tour guide steered the motorboat to an area where the sea bottom was close enough to the surface that by swimming around with our snorkels, we could see a host of amazing sea-life below us. The water was as clear as glass, and the scenery below did not disappoint us, resembling the colorful contents I had observed only at the San Francisco Aquarium before coming to Africa.

The guide had urged us to be careful to stay on the surface of the water so that the black sea anemones could not shoot us with their darts (stinging cells). However, two of us realized when we got back in the boat that we had each been stung in the ankle, a temporarily painful experience alleviated by removing the stinger and applying periodic applications of ice. The following day, our ankles were super itchy, but the effect wore off within a few days.

One day when we were lounging by the beach, we saw a man leading two camels along the shore. A while later, we saw another man headed the opposite direction, leading his camel with a large sign on the side of the camel's body which advertised, "Rent A Truck." We thought the sign was hilarious, so I walked down to the handler and asked if I could take a picture. He readily agreed, but after Lena took a photo of him and me and the camel, the man asked if I would like to ride the camel for a fee. That possibility was certainly not my intent, but when he told me the price I could not resist—I would soon regret that decision!

When the camel knelt down and I climbed on the saddle, the handler directed him to stand and then immediately began running him along the beach's edge as fast as the man could run. I kept calling out, "Slow down! Slow down!!" and I hung on for dear life. Unlike my previous ride in Niger, this one was not a relaxing experience. Camels are very tall, and I knew if I fell off, I would probably be badly injured. The man just laughed and kept running the camel. When he finally stopped, the camel knelt down and I could not get off of him fast enough. The look on the man's face was quite smug as I walked back to my companions.

We were staying in a very ritzy hotel with most of the tourists appearing to be quite wealthy, so I wondered if he had grown weary of spoiled travelers. Perhaps he had decided to have a little fun at my expense.

Whatever the reason for his action, he was long gone and I was just glad to have both feet firmly planted on the sand again.

About a year later, we returned to Mombasa with a larger group of people and with accommodations that better fit our missionary budgets. We (four young women, three young men, and I) rented a house for a few days. Our mode of transportation from Nairobi to Mombasa was also more budget-friendly—we rode an all-night bus. Kenyan buses did not have air-conditioning or bathrooms, so every few hours, the bus driver would pull over and stop at the side of the road. Those individuals who needed to relieve themselves stepped outside in the dark and quickly took care of business.

In Niger, I had learned to always wear a long dress in unfamiliar situations so that if the need arose, I could discreetly squat to relieve myself. However, I had not been warned that the passing driver of an eighteen-wheeler might flash his lights and blast his horn when he saw moving shadows next to the stopped bus. Thank you, Lord, for long dresses and a sense of humor!

On our second trip, we mainly ate, relaxed, and visited with one another. We also had the opportunity to go snorkeling along the beach's edge. I planted myself near a large, deep tide pool to allow the others to explore farther without my slowing them down.

While snorkeling in the tide pool (the size of a small pond), I saw many beautiful fish, including a small white octopus, an orange pufferfish who was puffed up in all his glory, and a royal blue angel fish. These sights were so exciting to me, until a Kenyan man dove down and speared the octopus! I suppose he wanted it for dinner, but I was sad to see something so beautiful destroyed only moments after I had admired it.

At the end of our stay, most of us chose to return home on a train while a few opted for the bus. The majority reasoned that the train would be a much shorter and more comfortable trip. We said our farewells to those who chose the bus and then headed for the train station. Our train departed in the early evening. However, an hour into the trip, the train simply stopped on the tracks. Eventually, a train worker came back to tell us that the tracks would have to be cleared of debris before the train could proceed.

We had a few leftover snacks with us which served as dinner, and as the evening grew darker, we settled down to nap a while. We ended up spending the entire night sleeping on the unmoving train. The bonus of that setback was that when the train began to move in the early morning, we had a ring-side seat for the display of animals outside—elephants, ostriches, dik-diks, and gazelle were the stars. If, as planned, we had ridden home in the dark the night before, we would have missed that incredible animal show only a few feet away. God truly works all things together for good! Ironically, those who had taken the bus arrived back in Nairobi long before we did.

Malaria!

The Lord sustains them on their sickbed
and restores them from their bed of illness.
—PSALM 41:3

Shortly after our return from Mombasa, Makena began to exhibit signs of malaria. Because Nairobi was considered a relatively malaria-free zone, we were encouraged not to take prophylactics on a daily basis. However, in the event of traveling, most of us took them as a safety precaution. We knew full well that we could still contract the disease, but hopefully the prophylactics would lower the possibility and the severity. Basically, a person could be bitten by malaria-carrying mosquitoes two or three times in one day and still escape a response, but if the person were bitten four or more times, the chances were high that he or she would get malaria.

Makena developed a high fever for several days, and the fever caused her to hallucinate and ramble nonsensically. Though her conversation made very little sense, she was incredibly funny! We had to convince her that she needed to go to bed and stay there until the fever passed, and within a few days, with the help of Doxycycline, rest, and lots of clear liquids, she was back to her normal self.

I would guess that most of us had malaria at one time or another. As soon as any teacher began to exhibit symptoms (fever, chills, nausea, diarrhea, body aches, severe sore throat, or weakness), the principal would dispense a few pills of Doxycycline, which he kept at the school for that purpose. Consequently, when most of us showed symptoms, we were not tested for malaria but recovered fairly quickly.

Intestinal parasites were another common cause of illness. Even with careful food preparation, we occasionally contracted some nasty intestinal bug. At one point, I was hospitalized for a few days and learned that patient care standards in Africa were a little different than the U.S. Whereas American hospital rooms usually include a bathroom for each room, the Kenyan hospital had one multi-stalled bathroom for the entire floor and I was expected to get myself there and back as needed, dragging my IV pole along with me.

I also discovered that a patient would not be discharged unless he or she was able to pay the full hospital bill before departure, a requirement that was not an issue for me, but definitely a serious issue for most Kenyans. The entire bill was only $300-$400, so I could afford to pay it, but that amount would have been daunting for most Kenyan families.

Regarding medical expenses, I had had a minor outpatient surgery performed during my second year in Kenya. Unbelievably, the entire medical bill was $400! Kenyan hospitals in Nairobi were always spotless and the care was excellent. Most of the doctors and nurses were of Indian descent, well-trained and personable. I came home thanking God for the reasonably-priced quality care, wondering how the U.S. could rationalize charging ten to twenty times more for the same services.

Weddings

... a man will leave his father and mother and be united to
his wife, and the two will become one flesh.
—MARK 10:7–8

Those of us who lived in the teacher house often joked with new arrivals that if they wanted to get married, they should move in with us. The first year resulted in an engagement between an American woman and a Kenyan man, the second year was an Australian woman and a Kenyan man, and the third year was a Canadian woman and an Australian man.

Only the second couple was married in Kenya, so that was the only wedding I attended. The event was visibly, relationally, and spiritually memorable as the families of two drastically different cultures came together to celebrate their children's union.

The ceremony was performed on the school grounds, outside in the shade of a few trees. Walking barefoot in the wedding procession, the bride wore a traditional white lace gown while her barefoot groom and his groomsmen awaited her in matching Kenyan shirts and dark pants. The two little flower girls, one Kenyan and one American, wore elaborately frilly dresses and shiny shoes. The ceremony was moving and Christ-centered with the couple dedicating their lives to His service. The reception had a few awkward moments as the oldest Kenyan relative noticeably separated herself from the 'foreigners' and her own family, but a compassionate American quietly moved her chair next to the old lady to silently convey the message that everyone was welcome at the Lord's table.

The first couple left SIL and moved back to the United States, the second couple is still serving in Africa, and the third couple served many years with MAF (Mission Aviation Foundation) in Africa before returning to Canada for the children's schooling.

"Mixed marriages" were understandably common overseas and were accepted with mixed reactions, some welcoming and some condemning, both among family and friends as well as among strangers in public. In entering such a union, each couple had to be certain that the Lord was directing their steps. They had to seek His wisdom for how to successfully combine their two cultures while coping with whatever family reactions they might face. For most couples, family peace and acceptance usually came with time.

Summer Visits

Children are a heritage from the Lord,
offspring a reward from him.
Like arrows in the hands of a warrior
are children born in one's youth.
—PSALM 127:3–4

Missing my two sons was the greatest sacrifice I endured while serving in Africa. Shortly after the Australian-Kenyan couple were married, they flew to Australia to meet the other half of their extended family. Meanwhile, I, too, climbed on a plane to head back to California. Because I was a school teacher, I had the treasured privilege of returning to the U.S. each summer for six weeks, a sweet time of reconnecting with family and friends.

Those weeks were precious to me, allowing me quality time to love my family, and allowing me time to connect with my supporters by visiting churches and small groups to update them on the work through photo presentations and stories.

Leaving my family for the majority of the year was incredibly painful, but those summer visits made the sacrifice more bearable. I thanked God that He knew my heart well and had provided a way for me to serve Him whole-heartedly without having to give up my family forever.

The Mother Teresa House

For I was hungry and you gave me something to eat, I was thirsty and you gave me something to drink, I was a stranger and you invited me in, I needed clothes and you clothed me, I was sick and you looked after me, I was in prison and you came to visit me ... Truly I tell you, whatever you did for one of the least of these brothers and sisters of mine, you did for me.

—MATTHEW 25:35–36, 40

Coping with frequent back pain, I occasionally hired a Kenyan woman to give me a massage. Jane was a great masseuse and we enjoyed conversing with each other while she eased the pains in my back. One day, she mentioned that she used to work in the Mother Teresa House in Nairobi. What?? I did not know there was one in Kenya. In my ignorance, I had thought they were found only in India.

I was fascinated and asked her a million questions. I shared with her that the major reason I had become a missionary was because I was inspired by reading of Mother Teresa's ministry in India. Jane told me a lot about her years working with the Sisters of Charity, and then she invited me to go with her to visit the site. I readily accepted! I shared the news with my two housemates and they decided to come along.

Soon thereafter, one Saturday morning, Jane and her son and two granddaughters came to pick us up at the house. We drove together for a long time, passing through unfamiliar areas of Nairobi when, to our surprise and consternation, her son drove the car right into the Kariobangi slum. The three of us expressed our discomfort with entering Somali territory, but Jane assured us that we were perfectly safe while accompanied by Kenyans.

The traffic was bumper-to-bumper as we slowly inched along. At one point, I looked out the window and saw an adolescent boy lying unconscious along the side of the road. He was sweating profusely and people were walking past him as if they did not even see him. I said to Jane, "We have to help him! At least we can move him into the shade at the side of the road."

But she replied, "He's probably a drug addict. If you get out of this car, you will be killed. Do not open that door." I found the situation gut-wrenching, but I could not put six people in jeopardy when our hostess forbade me to take action. We continued on our way and prayed for the boy; I could not get the image of his unconscious body out of my mind.

When we finally arrived at the Mother Teresa House, we were admitted through locked metal security gates. The entire complex was surrounded by an unusually tall protective wall. We entered a large courtyard with a long L-shaped building beyond it. We were met by several nuns who warmly greeted us.

After initial introductions, we began the tour. First, we entered a large room full of adult women. The nuns explained that these women were societal rejects. Many were mentally challenged, disabled, weak, or elderly. One woman walked over to me and began petting the top of my head. I asked the nun why the woman was stroking my hair and she answered that the woman had never before seen straight hair. The nuns were wearing traditional Sisters of Charity habits, so their hair was always covered. The curious woman was fascinated that my hair was so smooth, unlike the kinky or curly hair of her Kenyan peers.

When we entered the next room, there were young children lying on mattresses all over the floor. These children were also considered social rejects because of their disabilities. There were several women sitting along one side of the room, and their job was to take care of the children. Lena, Penelope, and I spread out and got down on our knees to pass from one child to another in greeting. As we did, we each touched and prayed for the child before us. The children just silently stared at us as we moved about the room. The experience was dramatically moving as I felt the presence of God passing through me to each child I touched. We could not verbally communicate with those precious children, but we could convey the love of God through touch and prayer.

The next room contained about ten small infant beds, each one holding a tiny baby. Several nuns were checking on them, rocking them, feeding them, and changing their diapers. My mother's heart wanted to take one of those little ones home with me, though I knew my desire was unreasonable. I found it heart-wrenching to see so many sweet babies who had been deserted at birth. The nuns explained that they would often find a tiny newborn left at the gate overnight. Like Mother Teresa, the sisters were committed to providing love and care for the sick and dying, as well as for those whom society had rejected.

The fourth room was filled with lively, happy children of all ages who flocked to us with excitement, laughter, and joy! The nuns explained that these healthy children would be housed and schooled until they reached the age of eighteen, and then, hopefully, each one would be placed in an apprenticeship or beginning job somewhere in the city.

As we left the building, the nuns asked us to support the Mother Teresa House by contributing clothing, food, or money, and each of us readily gave whatever money we had with us that day. I realized as we said our good-byes that the nuns had been wise in allowing us to see the healthy children last, leaving us with a sense of hope and encouragement.

The tour had provided clear evidence that any unwanted or broken person was welcome in their midst. Like Mother Teresa, these women were demonstrating the love of Jesus to the poorest of the poor. I thanked God for the opportunity to see the work in person and to meet some of the individuals who were devoting their lives to ministering in the name of Jesus.

The unexpected bonus for Lena, Penelope, and me was that by taking us back to Kariobangi slum, the Lord had shown us that even in the midst of devastation and darkness, He can raise up beauty and hope. One woman's love for Christ and her compassion for the poorest of the poor had ignited a movement that has spread throughout the world and has blessed more people than she ever could have imagined.

Scalding Water

Heal me, Lord, and I will be healed;
save me and I will be saved,
for you are the one I praise.
—JEREMIAH 17:14

One day, during our before-school prayer time, we were asked to pray for Joel's toddler son. We were informed that while upcountry, his family cooked over an open fire, heating water in a large pot placed over the flames. Their child had stumbled and fallen into the scalding water, which immediately burned off much of his skin. The child had been rushed to a hospital for burn care, and then he had been released to his parents for recovery. Joel and his wife had returned to the school with their injured child.

My heart broke to hear of this tragedy. We learned that such burns were all too common. I had known of a similar case in Niger, but had not realized then that childhood burns were a frequent occurrence. In Niger, one of the girls in my class had been carrying a bucket of boiling water when she tripped and fell into it. She, too, was quickly treated for burns, and she had recovered well. I prayed that this child, too, would recover well.

In God's perfect plan, I had brought a first aid kit with me when I moved to Kenya. In it, I had included some xeroform burn dressings left over from my own use years ago. The dressings were designed exclusively to encourage new growth when skin needed to regenerate, whether that need was from a burn or from the removal of skin for a skin graft (as in my case).

After school, I went home to get the dressings and returned to the campus where Joel and his family were living in a tiny house. I visited with them briefly, offered them the burn dressings for their son, and prayed with them intensely that the Lord would heal the boy and give them hope for his recovery.

I never saw the child again, but I believe Joel remained in the employ of the school for some years, so I would guess that, like many of his peers, the child wore the burn scars on his body but carried on a relatively normal life. I hope and pray that since that terrible day, Kenyans have found more effective ways to avoid such tragedies among their young ones.

The Elephant Orphanage

On several occasions, a number of us teachers visited the elephant orphanage that was located nearby. David and Daphne Sheldrick were world-famous among animal lovers; they had created a safe haven for baby elephants whose mothers had been killed by poachers. They had also trained a few Kenyan men to be the babies' surrogate parents, caring for their every need.

During my third year in Kenya, I had become good friends with the Kiswahili teacher, a Kenyan man who was married and was the father of one set of twins already. His wife was expecting their second set (twin births were very common among Kenyans). He had invited me to come visit his family for the day. He had made me a map and given me detailed directions on how to reach his home.

I drove there alone, not realizing that his house was a far distance from the school and familiar surroundings. When I arrived, I met his family and we visited briefly. He said the children would like to go to the elephant orphanage, so the four of us packed up and headed out while his wife remained at home.

The children were thrilled with seeing the baby elephants, and on that occasion, there was also a baby rhino who had been found alone and starving. He had been adopted into the family of elephants. We watched, entranced, as the keepers played with the baby animals. They had a variety of large toys that the babies enjoyed throwing with their trunks or kicking with their front feet. Then the keepers fed the babies with large baby bottles while an announcer shared interesting facts about each individual animal. Then we watched as the keepers washed the animals, an activity that seemed much to their liking.

We were also given a tour of the elephant nursery, where each animal had a large stall with fresh hay laid on the ground. Each keeper was assigned to a specific animal, and the keeper would sleep on the ground next to his ward. There were two keepers for each baby so that the two men were able to take turns with the day and night duties. We watched a brief movie about the establishment of the nursery and then visited a small store with elephant-themed souvenirs. We were each given a postcard with further information about the nursery and its needs.

And then we returned back to my friend's house to share a beautiful meal made by his wife in our absence. After a good visit, I said good-bye to his family and headed home. When I reached a familiar area, I pulled in to a gas station to fill up our gas tank.

The station attendant checked my tires because he said one of them looked low to him. He found that I had a large metal barb in that tire. He said he was surprised the tire had not gone totally flat, and that I was truly blessed. He said the area from which I had just arrived was notorious for street thieves who would put the metal barbs on the dirt road so that when a visitor's car was stopped for a flat, they could rob the person. Once again, I was made aware of the Lord's protection over His beloved child (me). Thank you, Lord! I wonder how many times our Father rescues us without our ever knowing it.

Masai Mara

And God said, "Let the land produce living creatures according to their kinds: the livestock, the creatures that move along the ground, and the wild animals, each according to its kind." And it was so ... And God saw that it was good.
—Genesis 1:24–25

One school break, five of us women headed out to visit Masai Mara. We had booked accommodations in an incredible "tourist camp" where each of us had our own large, luxurious tent with a concrete floor, separate bathroom, large soft bed, and attractive furnishings. The bathrooms all had walls of individually set stones and showers with hot water (not always the case in Africa). The tents were unusually spacious. The walls were made of a thick white canvas material, but from inside, the accommodations looked more like motel rooms than tents.

Outside, there was a central lounging area with a hammock and some small tables and chairs. There were a few tamed animals who wandered about at will. One day, Penelope was lying in the hammock reading a book when an exceptionally large warthog walked right under the hammock, scraping the bottom of the hammock with his back. Penelope was not sure whether to remain still or attempt to flee, but a nearby camp employee assured her that she was safe. The employee said warthogs were generally shy, but that those in the camp were quite accustomed to people, so they were totally unafraid of coming near. She said that warthogs were generally unaggressive, and that these domesticated ones were of no danger to the guests.

At the camp, we had hired a tour guide to take us to a Maasai village (Masai is the place, Maasai is the people). When he arrived, he piled us all into his Rover and took off across the vast yellow plains of dried grasses and occasional trees and bushes.

When we arrived at the village, a man from the tribe met us outside. He was wrapped in a red plaid blanket, the traditional garment of the Maasai men. The day was intensely hot and he was sweating profusely. He explained that it was not the climate that was causing him to sweat, but rather he was running a fever because he had malaria. He started the tour by walking over to the nearby bushes and explaining that his people made a brew out of the leaves of the bushes to treat malaria. He was completely confident that he would be well in a few days.

Then he took us inside the Maasai village. Maasai men used to be lion-hunters. They believed that lions were afraid of red, so traditionally all Maasai men and women wore red clothing. The men also painted their hair and bodies with a red dye made from mud. They grew their hair long while they were single, then cut off the long plaits and kept their hair closely cropped after they were married.

In contrast, the women and children always had closely cropped hair. The women wore many heavy circular metal necklaces around their necks. The necklaces looked almost as if someone had cut a hole in a thin metal dinner plate and then decorated it with beads. We would see later that when the women danced, the decorative necklaces would bounce up and down. We asked about the weight of the necklaces, because they appeared to be quite heavy. Our guide told us that the women often applied a special gel to their necks to protect them from the weight and the chafing of their skin.

Since Maasai men were no longer allowed to hunt lions, they had become cattlemen, and because cattle were considered prized property by several opposing tribes, the Maasai tribes built their villages protectively. They placed their mud huts next to each other in a circular fashion with all the openings facing inward. There was a large open courtyard in the middle. Behind the huts, they had planted a thick wall of sharp thorny bushes. At night, the cattle were brought in to the enclosure and a gate of sharp thornbushes was closed to keep thieves out.

When we walked through the opening into the Maasai village, the strong smell of cow dung was overpowering. Our guide escorted us into one of the huts, which he explained was built of mud made from straw and cow manure. We entered the large room inside which served multiple purposes with a kitchen area in one corner and a bedroom area in another. There was only one large bed where all the family would sleep together.

The man introduced us to a woman who was cooking over an open fire in the corner. The temperature outside had been high, but inside we found the air to be stifling, both because of the higher temperature created by the cooking fire and the stench of cow manure. After listening to a brief description of life in a Maasai village, we were relieved to be escorted back outside.

The courtyard area in the middle was carpeted with layers of cow dung, and the flies were thick and aggressive. As we walked across the yard, I was most uncomfortable when several flies flew up from the dung into the inside of my long dress. I quickly and discreetly pulled open the neckline, and, much to my relief and embarrassment, the flies flew back out of my dress. That little experience gave me the creeps!

We noticed a group of seven young children who were gathered near one of the huts. They were totally engrossed in watching us visitors, at least until we asked and were granted permission to take a few photos with them. As each of us stepped forward for our turn to pose with them, some of the younger children hid behind their older siblings or friends. Not wanting to frighten them any further, we took our pictures quickly and moved on.

Next, we were escorted to a shaded area outside of the village, where many of the tribesmen and women were waiting for us with a large display of clothing, jewelry, and souvenirs spread out on the ground. The traditional clothing worn by our hosts was noticeably threadbare. Each of us sought to find some item to buy, primarily to show honor for their hospitality and to contribute to the village's obvious need for funds. Then we packed up and headed back to our camp for the night.

The following day, we had booked a tour guide to take us on a two-day photo safari of the region. What an amazing experience that was! The guide picked us up in what looked like an elongated Jeep with three rows of seats, each row being a bit higher than the row in front of it so that all passengers had a clear view of the terrain. The jeep was open to the air, but there was a flat canopy above the seats to provide some shade.

At the younger teachers' insistence, I sat in the front row with the guide. Before he began to drive, he gave us careful instructions regarding our proximity to the animals so that we would not disturb them or cause any unfortunate incident. He said to be very quiet, whispering only, and that if an animal should come near or climb on the vehicle, we should remain calm and still, keep our hands inside the vehicle, and make no sudden movements or noises. With those instructions, we headed out into safari country for the day.

We saw a lion pride with the father, two females, and several cubs, a rhino standing in the shade, a number of Cape buffalo, zebras and elands grazing together, multiple gazelles, a lioness and her babies resting in the top of a tree, and several elephants. We saw one elephant with her one-week-old baby carefully protected at her side. Her sister and her young elephant niece stood nearby. But for me, the highlight of the day was the mother cheetah and her babies.

After we had seen most of the other animals, the guide asked if we were interested in searching for a cheetah; he thought he might know where to find one. We all answered in the affirmative, and off he went, traveling for some distance before he parked near several trees. Then he silently pointed to the scene unfolding before us.

There was a mother cheetah lying in the shade, teaching her three babies how to climb a tree. She would nudge one of the cubs over toward the trunk of the tree and gently push the baby upward with her nose. The baby would begin to climb the trunk and, after a few tiny steps, it would fall back onto the soft grassy ground below. Unlike cats, the babies did not land on their feet, but on their backs. Each time a cub fell, Mama would gently nudge that one or a sibling to give it another try.

We watched in silent wonder for quite a while, and then the mother cheetah calmly got up and walked toward our car. She jumped up on the hood and sat there scanning the high grasses in front of the vehicle. The guide whispered that she was hunting for game. But her babies were not happy with her being out of reach. They unsuccessfully tried to jump up on a front tire, but they met with no success. Then they all began to cry.

Initially, we did not recognize that the sounds we heard were coming from the babies. We heard what sounded like birds chirping, but when I asked the guide what the sound was, he whispered that the babies were crying. The cubs continued to jump and paw the vehicle, but their mama was entirely focused on the field.

Mama Cheetah stayed on our vehicle for about thirty minutes, allowing us ample time to get plenty of amazing photos, including one of me in the front seat and her on the hood directly behind me. We were separated only by the short front window of the Jeep. Eventually, she jumped down and slowly walked away, with three adorable cubs happily bouncing in the tall grass, following close at her heels.

We resumed our travels, passing various herds of animals along the way, and then we stopped for a picnic lunch out on the open grasslands. Sitting next to the Jeep on a blanket spread with an array of foods, we ate our lunch in sight of various wild animals grazing nearby.

The following day, our guide took us out for a second safari and we saw many more amazing scenes, but he was disappointed that we were never successful in spotting a leopard. The guide told us that the "top five" animals sought for photo safaris were the elephants, leopards, lions, Cape buffalo, and rhinos. Personally, I was quite content with having seen four of the five animals I had never expected to see outside of a zoo. In the United States, Germany, and Spain, I had always loved visiting zoos, but seeing the animals in their natural habitat was a truly magnificent experience.

When we returned to school after the vacation break, we all shared our favorite highlights of the trip with the staff members who had not gone along. When I shared that I found being that close to a cheetah an amazingly peaceful experience, Penelope responded, "Maybe for you!"

I was surprised at her response since she had been sitting in the far back of the vehicle. Nonetheless, I was grateful that she had remembered the guide's instruction to remain calm and quiet. Thank you, Lord, for the peace I experienced and for Your gentle hand upon the one who was afraid.

Nairobi Game Park

Now the Lord God had formed out of the ground all the wild
animals and all the birds in the sky. He brought them to the
man to see what he would name them; and whatever the man
called each living creature, that was its name.

—GENESIS 2:19

A few weeks after our adventure in Masai Mara, Lena, Penelope, and I decided to check out the wildlife in our own back yard. For five hours, we drove around in the Nairobi Game Park, seeing many of the same animals we had seen on safari. The Park covered about forty-five square miles and was enclosed by electric fencing on three sides and a river on the south side, thus allowing migratory animals to freely move in and out of the park.

The only scary moment was when we rounded a bend and came upon a rhino a little too close for comfort. We had been informed that though they have very poor eyesight, rhinos have an excellent sense of smell. We had been advised that they could be dangerously aggressive when annoyed. We prayed that the wind would not carry our scent in his direction. We held our breath while Lena quietly backed up the car and rerouted us to safer ground. Thankfully, we had not disturbed his repose.

As we wandered throughout the park, we found it mind-boggling to realize these creatures lived so near to a booming city of millions of people. We even managed a few photos showing the wildlife in the forefront with the city skyline in the background. Wonder of wonders!

Tsavo Game Park

Great are the works of the Lord;
they are pondered by all who delight in them.

—PSALM 111:2

My last outing in Kenya was a trip to the Tsavo Game Park during our Christmas break in 2003. Four of us ladies had headed out to spend a few days in a luxurious resort where the open-air dining room overlooked two natural waterholes. As we ate our meals, we could watch the animals gathering for a drink: elephants, zebras, ostriches, Cape buffalo, giraffes, impala, warthogs, dik-diks, bushbuck, African wild dogs, and other animals came at different times of the day, some sharing the space and some waiting until the other animals had left. We even saw an occasional big cat towards the evening when all the other animals were gone.

We soon learned that the waterholes were not the only draw for wildlife at the resort. Whenever we sat on our back patios to lounge and snack, we were joined by a number of hornbills. Hornbills are big birds with lots of personality! They were not too shy to land on the low dividing wall along the back of the patios to feast on the crumbs we set out for them. In the afternoons, we could sit there feeding the birds and gazing up at Mt. Kilimanjaro in the distance. What a majestic sight! I had read about that mountain in my teen years when I was an avid Ernest Hemingway fan, but I had never dreamed that I would see it in person. I had written in my journal,

> December 28, 2003: Thank you, Father, for the beauty of this place and the healing effect your creation has upon me. Thank you for the opportunity to step aside from the demands of daily life to drink in the beauty and peace all around us. Your creation is beyond description—mountains of varying hues and shapes, foliage plentiful and sparse, birds singing of your constant care, animals meandering on the plains of your provision. To see your creatures in their natural habitat is such a gift!

In advance, we had booked a tour guide to take us out into the bush to search for the elusive Top Five. At this location, the safari vehicle was a small closed tour bus with massive windows all around. Being the only clients in the bus, when an animal was spotted, we could easily move closest to the window with the best view.

On the first trip out, our guide took us to a river where there was a footbridge over the waterway. As we walked over the bridge, below us were more than twenty hippos lounging in the shallow water. Our guide informed us that hippos kill more people in Africa than any other animals. Hippos are naturally territorial and it is dangerous for a person to get between a hippo and a body of water. Their primary means of killing people is by drowning them.

We also saw some Cape buffalo, which we had seen in the past, but we had not known before how dangerous they can be as well. Our guide informed us that a Cape buffalo should never be approached because it could attack by head-butting, often killing the victim.

As we traveled, we had seen frequent mounds that appeared to be made of mud. We learned that the mounds were anthills, often almost as tall as I was. We stopped to get photos of the anthills, but after my experiences in Niger, I was extremely careful not to get close enough to get bitten.

Next, we took a short walk through a forested area. The guide carried a rifle while we walked along the pathways. There was a small body of water beyond the trees where a few crocodiles lazed in the sun. Our guide pointed out several baboons lounging in a large tree and explained he was carrying the rifle to protect us, just in case the baboons headed our direction.

A few minutes later, he pointed out a mother monkey and her baby well hidden among the branches of a tree. The baby was clinging to Mama's chest and Mama was keeping a close eye on us. The guide reminded us that monkeys have sharp teeth and a mother monkey can be quite ferocious.

We saw a full-grown ostrich strolling across the road, and again we were advised to be cautious; ostriches can be quite aggressive. I was beginning to wonder if there were many animals that were not dangerous in Kenya!

Over a few days' time, we made a number of excursions out into the bush, both in the mornings and the afternoons. The second or third day, I was too tired to ride on one more safari drive, so I remained at the resort when the others took off in the morning. After a leisurely breakfast, I was walking back to my room when I spotted a large turquoise, blue, and purple lizard who was enjoying his grasshopper lunch on the side of a tree out in the middle of a grassy area. Wearing only flip flops, I had carefully picked my way through the tall green grass to get a closer look at him and to take some photos.

Suddenly, I heard a Kenyan woman calling out to me, "Madam! Madam! Come away from the tree! You are standing in the grass where the snakes live!" Needless to say, I deserted my photo shoot and sprinted back to safer ground in a flash—but I still have a great photo of the lizard and his lunch!

When the others returned, they excitedly reported that they had seen a leopard in the wild. Charlotte was quick to report that when Joyce spotted the leopard, she started shouting, "Leopard! Leopard! Leopard!" and the big cat quickly disappeared into the nearby foliage. In her excitement, she had completely forgotten the instructions to always speak softly on a safari. During the rest of the trip, the others repeatedly teased her about her momentary indiscretion, shouting "Leopard, leopard, leopard!" and laughing gleefully.

On the last night of our adventure, we attended a presentation of Maasai warriors singing and dancing in their full regalia. We had seen Maasai dancers before, and these men were equally impressive, but somehow watching them dance and leap inside a plush hotel lobby was not the same as seeing them in a more natural setting. Nonetheless, we thoroughly enjoyed their presentation.

The next morning, we packed up and returned to Nairobi, content and refreshed, to spend our last few days of vacation preparing our lesson plans for the next week's classes.

Mama Mary and the Water Pump

Now to him who is able to do immeasurably more than all we ask or imagine, according to his power that is at work within us, to him be glory in the church and in Christ Jesus throughout all generations, for ever and ever! Amen.

—EPHESIANS 3:20–21

Whenever I had moved in the past, one of my first goals was always to find a good church. Nairobi was no exception. Lena and Trudy had chosen a church downtown while Penelope and I had become involved in a large church in our community where the congregation consisted of both Kenyans and missionaries.

The services were invigorating every week, so I must admit I was a bit surprised when Easter Sunday was not even grander: no fanfare, no unique choice of clothing, no mention of resurrection. I guess if a congregation is actively celebrating every week, one could say they were always exercising the joy of Easter. And, in fact, they were! The only time I saw a livelier service was once when I visited an indigenous Kenyan church where the pastor literally instructed everyone to stand and dance during the worship songs. What fun!

The first time we attended a women's group at our church, we marveled at the depth of their faith and strength in prayer. Those women could pray portions of Scripture back to the Lord like nothing I had ever heard. The first few times I joined with them in prayer, I was hesitant to pray aloud because of their prayer expertise. Their devotion to prayer and their commitment to memorizing the Word humbled and challenged me to stretch and grow in my expressions of love for the Lord.

Penelope and I became good friends with a few of the Kenyan women. One Sunday after church, one of them invited us to go with her to help out at a local orphanage, another experience that proved to be humbling and eye-opening.

When we arrived, Mama Mary, the director of the orphanage, assigned each of us to specific tasks involved in bathing all the children. The children were lined up in two long rows, all of them stark naked. As they reached the front of the line, two of us were assigned to submerge a washcloth into a bucket of sudsy water and wash down the child's body, then rinse with clean water and wrap a towel around the child. The next two women would pat them dry, and the last two would apply Vaseline to their naked bodies. We were informed that the Vaseline protected the children's skin from the harsh elements of the environment. Then the children chose a few items from a pile of clean clothing and dressed themselves.

Having always been a modest person, I found it confronting that these children were allowed no privacy whatsoever. In their culture, or perhaps growing up in an orphanage, the practice of group bathing may have been common, but from the looks on some of the children's faces, the practice was not a welcome one. I tried to bathe each child quickly and discreetly, allowing him or her to use the washcloth independently for more private areas. The children and I did not make eye contact during the entire process.

By the time we finished, all the children were fully dressed and the bathing brigade had been disassembled. The children sang a few songs, Mama Mary thanked us for our help, and we drove back to our own house. But the sight of those beautiful little people who had no mothers or fathers had touched my heart deeply. On the way home, Penelope and I discussed our reactions and decided we would return at a later date to ask Mama Mary and her daughter, Jane, if there was a way we could help out on a regular basis.

So began a beautiful and rewarding relationship with Mama Mary, Jane, and their precious wards. There were 110 children from the age of six weeks to nineteen years of age. The first few times we visited, we were asked to hold and rock the babies, who needed as much physical contact as possible to be well socialized and emotionally healthy. There were two Kenyan women whose full-time job it was to care for the babies, so they were especially grateful for reinforcements.

Mama Mary explained that some of the babies and children were actually the sons and daughters of prostitutes who could not afford to care for them, but their mothers would occasionally visit them. However, the majority of the children were the orphans of parents who had died of Aids. In the early 2000's, Aids was sweeping the continent, creating widespread devastation throughout Africa.

Jane was a trained nurse who ran a much-needed Aids clinic next door to the orphanage. Her knowledge of the disease was extensive and her desire to educate her neighbors was sincere. She felt personally committed to helping every Aids patient develop the best quality of life possible while she also sought to educate her vulnerable neighbors on the pros and cons of adequate protection against the disease.

Sometimes when we visited, we played with the children, and sometimes we helped Mama Mary with whatever task she was undertaking. Mama Mary and Jane were always working and always ready to share about the orphanage and its children. Penelope and I were getting an up-close education about the reality of poverty, disease, and their long-term effects.

On New Year's Day, 2004, Penelope and I took two friends along with us to visit the orphanage, but when we arrived, the scene was not a happy one. Mama Mary, Jane, and all the children were spread out in the large open area, sitting on the sandy ground and looking miserable. When we asked the women why everyone was so sad, Mama Mary explained that their water pump had broken on Christmas Day and they had had no clean water since then. The pump was old and they would need $4000 to replace it, a sum far beyond their reach.

For seven days, the children had been searching for nearby water sources. They had walked long distances while carrying empty buckets and food containers for scooping up water from mud puddles or any leaky faucet they could find. They were tired and discouraged, and if they did not get clean water soon, surely some of them would become ill.

Like Job's friends, we sat on the ground with them and grieved deeply for a while. Then we decided to pray together for the Lord's wisdom. We all sat there for a long time, verbally and silently praying, and then we discussed various ways we might be able to raise the funds for a new pump. But none of the ideas we considered were likely to raise that much money.

Then one of us suggested that maybe Mama Mary could hire a water truck to fill the two storage tanks so that at least they would have some water in the interim while we tried to find a more permanent solution. Mama Mary and Jane were doubtful that plan would work, and where would they get the money for the interim water? We returned to silent prayer.

And then the Lord moved in an unexpected way. As I was praying silently, the Lord reminded me that about a month earlier, one of my financial partners had sent $1000 to my Wycliffe account, instructing me to use it for a special project. I had been waiting for the Lord to reveal what that project might be, and now He had shown me!

I excitedly told the other adults of the Lord's reminder and suggested that we could use the $1000 as seed money to raise the other $3000 we would need for a new pump. I told them that I was willing to write to all my prayer partners and financial partners to tell them of our dilemma and ask for their help.

I suspected that raising the money would take a considerable amount of time. We discussed the possibility that maybe Mama Mary could promise to pay 50% of the money up front and then request monthly installment payments for the next five months; that plan would give us longer to raise the full amount. The others agreed that the plan might be worth trying. We prayed some more with Mama Mary and Jane, asking for the Lord's blessing on our plans, and for His touch on the hearts of those He had chosen to help us.

The next thing I knew, Mama Mary had announced to all the children that I would be buying them a new pump! I had thought we were still discussing possibilities, and suddenly the responsibility of raising the funds was placed firmly on my shoulders. I urged her to make it clear to the children that we were still seeking solutions and that I did not have $4000.

The four of us visitors left the orphanage excited and encouraged, though I was sincerely hoping I had not gotten in over my head. I spent the rest of the day preparing a letter to email to all my supporters, and I sent it out at midnight that night.

The very next day, one couple sent me notice that they had contributed $2000 to my account, and within three days, I had received notices of contribution amounts that added up to the remaining $1000 we had needed. Praise God from Whom all blessings flow! We had raised the full amount in three days. God alone had demonstrated His love and provision much faster than we ever could have imagined. But He was not done yet! The money kept coming, so we were able to buy the orphanage a new washing machine as well.

I contacted my Kenyan friend who had first connected us with the orphanage, and she was invaluable in instructing me on how to successfully procure a new pump. She warned me that Kenyan businessmen could often be extremely fickle, especially if the cash was presented prematurely. She urged me to keep the money safe in my possession, go with Mama Mary to the pump engineer's office, and make it very clear to him that the money would not be released until the pump was successfully installed. She warned me that paying even a deposit in advance could be unwise, and that I needed the agreement in writing before any work was done.

I am not a particularly business-minded person, so the idea of meeting with the engineer was quite intimidating for me. I knew I would need to be fully dependent on the Holy Spirit's guidance. When we met in his office and presented our proposition, he flatly refused to accept monthly installments. He insisted on 50% down and the other 50% within thirty days. I think he was as surprised as I was that, with the strength of the Holy Spirit, I was able to make and hold my stand for the sake of those precious children. He eventually agreed to 50% when the pump work began and 50% when it was completed.

The pump was installed and inspected by the appropriate authorities, and then the first water was drawn as the children cheered and held up the empty containers they would no longer have to fill with dirty water. The Lord had performed a miracle, and every person present was fully aware of that fact. He had proven again that nothing is impossible for Him (Jeremiah 32:27 and Luke 1:37). Sing alleluia to the King!

Prayer and Fasting

But when you fast, put oil on your head and wash your face,
so that it will not be obvious to others that you are fasting, but
only to your Father, who is unseen; and your Father, who sees
what is done in secret, will reward you.

—MATTHEW 6:17–18

Penelope was the first person I ever knew who faithfully followed this command. I had not been trained to make fasting a part of my prayer life, but she consistently and quietly fasted every Friday for twelve hours while teaching school all day with a smile on her face and a bounce in her step. I was definitely impressed; she made it look so easy. Nonetheless, I was not eager to try it myself.

But a dear friend at church had other ideas. When I had shared with her my concerns for my mother, who had left her faith when my sister died young, my friend insisted that if I wanted to see my mother come back to Christ, I must spend time in prayer and fasting. She challenged me to join her in fasting for twenty-four hours and then to come to her house for a morning of praying together. She was quite persuasive, and she made it very clear that refusing was not an option.

Fasting was harder than I thought it would be, but I lasted for twenty-four hours on only water, and then I drove to her house that Saturday morning. When I arrived, I met her prayer partner, who had decided to join us for the day. Together, we spent the next three hours praying for my mother's broken heart and for her salvation. I was blown away by the intensity of their prayers, and again by their ability to call up the perfect

Bible verses from memory. The morning was exciting and exhausting as the three of us lay our petitions before the Lord.

When the two other women felt we had completed the Holy Spirit's agenda, we began to rejoice, thanking the Lord and singing praise songs. Then they invited me to join them for a celebratory meal. To my amazement, my hostess filled a large rectangular table with multiple bowls brimming with delectable African delicacies. The two of them eagerly began eating everything in sight, but after fasting for twenty-four hours, I found that my stomach was not in a big hurry for a large meal. I nibbled at this and that, enjoyed interacting with the two of them, and when it was appropriate, I thanked them for their prayers and returned home.

My heart was full and hopeful. I had been praying for my mom for many years, but for two strangers who would never meet her to have cared that deeply and to have invested their time to pray for her had blessed me beyond description.

The answer to our prayers did not come right away, but it did come in God's time. I am reminded of the verse in Revelation describing bowls in heaven filled with the prayers of the saints (Revelation 5:8). I know that day of prayer contributed to the bowl filling up with prayers for my mother. God used that day and those two women to teach me the importance of praying continually (1 Thessalonians 5:16-18).

Lamu: Bringing Light to Dark Places

Your word is a lamp for my feet,
a light on my path.
—PSALM 119:105

April 14, 2004, was the most memorable Easter I have ever experienced in my life. At the time, I was on the island of Lamu off the coast of Kenya. The appearance of the island reminded me of Venice with narrow streets, buildings closely packed together, and the city being surrounded by water, but there the similarity ended: on Lamu, all adults were in Muslim apparel and the only means of land transportation beyond walking was riding donkeys.

Six other missionaries (three young men and three young women) and I had traveled there for a much-needed vacation. In God's perfect way, on the first day we just 'happened' to meet a young couple who had moved to the island two years earlier with their two little daughters; they had come to plant a Christian church. They invited us to join them for an Easter service the following morning. They told us that historically, the island had been 97% Muslim, but recently the percentage had dropped to 90% and the percentage of Christians had slowly begun to increase.

Early Easter morning, Steve and Jenifer (the pastor and his wife) and their daughters (ages six and eight) came to our guesthouse to walk with us to church. We walked through narrow streets surrounded by closely-packed little homes. We saw few men along the way, but the women were dressed in all black from their heads to their toes, with veils covering the lower half of their faces. Their children looked the same as children everywhere, frolicking happily with their neighbors. With six of us having white skin and all seven of us wearing colorful clothing, we felt totally exposed, and because we were carrying Bibles, it was readily apparent that we were Christians.

I assumed we would arrive at a private home where a few individuals had cautiously and quietly gathered, but instead we could hear the music and singing before we even saw the building. When we arrived, we entered a recently-built structure with a large sanctuary, concrete floors and backless wooden benches, a powerful sound system, and a few smaller rooms for Sunday School, food preparation, and meetings. There were many people already gathered, and the celebration had begun.

The service officially began at 9:30 a.m., and it finally ended at 6:30 p.m.! In that time, we sang beautiful praise songs, read Scriptures, listened and watched the choir sing and dance, listened to the pastor's sermon about that first Easter morning, and dedicated several new believers. We worshiped enthusiastically, in Spirit and in truth!

For us mazungus (white people), key parts of the Kiswahili were translated into English, but I realized when I heard the translation that the Lord had temporarily given me the ability to understand most of what was being said without hearing it in English.

The sense of corporate worship and God's presence was strong. Many individuals gave their personal testimonies about being delivered from

128

the traditions which had bound them—for example, one woman said that through prayer and the teachings of the church, she had developed the courage to remove the charm that had been tied around her middle when she gave birth to her first child. She rejoiced in new freedom for herself and her family. Many others shared similar stories of joyful redemption.

For me, time passed without notice, but for my companions, the time moved all too slowly. They grew steadily more restless, for they had planned to go boating in the afternoon. Except for the one Kenyan among us, the others were not experiencing my same God-given ability to understand the language around them. When they informed me that they had decided to leave the service, the Holy Spirit whispered to me: "Stay. And learn." They were surprised at my decision, but quickly and quietly left the sanctuary around noon.

Little did I know that the day was just beginning. While the choir had been singing and dancing, I had noticed one woman with a badly deformed face. She appeared to have a large tumor in her left cheek. I kept sensing the Lord's direction to pray for her, and when I told the pastor's wife, she passed it on to her husband. The pastor followed me outside to say goodbye to my companions while his wife summoned the woman to join us outside.

After saying our farewells, the pastor introduced Lydia to me and explained to her in Kiswahili that I felt led to pray for her. We moved behind the building where we could not be observed by others. He and his wife laid hands on her shoulders and I placed my hands on her face. We prayed and praised at length in tongues, English, and Kiswahili, and soon she was slain in the Spirit. She gently collapsed to the ground as the pastor supported her body. We continued praying for a while, and when Lydia got up, she gave me a big hug. The pastor encouraged her by saying her healing would take time, but that it had begun. Praise God! Then we all returned to the service inside.

Shortly after we went back inside, the pastor gave his sermon and the congregation received communion. Then three people who had been baptized were dedicated to the Lord. And then things took an unexpected turn (at least for me). The elders had asked for people to come forward if they wanted prayer, and after several others had been prayed for, another man came to the front.

When he quietly told the elders why he had come forth, they immediately began to pray for his deliverance. While we watched, he literally vomited out some of the evil that was being removed from his body. Then the elders took him into another room with all the other men. As they left, the pastor asked the women to remain in the sanctuary to back up the men in prayers for deliverance and salvation.

In the next few hours, I experienced the meaning of the Body of Christ in new and powerful ways. This type of prayer was fairly new to me, though I had witnessed a deliverance among charismatic Catholics some years before, an experience that had thoroughly frightened me. But as the prayer continued, the Lord kept whispering to my spirit, "Stay. Observe. There is no reason to be afraid."

The men all prayed in one room while the women prayed intensely in the sanctuary. We prayed individually, in pairs, all together, with prayers, songs, and Scriptures. At times, we heard the men shouting, "in the name of Jesus!" and periodically, someone came to report to the women what was happening.

We learned that initially, the man had indicated his need for deliverance. During his prayer time with the men, he gave up many of his charms, which were promptly burned. One charm was about the size of a quarter, but when they placed it on the floor to burn, it turned into a large black beetle four times the size of the coin and it quickly scuttled away.

The man also confessed that he had placed a cursed charm in the offering plate, a charm which was retrieved and destroyed. At various times, the men heard different demons speaking from the man's mouth. Eventually, he was delivered of seven demons, leaving the three strongest ones still within him. The men continued to pray fervently, as did the women in the other room.

But sadly, after much more prayer, the man confessed that he was a willing channel for demons, being paid by individuals from the mosque and the Jehovah's Witnesses church to sow division in Christian churches. He confessed that he had already been to the Methodist church and that he had every intention of returning there when he had finished his work in this church.

It was then that Steve (the pastor) sent for Jenifer and me to join the men in the prayer room, and he also sent someone to bring two elders from the Methodist church. I was puzzled at being asked to join the men, but obediently followed Jenifer to the room. As I entered, the demon-possessed man totally focused on me, and I could see pure hatred in his eyes. I recognized that as one of only a few whites on the small island, I would be very easy to find, and I prayed for the Lord's protection.

Upon arrival, the Methodist elders confirmed that this same man had been banned from their church. Then the demon-possessed man stated that he had no intention of becoming a Christian and that he preferred to remain in the employ of the devil. He even demanded his charms back, saying (in his language), "You've taken all my powers!"

The men continued to converse with him and to clearly present his two options: heaven or hell. He replied that he had been to hell already and that he chose to continue working for those who paid him to sow division because they brought him women. I was stunned that anyone would choose the devil over Jesus. Finally, the men acknowledged his choice and stepped aside.

As we all left the prayer room, the children joined us from the Sunday School room. The demon-possessed man walked straight to the back of the sanctuary, picked up a long walking stick, and began to WHACK it hard across a back bench. He shouted something in Kiswahili and left. The pastor laughed and said that the man had just cursed us all, but we were covered by Christ. There was no reason to fear! Families began to say farewell to one another, and the sanctuary slowly emptied.

As we prepared to leave, one of Steve's daughters asked to carry my Bible. She was thrilled when I handed it to her. I marveled at this child's faith—like her father and mother, she was totally unafraid. She gave new meaning to the Scripture stating that "a little child shall lead them" (Isaiah 11:6). I was humbled by her courage.

As we walked through the maze of tiny streets, I was acutely aware of the Muslims all around us, their watchful eyes and silence, and the devastation of their lostness. I was greatly relieved that we were not confronted or assaulted by anyone along the way.

Steve's family dropped me off at the guesthouse where I awaited the return of my companions. When they arrived, we had a nice dinner together. They excitedly shared the details of their day, though I said little or nothing about mine. Then we headed to our separate sleeping quarters for the night.

Because my back was bothering me, I pulled my mattress off the bedframe and laid it on the floor. As I did so, a large black beetle crawled out from under the bed and scuttled across the floor. Disliking all bugs, Penelope was quite upset by the sudden appearance of a beetle, and she voiced her concern about my sleeping on the floor. But I was still enveloped by the Lord's peace, which had been so strong all day. I slept soundly without incident.

The following day, my companions and I rode donkeys to the other side of the island. After several hours of our wandering through tiny shops and walking along the beach, the young ones decided to swim in the ocean for a while and I returned to our guesthouse by boat.

Quite by accident (in God's perfect way), my friends met up with Steve and Jenifer after I had left. The pastor and his wife shared the details of the deliverance ministry that had occurred the day before. Later, when Penelope returned to our room, she expressed her surprise about what she had learned from Steve and Jenifer. She asked me how I could sleep on the floor after witnessing the deliverance ministry and seeing the beetle in our room. I did not really have an answer for her, perhaps because I was still digesting all that I had witnessed.

In fact, it took me several weeks to absorb the many lessons the Lord had taught me in those nine hours. I could not begin to list them all now, but, perhaps most importantly, I had learned that God is more powerful than we could ever imagine, that He alone can heal and protect His children, and that He gives us free will to follow or fall away. I learned that true worship transcends time, thirst, and hunger, and that if we truly care for our lost loved ones, we need to pray for them without ceasing. I have never forgotten that crash course in spiritual warfare, and the Lord has definitely used it to intensify my prayers for those who do not know Christ.

The personal bonus for me in the midst of all the other lessons was that the Lord answered a question I had been asking for several months. I had been wrestling with my feelings about ongoing digestive and breathing problems; I had been wondering if I should remain in Kenya. When we returned from our trip, I was meditating on the lessons I had learned in

Lamu when I heard the Holy Spirit whisper to my heart, "You are exactly where you belong. It isn't about health or work but about Me. It is all about obedience. I can use you, if you are willing." My answer: "Lord, I am willing!"

Apartheid

There is neither Jew nor Gentile, neither slave nor free, nor is there male and female, for you are all one in Christ Jesus.
— GALATIANS 3:28

Apartheid has many faces, and none of them are pretty. Most of us associate that word with South Africa, Nelson Mandela, and the horrendous history of racial mistreatment in years past. But the attitudes of apartheid were subtly present in other African countries as well. I learned that sad truth through personal experience in Kenya.

I had noticed small signs along the way—the Kenyan workers were pleased but surprised when I daily greeted them in Kiswahili and briefly engaged them in conversation; the Kenyan couple whom we invited to dinner was noticeably uncomfortable and confessed they had never before been invited into a white person's home; the neighborhood children lined up to watch me prune some bushes one day, and when I asked our guard why they were watching me, he said they had never before seen a white woman work. What?? Kenya had been an independent nation since the 1960's, and the whites were still viewed as the 'masters?' What's wrong with this picture?

I also overheard a school administrator shouting at the workers a few times after school when most teachers were no longer within earshot. Sadly, I witnessed one situation that especially distressed me: one of the workers was fired because he did not show up for work for several days. Even though he explained that he had been home with malaria and had no access to a phone, he was fired on the spot.

And then the issue became personal in my third school year. Housemates had shifted at various points as girls became engaged or married. The third year, two new American teachers moved in with Penelope and me: one was super young and one was sixty-five years old. We were just beginning to become a new family when our housing situation was suddenly turned upside down.

One morning during the staff prayer meeting, the principal announced that he had decided to close the teacher house for various reasons. Consequently, we would all need to move. At first, his words did not even compute. Was he serious?? We all stared at him in silence and disbelief.

He went on to explain that he had already spoken with the older woman and the younger one and that he had found each of them a new housing arrangement. He further announced that he wanted Penelope and me to move as soon as possible so that the teacher house could be sold.

The next few days were horribly stressful. The older woman moved immediately and the younger girl moved in with a friend shortly thereafter, leaving Penelope and me alone with the added responsibility of helping to close down the house while searching for new housing and working full-time.

Penelope wanted to live in an apartment with Kenyan neighbors while I decided to move into a small house that was available directly across the street from the school. However, to live there I would need a housemate to share the rent. I invited one of the Kenyan teachers to move in with me. We were both quite excited about living together.

I lived in a large missionary community where there were no secrets for long. When one man learned that I planned to live with a Kenyan woman, he emphatically voiced his disapproval. He told me flatly that I could not live with her. I tried to gently remind him that who I lived with was my choice and was not of concern to him. But my answer did not sit well with him, so he began to verbally harass me whenever others were not near enough to hear his words.

The Kenyan woman and I were delighted to move into our new home. It was a cute little cottage with a small living room, a tiny kitchen, three small bedrooms, and a bathroom. Outside, there was a beautiful garden with flowers of every possible color and description, some tall shade trees, and little pathways wandering throughout the small yard. The house came with a guard dog, a day guard, a silent security system, and the usual thick white walls and metal gate.

The two of us thoroughly enjoyed living together. She was passionate about her call to teaching, she had a great sense of humor, and she was a good cook. She taught me about many of the surrounding tribes and about her family history growing up in Kenya. She shared that she had gone to the U.S. for advanced education and had remained there to teach in an American university for several years. But she had missed her family and her home! She had returned to Kenya at great financial loss, but did not regret her decision.

I loved waiting to see her return from the hair salon every few weeks. The hairstyles she chose were spectacular, setting off her beautiful face; they were unlike any hairstyles I had ever seen before. Her hair texture naturally allowed for elaborate hairstyles.

When Penelope gave up trying to find an apartment with Kenyan neighbors, we invited her to move in with us. The three of us made a great team; life might have been close to perfect, if it had not been for the ongoing tension created by our disgruntled neighbor.

Sadly, he not only continued to harass me privately, but he also found not-so-subtle ways to create situations that stressed all three of us. On countless occasions, we sought the Lord's help. We made every effort to seek peace with our neighbor, but he would not have it.

Finally, I reached the breaking point when he sought to undermine my good standing with SIL. After much prayer, I called my SIL contact, told her what was happening, and requested a transfer to a different school. Over the next few days, we talked on the phone many times as she counseled me regarding my dilemma and possible solutions. When it was decided that my leaving the school was the best option, I turned in my written two-week notice of resignation to the principal, giving no specific reason for my decision.

During my remaining days at the school, my neighbor continued to harass me unmercifully. The school found a replacement teacher, and together the two of us began the transition phase to gently prepare the children for my absence and her presence. In late October, I tearfully said good-bye to my precious students and walked away from the job I had loved. I have no idea whether or not the harassment stopped after I had left, but I do know that both of my housemates resigned and moved away at the end of the school year.

Uganda?

Whether you turn to the right or to the left, your ears will
hear a voice behind you, saying, "This is the way; walk in it."
—ISAIAH 30:21

Our God is gracious, and He is faithful to keep His promises; I knew I could trust Him. Shortly after my job had ended, my SIL contact called to say she wanted me to make a trip to a small school in Uganda where they needed another teacher. Consequently, I bought a ticket and flew to Uganda in early November to meet with school personnel for several days.

When I arrived early in the day, I was warmly welcomed. I was provided with a beautiful guesthouse room near the shore of Lake Victoria. The scenery was magnificent with the edge of the lake at the bottom of the hill and the green foliage and colorful flowers in abundance along the street. Since I would not be connecting with the school personnel until the following day, my hostess suggested that I should catch a "dolla dolla" to go visit the local marketplace. She explained that dolla dollas were small motorized scooters used as taxis throughout Uganda, and she assured me that the mode of transportation was considered perfectly safe for a single woman.

I walked to the nearby departure point and waved down a passing dolla dolla. The driver motioned for me to sit side-saddle on the back of the scooter, which I did, but when he took off driving fast, I asked him to stop so that I could swing one leg over the back of the scooter. He was surprised at my request—ladies did not ride that way—but he complied and tolerated my atypical riding form. We had one wild ride to the market! I hung on tightly to his waist, and I was very glad that I was not riding side-saddle! I felt again like I had entered a storybook fantasy. How could I be riding a scooter with a total stranger in the wilds of Uganda, Africa?

The taxi driver delivered me safely to the market, and I began a delightful afternoon of wandering around the marketplace. I found a spectacular array of colorful cloths spread out on the ground to display a variety of enticing wares. When I had finished, I flagged down another dolla dolla for the trip home—but this time, I started the journey with one leg on each side of the scooter. I am guessing there may have been two dolla

dolla drivers that night who amused their families with tales of the odd American woman who had not known how to ride on a scooter correctly.

The next day, I was escorted to the school where the staff were kind and welcoming. The school building was a private home that had been converted into many small classrooms. I visited the school for a few days, interacting with the students and the staff, while asking and answering the questions that arose. The setup was much smaller than the school in Kenya, but I was open to moving there, if the Lord confirmed that Uganda was His choice.

Surprisingly, on the third or fourth day, I learned that their situation had unexpectedly changed because they found out several families would not be returning in January. Consequently, the student numbers were dropping and they no longer needed another teacher. Since I had made travel plans to stay a few days longer, one of the teachers suggested I should walk to a nearby botanical garden to tour the area.

Her directions were simple and I readily found the place, which was like a huge park. I wandered around for a couple of hours admiring the incredible landscape of lush foliage, colorful birds, a few monkeys, and even a large monitor lizard. I whipped out my camera to take his picture, but he quickly slipped under a rock, leaving me a photo of only the rock with his tail sticking out from underneath it.

I decided it was time to retrace my steps to return to the school, but in making so many turns this way and that, I had become hopelessly lost. I quietly cried out to the Lord, asking Him to guide me back to the school. I walked for another hour or so, praying all the way, and eventually came out on the road where my guesthouse was, a long distance from the school. I called the school coordinator to let her know that I was all right, and I learned that they thought someone had taken me home, so no one had suspected I was missing. Thank you, Lord, for always watching over Your children! Once again, I had been rescued from a situation that could have turned out badly.

When I returned to the Ugandan school the following day, I was introduced to a school administrator from Tanzania, who had traveled to Entebbe to meet and confer with the local school officials. He said his school desperately needed more teachers. For several years, they had had a steady flow of young short-term teachers who came for only one to three months and then left, resulting in poor consistency in the instruction and a high level of frustration for the students. He asked if I would be willing to move to Tanzania; he told me he especially needed a second-grade teacher. He gave me his email address, asking that I prayerfully consider his invitation and let him know by email when I returned to Kenya.

Our God is so gracious. He often closes one door rather painfully to encourage us to seek the new door He has for us. After I returned to Kenya, I sought the Lord's face and experienced the peace of knowing that He had opened the next door for me. I emailed the administrator in Tanzania and accepted the position, sight unseen.

A Week at BTL

Serve wholeheartedly, as if you were serving the Lord, not people.
—EPHESIANS 6:7

After resigning my position at the school and accepting my next assignment in Tanzania, I found myself with a full week clear of commitments. In praying for the Lord's guidance regarding how to spend that week, BTL came to mind.

BTL was a large two-story building in downtown Nairobi that housed many missionary teams involved in Bible translation and literacy (thus the acronym BTL). Each team served specific language groups that were located throughout Kenya and many other African nations. Most of the teams consisted of both expats and indigenous individuals working together to produce small printed copies of individual books of the Bible. Then when all the individual books were completed, the team would compile their content to create hardback Bibles which were printed in Korea and shipped to the specific country where they would be distributed.

I had seen some of the finished individual books in Niger and had been highly impressed with the efforts being made to make God's Word available to every tribe and nation. Consequently, I jumped at the chance to volunteer in a production room for the week. I contacted the father of one of my previous students since I knew his team worked at BTL. When he heard my offer, he enthusiastically welcomed an extra set of hands for his team.

He and his team were actively dedicated to creating publications for many people groups throughout East Africa. Besides the Bible, they often published traditional local stories, health booklets, and other materials that were aimed at improving the daily standard of living in those communities. At the time, SIL was the top organization in the world for research and development in the field of linguistics.

I spent the week cutting huge piles of paper in a special machine, collating pages, folding and stapling small booklets written in a foreign script, wrapping up the booklets in small bundles, and loading them into large boxes to be shipped to Tanzania for the Giryama tribe. The translation team was in the final phase of creating an entire New Testament for that people group, but in the meantime, they were delivering the individual books as each one was completed.

Though I had always viewed my teaching role as supporting Bible translation, I was thrilled to have the opportunity to actually put my hands on the materials being produced for people who were just beginning to learn about the gospel. My contribution was ever-so-small, but the experience ingrained in my heart a sense of thanksgiving for those individuals who were willing to devote their lives to performing whatever mundane tasks were necessary to bring the gospel to those who had never heard.

Farewell Ritual at the Giraffe Centre

Finally, brothers and sisters, rejoice! Strive for full restoration, encourage one another, be of one mind, live in peace. And the God of love and peace will be with you.

—2 CORINTHIANS 13:11

One of my first group trips in Kenya had been to visit the Giraffe Centre in Nairobi. It was a sixty-acre sanctuary with wide open spaces for the giraffes, a beautiful gift shop, and a tall lookout building with a small museum room and an outside platform for viewing or feeding the giraffes. There was also a space along the front perimeter of the sanctuary enclosure where visitors could admire and feed the giraffes. Along that edge, there was a stone divide that separated the giraffes from the people. The stones formed a wall which was only about three feet tall and four feet wide, but the giraffes seemed uninterested in escaping their side of the divide.

The Giraffe Centre had been originally created by a Kenyan man of British descent and his American wife. They were acutely concerned about the possible extinction of giraffes. The animals' natural habitats were being progressively compromised or destroyed, leaving little viable land for the tall creatures to inhabit. The couple had spear-headed the creation of the African Fund for Endangered Wildlife (AFEW), a Kenyan non-profit organization that developed an American counterpart to help with funding.

AFEW was instrumental in creating awareness and solutions for the giraffes' long-term survival as a species. A major purpose of the organization was to educate Kenyan school children, as well as both local and foreign visitors, about Kenya's wildlife and environment, and about the crucial need to protect them.

My friends and I loved going to the Giraffe Centre periodically. From what we could see, giraffes appeared to be quiet, peaceful animals. Little did we know that a grown giraffe could kill an attacking lion by kicking it to death. The giraffes we observed were so tame that when a visitor would hold out a Centre-approved food pellet, the giraffe would lean its head toward the visitor and lick the treat right out of the visitor's hand.

The first time I went along, our friend, Charlotte, demonstrated that if she put the pellet between her teeth, the giraffe would literally lick the pellet right out of her mouth! When I saw her do that, I assumed her bold behavior was a fluke, but later I learned that whenever a teacher was preparing to leave Kenya, the others would escort her to the Centre to kiss a giraffe goodbye. Consequently, as the time grew close for me to leave Kenya, we made another trip to the Giraffe Centre.

When my turn came, I found being kissed by a giraffe was actually rather fun. A giraffe's grey tongue is eighteen inches long, soft and slimy. I got my face washed as he scooped up the treat that I was holding in my teeth. The experience reminded me of being licked by my cat when I was a child, but a cat's tongue is much smaller and rough while the giraffe's tongue was long and soft. To this day, I grin appreciatively when I notice the large photo on my wall which aptly displays my farewell to Kenya.

Car Accident!

For he will command his angels concerning you
to guard you in all your ways.
—Psalm 91:11

After receiving an urgent call from a family member, I had made the decision to fly home to California for a month while the Tanzanian school was on Christmas break. Penelope and I were driving downtown to pick up my plane ticket when we became hopelessly lost in a web of unfamiliar streets. I was driving the car and I had pulled over to the side of the road for us to discuss what to do next—proceed toward downtown or return to our home?

We decided to return home, and though I had looked both directions before pulling out from the curb, we were side-swiped by a fast-moving matatu (taxi). Matatus were famous for causing car accidents because the contracted taxi drivers would compete for the fares, racing from one stop to another to beat their competitors to awaiting customers.

Matatus were van-type vehicles seating ten or twelve passengers at any given time. Evidently, the matatu that had been parked a fair distance behind us had pulled out at the same moment that I did, and WHAM! He hit the front right side of our car so hard that the tire and axle were forced completely underneath the car. Needless to say, we came to a crashing halt.

Even though it was obvious that the matatu had crashed into our car, the driver jumped out and started yelling to the Kenyan bystanders that the crash was my fault. Then he began ranting to them in Kiswahili. There were many angry men standing with folded arms, staring at the two white women in the car. We locked our car doors, kept the windows up, and one of us called the school while the other called the police.

The policeman arrived first. We were so relieved to see him! He asked if we were injured and we both said no, though I knew I had injured my back. I kept silent about the pain because the situation did not feel safe to me. The officer asked for my driver's license, but when I presented it to him, things began to go sour. I had foolishly assumed that all driver's licenses were good for four years, but in Kenya, they were good for only two years. Mine had expired.

My license was seized and we were ordered to report to the police station immediately. When our friends from school arrived, we got in their car and followed the policeman to the station, where I was reprimanded and ordered to appear in court the following day.

Of course, I immediately notified SIL of the accident. The next day, they sent a driver to accompany me to court. He picked me up at 8 a.m. to begin the ten-hour ordeal. He drove me to the courthouse and sat with me in court, a great comfort since I was the only white face in a room of approximately sixty Kenyans. We waited for hours as the judge heard each case and immediately declared the judgment or sentence.

When it was my turn to be called forth, I was hoping for leniency since the judge was a woman. But she proved to be hard as nails. After she asked me a few questions about why I was driving with an expired license, she berated me in no uncertain terms for being stupid and irresponsible, and then she ordered me to go pay a fee in a different building.

The Kenyan driver kindly accompanied me to the second building. Again, we waited a long time for my turn to enter the small office. I paid the fee, got a receipt, and then I was instructed to drive to the Department of Motor Vehicles to apply for a new license. The driver patiently drove me to that building, which was clear across town.

Somewhere in the midst of our travels, the driver had stopped to purchase some water and a quick snack to sustain us. Again, he accompanied me as I filled out the proper paperwork, paid more fees, and was issued a new license. Then we had to return to the courthouse to present evidence of my having paid all the fees and renewed my driver's license.

By the time we returned to my home, it was 6 p.m. Thank you, Lord, for carrying me through a very tough day, and for giving me a companion to encourage and protect me along the way.

Penelope's license was also expired, but thankfully the officer had not asked to see hers. If I remember correctly, Lena and Trudy also had expired licenses, so the three of them went together to renew them shortly thereafter. Obviously, I was not the only one who had falsely assumed that a driver's license was good for four years. Nonetheless, we were all legal drivers once again, and life went on.

In early December, I flew home to California to spend a month with my family. While I was home, I learned that I had broken several ribs in the car accident.

January-May 2005

CHAPTER FIVE

TANZANIA, EAST AFRICA
(JANUARY-MAY, 2005)

||||||||||||||||

Another Beginning

And we know that in all things God works for the good of those who love him, who have been called according to his purpose.

—ROMANS 8:28

After a refreshing month with family and friends in California, I arrived in Tanzania in early January to begin the next chapter of my days in Africa. Though it had broken my heart to leave Kenya, I trusted that the Lord had His reasons for moving me. Soon I would see that He had great things in store for me and for His other children in Tanzania. His plans are always perfect!

Traveling to Tanzania had been more of a trek than reaching either Niger or Kenya. To reach Tanzania, I had flown from the U.S. to London to Nairobi, and then I had caught a smaller MAF plane to fly from Nairobi to the city where I would be living. MAF (Mission Aviation Fellowship) was and is a mission organization that demonstrates the love of Christ by supporting other missionary groups through providing transportation to and from remote areas. The plane had the capacity to hold five or six passengers. I loved riding in small airplanes, and the scenes below me were breath-taking. Seeing the land and the animals from above was a rich adventure.

In 2005, the population in the city was roughly 150,000 people. African Tanzanians were primarily engaged in agriculture while Indian Tanzanians were the primary store-keepers and usually the more well-to-do citizens. African Tanzanians were members of the Gogo, Sanawe, Rangi, and Burungi people groups. The local SIL families were actively involved in creating Bible translations for each of these tribal groups.

I arrived in the Tanzanian city to find the temperature warmer than Kenya but cooler than Niger. I would guess the temperature was generally eighty to ninety degrees Fahrenheit during the days and maybe seventy to seventy-five degrees at night—perfect! I was welcomed with open arms and escorted to one of seven or eight apartments surrounding an open walkway in the middle of the buildings. Several of the young teachers lived in the same complex. I was given a few days to get over jetlag before seeing the school or beginning my teaching assignment. Meanwhile, my young neighbors were gracious and hospitable in providing fellowship and meals.

After I had had a few days' rest, one of the young women escorted me to the school on foot. None of the short-term teachers had cars, so we were all expected to walk to school. When we began to walk, I soon realized that the school was much farther away than I had anticipated. I managed to walk the distance that first day, but it was not easy. My companion and I were both aware that I would not be able to walk that far round trip on a daily basis. That afternoon after school, a parent drove me back to the apartment complex where my fellow teachers and I began to discuss possible housing solutions.

One of the young women mentioned that her friend lived in an apartment close to the school. She called him and he readily agreed to switch apartments with me. The switch was an easy fix, and both of us were happier with our new accommodations—now the young man was housed near several of the young female teachers and I was conveniently housed next door to the school. Furthermore, when I met my new neighbors, I found that most of them were closer to my age.

I had traded a large, spacious apartment for a very tiny one, but the size was of little importance to me. The young man, on the other hand, was quite delighted to have more space for hosting and hanging out.

Similar to the other complex, my new apartment was one of seven formed in a rectangle with a courtyard in the middle. Reminding me of Niger, the floors and walls were of concrete and the windows had only screens, no glass. Our apartments were attached to one another, so no one had any secrets; we could hear almost every word spoken in our nearest neighbors' homes.

The guards were super friendly, going by the windows and looking in at all hours of the day and night. I was a little startled when I often heard a male voice calling out greetings to me when I thought I was alone. At times, I felt like I was living in a goldfish bowl! Consequently, I resorted to keeping the café curtains closed over the bottom of the windows at all times so at least I had some semblance of visible privacy.

My apartment consisted of two rooms: a small living room which included a kitchen corner, and a tiny bedroom big enough for a single bed and a tall skinny dresser next to it. The bed and dresser were so close together that I had to sit on the bed to open a drawer. There was also a small skinny bathroom attached to the bedroom. Once again, the shower included a widow-maker, making bathing a daily trust-walk.

The city where I lived was a low malaria region, so I did not need to take daily prophylactics. In fact, the school administration recommended that none of us use them in that particular area. We were told the mosquitoes had grown resistant to the prophylactics, causing blood samples to inaccurately detect the level of disease in a person's blood. If a person contracted malaria, the lab needed an accurate measure of infection to be effective in treating the disease.

Though we took no meds, we did take regular precautions by always sleeping under mosquito nets. I soon noticed that there was a one-inch gap under my front door, so I usually placed a rolled-up towel across the opening in the evenings. However, in spite of my protective efforts, at night I often saw mosquitoes land on my arms, so I quickly killed them. The habit of smacking freshly-landed mosquitoes was commonly called the missionary dance! As time passed, I found that I 'danced' less as the futility of the effort became apparent. I knew I was being bitten fairly often, but I was pleased to remain free of malaria.

There was a farm directly behind our complex and a secular elementary school next to that. I loved listening to the school children reciting or singing their English lessons in the afternoons. The farm included a rooster, chickens, turkeys, and cows, so I also enjoyed the peaceful sounds of the animals each day, though I was a little puzzled one night when one of the cows mooed all night long. The mystery was solved in the morning when I looked out the window to see that she had a new baby calf at her side.

The town where I lived presented a unique medley of sounds, both day and night. Added to the sounds of children and animals, there were almost always the sounds of laughter, music, singing, and lively conversation, mixed with the peels of the Catholic steeple bells and the chanting of the Muslim calls to prayer. I also heard the taxis' blaring horns and the sounds of men and women engaged in the work of the day: chopping, hammering, raking, washing clothing, and calling out their wares. On Sunday nights and into Mondays' early hours, I was met with the added challenge of trying to sleep through the loud partying at the local bar. In time, I learned to sleep through just about anything!

Oddly enough, my next-door neighbor often added to the medley of sounds. She was a friendly British woman who was totally deaf. She had arrived shortly after I did. She left a loud clackety fan on day and night, and when she washed dishes, it sounded like she was beating the pans together.

But the pleasure of her company far outweighed any concern I had about the noise. She was a cheerful individual in her mid-forties who often joined us in the courtyard for brief visits, even though she had difficulty following the conversation. We quickly learned to face her when we were speaking, no matter who we were actually answering, so that she could read our lips.

Our new neighbor shared that she was working with a missionary group that was creating a Bible in sign language. I loved watching her gather under the shade of a tree with her team while they 'chatted' with their hands. I had hoped to learn to communicate in sign language, but that hope went unmet. Sadly, my neighbor remained in Tanzania for only a short while because of her difficulty in adjusting to the vastly different cultural norms. She soon returned to the UK, where she continued working on the sign language project from a distance.

Next to her apartment was a young German woman who had been invited to join the staff by old friends who were serving as missionaries to the Rangi tribe. She was thoroughly bilingual and a delight to be around. She spent much of her time with her best friend, a young Indian woman from the UK who lived next to our complex. Her best friend was also teaching at the school, though she was not a Christian believer. Consequently, the German girl taught the weekly Bible lessons in her friend's classroom.

I was surprised to learn that several of the teachers were not believers, a fact that seemed contradictory in a Christian school. I was reminded again that the Lord's ways are different than ours and that He can make the best of any situation. The young Indian woman was hearing Bible stories every week, and she had lots of questions about faith. Once again, I found myself in a mentoring relationship. She would often stop at my apartment on her way home in the afternoons to visit and ask questions about whatever biblical concept was puzzling her. I was not in Tanzania long enough to see a change in her beliefs or lifestyle, but I would guess the Lord continued to water the seeds that were planted during her time at the school.

Another neighbor was about sixty-five, and she was Australian. She had been serving at the school for several years. She was also one of the few staff members besides me who was actually a credentialed teacher. One weekend, she invited me to join her and her two friends for an evening of dinner and a game similar to Scrabble. The evening started out great as I got to know them during a tasty meal and friendly chatter, but when the games began, the atmosphere noticeably changed. I had never before witnessed such cutthroat game-playing in my life. For them, playing and winning were serious business!

The neighbor farthest from my apartment was a Russian-American in his forties. He taught in the classroom next to mine. He was a great neighbor, and he comfortably handled the fact that he was the only older single male among many older single females. He often arranged neighborhood game nights, which we all thoroughly enjoyed. We played a multitude of different card and board games over the months. He taught us one Russian card game that was complicated enough to require intense concentration and a long list of rules, but we all made the best of it that night. Not surprisingly, that particular game did not become a group favorite.

Another apartment housed a missionary doctor and his wife and children. They spent most of their time traveling from village to village to minister medical services to the local people. Consequently, they were seldom home and I had little opportunity to get to know them.

The last apartment was also empty most of the time because the missionary who rented it was usually out working on language survey.

As in other African countries, I was expected to hire a local person as my contribution to the local economy. I hired a wonderful woman who served me weekly as a house-girl. She cleaned my apartment and did my laundry by hand, but she did not cook for me. We became good friends, and she readily shared about her life.

In each African country where I had lived, I had been blessed and humbled by witnessing the deep faith of God's people in another culture. Because they faced the daily reality of possible death by disease, their devotion to the Lord was unshakable. My house-girl was no exception to that description. She often shared about her family's struggles or losses as malaria and Aids took their toll among her loved ones. I was honored that she occasionally allowed me to help by supplying food or clothing for the suffering families. She was very matter-of-fact about disease and death and was entirely confident that the Lord held her and her loved ones in the palm of His hand. Her demonstration of faith positively stretched and impacted my own.

New Nation, New Challenges

Sing to the Lord a new song;
sing to the Lord, all the earth.
Sing to the Lord, praise his name;
proclaim his salvation day after day.
Declare his glory among the nations,
his marvelous deeds among all peoples.

—PSALM 96:1–3

During my days in Africa, change seemed to be the name of the game, so here I was in Tanzania, facing my third set of unfamiliar cultural expectations. The first challenge I had to tackle was one involving workable transportation. Since none of the short-term teachers had vehicles, we were understandably dependent on other forms of travel: walking, hiring a taxi, or hitching a ride with a family. Perhaps because of my foot disability, the headmaster had sent me an email in Kenya saying that he had decided to lend me a scooter to use while I was teaching in Tanzania.

When he had written, I had pictured a small, lightweight scooter like the ones I had seen in Uganda, but when the headmaster brought it to my apartment, he arrived with a massive scooter that more closely resembled a motorcycle. When parked, the scooter leaned to the left. To ride it, the driver had to pull it up straight, mount the seat, push down the pedal to start the engine, and pull up the second foot onto the running board while still balancing the vehicle.

With my foot disability, balance was less than ideal anyway, and trying to press down the gas pedal while pulling up my other foot was not an easy task to accomplish. After multiple attempts, I determined that the scooter was simply too heavy for me to safely maneuver. I thanked him for his kind offer, but informed him that I would prefer to walk or depend on taxis.

Taxis were incredibly reasonable to hire. I could go just about anywhere in the city for the equivalent of $1.50 in American money. After a few awkward encounters, I just 'happened' to find a taxi driver who spoke a little English and understood my limited Kiswahili (Thanks, Lord). Together, we managed quite nicely as we each "negotiated language." He was pleased to have a regular customer and I was relieved to have a regular source of dependable transportation.

About a week after I passed up the offer to borrow the scooter, one of the young teachers arrived at school with one of his legs in a brace from ankle to groin. He told me the headmaster had lent the scooter to him and on his first trip out on the road, a bus had side-swiped him and injured his leg. He was a quick healer and not discouraged by the accident, but I was doubly glad that I had had the common sense to say 'no' to the scooter.

The next challenge was the need to improve my language abilities. I had managed with minimal Kiswahili in Kenya, but in this part of Tanzania, knowing the language was a must. Very little English was spoken anywhere in the public arena. I emailed my prayer partners to ask them to pray that I would pick up the language quickly. Then, to achieve that goal, I hired a local tutor to begin weekly lessons in my home.

Surprisingly, improving my Kiswahili was not the only language obstacle that I faced. When I first arrived, I could barely understand most of the other teachers, though they were all speaking English. Other than my one American neighbor, the rest of the staff members were from Tanzania, Australia, and New Zealand. With their unfamiliar accents, pronunciation, and vocabulary usage, I had my share of puzzling moments.

I remember when I first recovered from jetlag, one of the women asked me if I was "feeling bitter." I assured her that no, I was not feeling bitter; jetlag was just a fact of life. But she asked me again, "And you're not feeling bitter yet?" I gave her a puzzled look, causing one of the other teachers to spell the word 'better' aloud. Oh! Yes, I felt better. We all laughed at my obvious confusion. Thankfully, I soon developed an ear to clearly understand the English being spoken around me.

Whereas the first and second schools had been following the American system of education, the school in Tanzania was following the British system. American schools classified students as Elementary (grades K to 6), Intermediate (grades 7 and 8), and High School (grades 9 through 12) whereas British schools classified students as Primary (Reception/ages four and five and Standards 1 through 6), Secondary (Standards 7 and 8), and Further Education (Forms 1 through 4). The terms were a little different, but the general curriculum was much the same.

When I first met with the headmaster, I was in for a big surprise. He informed me that I would not be teaching second grade (Standard 3). Instead, I would be team-teaching Standards 6 and 7. He explained that the school had just welcomed a newly certified teacher who had only one year of experience behind her. She had taught second grade for that one year, and she was not comfortable trying something new.

The headmaster had reasoned that since I was an experienced teacher, I could more readily make the switch to another level. I took a deep breath (gulp) and agreed to make the change. Back at Mexicali in the late 1990's, I had learned the importance of being flexible in any mission situation, and I was certainly experiencing that truth once again.

Whereas the school in Niger had been created solely for missionary kids and the school in Kenya had been created for both missionary and local Christian students, the school in Tanzania had been intentionally created to serve both as a Christian school for missionary kids and as an outreach to the local community. Our school included students from Christian, Muslim, and Sikh families. It was a treat to have the daily privilege of teaching about Jesus and the Bible to a group of children where some were familiar with the Christian faith and others were being newly introduced to its truths. Watching the Christian children share their faith with their unbelieving peers was a treat.

Mr. J, my new teaching partner, was a recent college graduate from England who had had no formal teacher training, but he was a natural with the students. I was quite impressed with his lesson presentations and his overall rapport with the students. The two of us made a good team, and I thoroughly enjoyed working with him.

Our students ranged in age from eleven to fourteen years old, representing a variety of home countries, including Australia, Germany, Holland, Scotland, Korea, Oman, India, and Tanzania. Many of the children came from missionary families, but we also had a few students who came from Muslim or Sikh families. One student from a Muslim family was confined to a wheelchair.

Afzal the Lion-Hearted

Everyone who calls on the name of the Lord will be saved.
—ROMANS 10:13

Afzal was a fourteen-year-old Tanzanian boy of Indian descent whose body showed the ravages of Muscular Dystrophy. He had been a normal, active child who loved playing soccer until the age of seven when the disease began to manifest its ugly symptoms. He had gradually lost balance, strength, and mobility, becoming a paraplegic by the age of twelve.

His grandmother lived with him and his family, and she, too, was in a wheelchair. In contrast, he had a younger sister who was in constant motion and was usually getting into mischief. His mother single-handedly cared for the family's daily needs while his father worked in a bigger city and sent home money to support his family.

The first time I saw Afzal, I was struck by how small and sad he looked in the dilapidated old wheelchair. He was slumped down with his expressionless face barely appearing over the surface of the large school desk. He was surrounded by a sea of lively movement and chatter from the other students around him, but he himself seemed unresponsive and invisible to them.

He did not speak or look at them, and they ignored him to the point of literally stepping over his wheelchair as if it were empty. I was horrified to observe how totally oblivious they were to his very existence.

As the new teacher joining an already established classroom, I spent the first few days primarily observing classroom format and learning the students' names, but as time passed, I became increasingly uncomfortable with Afzal's overall situation: he was obviously lonely, ignored, and discouraged.

One night, I was invited to an evening Bible study group that met near my home. Among the participants were several fellow teachers and the headmaster, so when the opportunity presented itself, I voiced my concerns for Afzal as a need for frequent intercession. Sharing my concern began a journey of committed prayer and action among the staff, a Spirit-led campaign that brought about major positive changes for this boy. Soon, both teachers and students were involved in bettering Afzal's daily existence.

While observing the class, I had seen that my teaching partner made lessons exciting and interesting. He found creative ways to engage most of the students in the learning process, but his efforts were totally lost on Afzal. Though the boy obviously loved Mr. J (and depended on him for the only attention he received), his motivation to successfully complete assignments seemed to be hampered both by his physical limitations and by his apparent belief that he had no worthwhile abilities. Basically, Afzal had given up, as evidenced by his minimal attention during lessons, his miserably poor test scores, and his infrequent completion of homework.

But our God is a mighty God, and no one He has created is useless! I was soon convinced that one of the major reasons the Lord had sent me to Tanzania was to use my Special Education training to encourage this particular student. God gave me a heart, a hope, and a drive to see things change for this boy, and soon others joined in my passion.

The headmaster not only gave me permission to use my Special Education knowledge to improve the situation for Afzal, but he also asked me to train his entire staff on how to incorporate a child with disabilities into a mainstream classroom. I jumped at the chance!

I made a trip to the open market to buy some sturdy wood, thick foam, and colorful cloth. Then the janitor cut the wood to size and we rebuilt the wheelchair seat to make it more comfortable and to better support Afzal's body. We raised the seat so that Afzal was at a more reasonable height, both for using his school desk and for interacting with his fellow students. When the wheelchair rebuild was completed, my teaching partner and I rearranged the entire classroom to make every area accessible to Afzal's wheelchair.

Afzal was thrilled with the physical changes to his wheelchair. Besides being more comfortable, he was now sitting at a height which allowed him to use his desk more effectively and to interact with his classmates at their shared eye-level. He gleefully announced, "I feel so tall!" and a great big smile lit up his face.

Coincidentally (in God's perfect way), Mr. J and I had planned to begin a new unit on teamwork. I had accepted the task of planning a weekly lesson to encourage greater unity among the students. A helpful teachers' manual was provided, and the Lord built the program from there.

We began the unit on teamwork with a group discussion about the "stars" in our lives, people we admire for various reasons. Then I asked each student to name one classmate who demonstrated strength. Most suggested one of the more obviously muscular boys, but after the students had exhausted their suggestions, I asked them to stretch their thinking beyond the obvious.

I described a boy who had demonstrated great strength in patience every single day. From some of the examples given, the students eventually realized that I was speaking of Afzal, and they began to recognize how long-suffering he had been in his enduring their inconsiderate behavior.

Over the next weeks, we discussed the importance of recognizing and accepting the strengths and weaknesses in one another. The students began openly exercising support and encouragement for one another in the classroom. Along the way, Afzal got the nickname of "the lion-hearted" because the students finally began to recognize the strength he had long demonstrated in his daily tolerance of their poor behavior. Thankfully, their attitudes toward him began to markedly improve.

New rules were established about honoring Afzal's space: there would be no more climbing on the wheelchair, he would be an equal member of the group, and he would always be transported to participate in every classroom or outdoor activity.

We also began an advocacy program. We posted a list of students on the wall, and each morning the arrow was moved to the next name on the list. All students were allowed an equal opportunity to serve as Afzal's advocate, a job considered an honor to be taken seriously. Each day, the advocate was responsible for transporting Afzal to and from all indoor and outdoor activities.

By the grace of God, Afzal's wonderful smile began to appear more and more often. Soon he was joking with others in the classroom, and he began to voluntarily participate in discussions and other activities. We discovered he was a creative fellow with an active imagination as he began writing and sharing some of his poetry and stories.

Before I had arrived at the school, the class had gone on frequent field trips, but they had always left Afzal behind. I was determined to break that unkind pattern. When Mr. J and I planned the next field trip, I contacted my favorite taxi driver and he was more than willing to transport Afzal and his wheelchair to the field trip destination. Afzal's advocate for the day was allowed to travel with Afzal and me in the taxi, making the trip even more of an adventure. That method of inclusion became our standard for all future field trips, and Afzal continued to grow in joy and participation. He finally felt like an equal member among his classmates.

Much to our amazement, Mr. J and I discovered an exciting secret in Afzal's classroom journal. His writings clearly revealed that he had grasped and accepted that Jesus Christ was Lord of his life. Coming from a Muslim family, he shared those stories privately with only Mr. J and me. We rejoiced at seeing the transformation brought about in his life by Jesus Christ, and we prayed that God would use his quiet faith as a witness to his entire family.

Life Comes with Surprises

I had been at the school for only a week or two when the headmaster came to ask me for a favor. He told me that the Reception (pre-Kindergarten) teacher had had a family emergency the night before; she had flown home to Australia immediately. That morning, he was in desperate need for someone to cover the class until her return, and he had no extra teachers. Standards 6 and 7 met all day, but he asked if my teaching partner and I would be willing to rearrange our schedules so that I could teach Reception in the mornings.

I had already become attached to the older students, but I readily sympathized with the headmaster's dilemma. Since I was more accustomed to teaching younger children anyway, I agreed to make the change. My teaching partner and I hurriedly met to rearrange the timing of the lesson plans we had written for the week, and I began teaching the four to five-year-olds in the mornings and the Standards 6 and 7 students in the afternoons. The schedule was workable, but definitely taxing because I taught all day without the normal breaks. Knowing the situation was temporary helped me push through each day.

I quickly came to love my new little students as well as the older ones, and I greatly appreciated that the Reception teacher had left thorough lesson plans for me to follow. Her advanced planning saved me a chunk of time that would have been spent on preparations in the evenings. However, I will admit that I found her plans for the reading program personally confronting. The British (or perhaps her personal) philosophy was drastically different than my own. I had been trained to teach reading through phonetics, whereas the lesson plans I was given followed a sight-reading procedure aimed at very young children.

Each day at the close of school, the children were required to take an assigned book home to "read" with their parents, and then the next day they were required to read the book to me. They had to take the same book home each day until they were able to successfully read it without error. From what I could see, most of the children were not ready to tackle reading, and only those with extremely good memories were able to pretend-read. For me, watching them struggle through the pages was painful.

I knew I was expected to follow the lesson plans prepared for me, so I swallowed hard and followed them to the letter. I did not teach Reception long enough to see if the system eventually paid off, but I sincerely hoped that the reading program involved more than was evident to me in that brief period of time.

My split assignment lasted for only three weeks, and then I was quite relieved to return to my own classroom full-time.

School Days in Tanzania

The layout of the school was perfect for me. The entire campus was on a flat piece of land. The buildings were all attached, connected in a long rectangular shape with one end open to the spacious play yard. The play yard was basically a huge sandy field. The middle courtyard among the buildings was paved with concrete around a large shade tree in the middle.

One long side of the rectangular building consisted of rooms for the Computer Lab, the Teachers' Lounge, and the Administration Office. The far end held a large room for Reception, and the other long side of the rectangle consisted of smaller individual rooms for the Standards and Forms, starting at the youngest next to Reception and consecutively moving toward the oldest by the play yard.

Every Friday morning, we met for Assembly, a time of Chapel for students from Reception through Standard 7 classes. We met outside in the cool of the morning, with the children sitting on mats on the concrete. Each week, one teacher led songs and presented a brief devotional.

On the other days of the week, Mr. J and I began our mornings with a class meeting for discussing any announcements or concerns, and for presenting daily devotions and group prayer. I was always touched to hear these young ones praying together, all in the name of Jesus, regardless of their parents' faith. Praying aloud was strictly voluntary, but most of the students participated. Starting the days with prayer set a peaceful tone for the day's activities.

Mr. J and I met up weekly to lay out the lesson plans for the week ahead. He especially enjoyed teaching Science, and I especially enjoyed teaching Language Arts. Computer Science was taught in the Computer Lab by a separate instructor, but we shared responsibility for the remaining subjects: various levels of Reading and "Maths," Social Studies, History, Art, and class meetings. We were also required to teach Family Life (sex education), so naturally, Mr. J taught the boys and I taught the girls. We were not required to help with recess duty since the school had volunteer mothers who served in that capacity.

When I had taught in the U.S., I had not enjoyed teaching Middle School grades, but overseas was an entirely different scene. The Standard 6 and 7 students were always respectful, cooperative, and personable, making teaching a joy. They were amazing in their openness and honesty about their personal adolescent concerns. Several of the girls shared with me about their religious traditions and their family life, their hopes and dreams. I thanked God for giving me a glimpse of life for a Muslim or Sikh child who obediently accepted the traditions of his or her parents. I also saw the heartache they endured when some students found themselves caught between the beliefs of the parents and the tenets of the school.

For Easter, the school had an annual tradition of creating a school-wide presentation to be performed for the students' families. Each class was required to present a song or brief drama. The year I was there, Forms 1 through 4 had created a choir. With all the students in white shirts and dark pants or skirts, they sang several beautifully harmonized Christian songs. Then all the lower classes performed their parts, and then our class presented the finale.

Our class had chosen to perform an abbreviated version of the musical, *Jesus Christ, Super Star.* The children had chosen several of the songs to sing, and they had woven the appropriate Scriptures around the songs to present the full story. We had spent weeks practicing the scenes and songs, and the students were understandably excited to perform for their parents. They brought their own colorful costumes, and they were spectacular in telling the story of Jesus Christ to an audience that included both believers and unbelievers.

Praise God for the opportunity to present the gospel to new ears! The presentation was well received by one and all. For many of us, our prayer was that the Lord would use the day's activities to plant seeds in the hearts of those who did not yet know Him. We could trust that His Holy Spirit would water those seeds over the seasons that followed.

The school also held an annual Sports Day similar to the one in Kenya, but in Tanzania the color teams included students aged three to sixteen and all staff members. We had running, hopping, and skipping races, three-legged races, "frog" and "crab" races, stationary competitions such as bean bag throws and boulder throws, high jumps and distance jumps, and team cheering competitions. Each team had created its own cheer to shout periodically throughout the day.

The judges counted up the scores, both for individuals and for the teams, including points for demonstrations of good sportsmanship and cooperation among team members. At the end of the day, first-, second-, and third-place prizes were presented to individuals, and the team with the highest score was recognized with loud clapping and cheering. Sports Day had been a marked success for everyone involved, including Afzal, whose team members had intentionally found ways to include him in the fun.

At the end of the school year, Standards 6 and 7 had the adventure of creating a program for the Standard 7 graduation. The ceremony was well-received by their families, and the students were pleased with their production. For reasons I will explain later, I was unable to attend the graduation ceremony, but Mr. J was thoughtful enough to email multiple photos and videos to me with an extensive description of the day's festivities.

Weekends in Tanzania

Game nights were not the only activity shared by school staff. We often came together for hosted or potluck dinners, an occasional outing such as going to the local open market, or a group hike ending in a simple meal cooked over an open fire.

Similar to Niger and Kenya, the open market was an adventure in itself. On Saturday mornings, the local vendors would all gather in one area to spread their wares out on colorful cloths. But in Tanzania, I saw something I had not seen up close before: the local butcher. At one end of the market, there was a long wooden table covered with huge sections of beef. The table was soaked with blood and the meat was covered with hundreds of large black flies buzzing about.

I watched as a customer stepped forward and pointed to a piece of meat, asking for the desired portion he wanted to buy. The butcher waved off the flies, cut and weighed a portion of meat, and wrapped it in a piece of newspaper. Before witnessing that scene, I had been primarily consuming a vegetarian diet with an occasional piece of fish, but after visiting the meat market, I seldom if ever ate meat.

Besides the open market, there was one small indoor market near us where we could buy a few canned, frozen, and packaged goods. The store was small and dark, and the back wall was covered with floor-to-ceiling wooden shelves where the sparse array of items was displayed. There was also a small freezer at one end of the shelves.

Fresh produce could be bought on the street outside where a few individuals displayed their particular produce: delicious pineapples, mangoes, and bananas were readily available, but the only watermelons I found were extremely small, and they proved to be totally tasteless—a big disappointment after the incredible watermelons in Kenya.

There were several of us who often went swimming on Saturday mornings. My sixty-five-year-old neighbor belonged to the local country club, which consisted of only a pool and a few outdoor tables with chairs. Because she was serving long-term, she owned a car. She loved gathering up a carload of women to join her for a refreshing and relaxing change of pace after a full week of teaching. Swimming was an activity I had enjoyed all my life, so I was usually among those who headed for the country club.

Once in a while, a few of us would go out to share a meal. In our immediate vicinity, there was only one restaurant available, so the choice of where to dine was made simple. The restaurant was so tiny that though the food was prepared indoors, the waitress would bring it to the customers at a few outside tables. The menu provided a limited choice of amazing Indian dishes, but one had to be careful to emphasize the level of spices desired or chance going home with a fiery mouth.

We did not know of any restaurant that offered traditional African dishes, but I often cooked Sukuma wiki and Ugali at home. On one occasion only, I was blessed to enjoy a home-cooked African meal when I went upcountry to visit my house-girl.

Faces of Worship

Come, let us bow down in worship,
let us kneel before the Lord our Maker ...
Let them praise his name with dancing
and make music to him with timbrel and harp.

—PSALMS 95:6 AND 149:3

I was aware of only two Christian churches within the city proper: the Anglican cathedral and the Catholic cathedral. Most of the missionaries I knew attended services at the Anglican cathedral, where the worship was unusually subdued compared to what I had experienced in Niger and

Kenya. Though I had often participated in contemplative services in the U.S., that worship style seemed unnatural to me in an African setting. My knowledge of indigenous worship was definitely limited, but what I saw in Tanzania seemed atypical to me. The liturgy was noticeably formal in style.

Generally speaking, the songs that were sung lacked the celebrative flavor to which I had become accustomed. As we sang, the congregation showed little, if any, outward response—no clapping, no swaying, no raising of hands and eyes to heaven. I felt like I had been transported to another continent. I missed the more expressive forms of singing that I had come to love in Niger and Kenya.

Evidently, Mr. J had had a similar response to the absence of true African flavor, so he took it upon himself to do something about it. He was highly committed to full immersion in the local culture, so he had become good friends with many of his Tanzanian neighbors. He had convinced some of them to join him in creating a more authentic African choir.

He and his friends had written worship songs together, and they had recorded them for sale. Their songs were lively, and the background accompaniment was provided by a number of traditional African instruments. Occasionally, their choir was invited to lead Sunday morning worship. When they did, those mornings were infused with a greater sense of celebration. Their lively worship style noticeably increased the congregation's enthusiasm and participation. For some of us, the choir's visits were far too infrequent.

But in contrast to the usually subdued worship style in town, I was blessed with one memorable visit to an indigenous church upcountry. One Sunday morning, I accepted my house-girl's invitation to join her in a service at her local church, an experience that proved to be eye-opening and personally invigorating.

I arrived by taxi to discover that my house-girl lived in a beautiful house much larger and more elaborately furnished than my own tiny apartment. After she showed me around, we walked to her church, which was located nearby. She introduced me to many of her friends, all of whom did not speak a word of English. I was glad I could at least greet them and respond to simple conversations in Kiswahili. Then we entered the small church building and we found two empty seats among the rows of fold-up chairs. I would guess there were forty to fifty people attending.

The entire service was in Kiswahili with no interpreter, so once again I caught only a few of the key words like Lord, Jesus, and Christ, along with the general theme of the sermon. Though I could not understand word for word, I picked up just enough to follow that we were talking about Samuel in the Old Testament. I was thankful that I had brought my Bible along and that I knew the story well. I could fill in some of the blanks as he spoke, and I could read the verses in English. The pastor was lively and engaging in his sermon, and then the worship began.

After a few songs were sung, the entire congregation burst into full-out worship mode: some were kneeling, some standing and dancing, some raising their hands or falling prostrate to the ground, some crying and some laughing, while the majority continued singing, clapping, and praising in tongues.

With everything happening simultaneously, one might think the scene was chaotic, but it was not. All the activities melded together into an incredible, harmonious demonstration of open worship. I marveled at the worshipers' ability to totally focus on the Lord and to forget those around them. In doing so, they created a symphony of heavenly music and a picture of devout worship.

Being exposed to a congregation where everyone was involved in demonstrative worship was a welcome and exciting change of pace for me. I had always enjoyed American praise songs, and I had occasionally participated in a Sacred Dance choir when a few of us danced to invite everyone into personal worship. But in Tanzania, every single person was equally involved in the physical as well as the spiritual act of worship. The Holy Spirit was the only worship leader, and God Almighty was the only audience that mattered.

For me, the worshipers' purity in focus brought whole new meaning to John's vision in Revelation when he wrote of every tribe and nation worshiping together before the King (Revelation 7:9). The congregants' honest abandon and whole-hearted worship that I witnessed that day must have been a sweet fragrance to our heavenly Father.

I was grateful for the opportunity to personally extend my understanding and acceptance of participatory worship. The longer I lived in Africa, the more I learned about the diversity of ways to truly worship our Father in heaven. Whether praising Him in stillness or open celebration, my African brothers and sisters reminded me that what mattered most in worship was focusing fully on the Lord.

Tough Choices

I keep my eyes always on the Lord.
With him at my right hand, I will not be shaken.
—PSALM 16:8

When I began teaching in Tanzania, my greatest need was to know that I was exactly where the Lord wanted me to be. In my first meeting with the headmaster and the personnel director, they had both urged me to give serious thought to serving long-term at the school, an invitation that was most confirming but also somewhat premature. While I was contending with jetlag and cultural adjustments, I was not in a frame of mind to give their request much thought.

Nonetheless, as the days passed and I settled in to my new surroundings, I recognized that my new home offered all the positives about living in Africa without the major negatives of a physically threatening environment and the stress it produced. Living in Tanzania, my whole body began to relax over the first few weeks, and the tense habit of constantly being on guard had gradually given way to daily thanking God for the peaceful environment around me.

Even though the city was home to Muslims, Sikhs, and Christians living together side by side, I had never before lived in any place that exhibited such open acceptance and respect for one another. There was an amazing sense of peace and communal harmony in my new surroundings. Before long, I met with the headmaster to indicate that I was willing to remain at the school for long-term placement, and together we began to make plans for the following school year.

And then the unthinkable happened: I attended an SIL meeting that changed everything. At the meeting, future plans for the SIL families in the area were discussed in detail. To my shock and dismay, I learned that

SIL had decided to move their local base for the translation teams to Dar es Salaam, a huge city along the coast of Tanzania. They estimated that the SIL office in our region would be closed within a year's time. They highly recommended that the families move to 'Dar' at the end of the school year.

The major reason I had been invited to teach at that particular school was because there were SIL students attending there. My presence meant that SIL families had received a reduction in tuition fees because their organization had provided the school with a much-needed teacher. I knew if all the SIL students were relocated the following year, SIL would have no reason to continue my placement at the school.

But during the meeting, it became evident that a few of the SIL families would prefer to remain at their present location for another year or two to avoid disrupting their children's present education. That reprieve would be only temporary, leaving my future much in question. I had written in my journal:

> March 1, 2005: Circumstances are changing around me yet again. I feel at home here, Lord, and had begun to make plans to return—and now I am learning of various circumstances that may make that impossible or unadvisable. Lord, direct my paths!
>
> Positives: I love the kids, I like working with Mr. J, I like this new locale, and I see that you are using me to minister to Afzal, and to witness to others. Negatives: Many teachers are not Christians, SIL is moving to Dar, and SIL families may leave.
>
> O Lord, I don't want to move again. I feel I've dealt with just about all the change I can stand for a while. Yet I hear your gentle reminder, "It doesn't matter _where_ you serve—it matters that you serve."
>
> I am basking in the peace of your presence in this season. And I am battling the little things: constant congestion and a sore throat, no transportation, I don't know the language well, I have to build a new set of friends, and I haven't found a church where I feel I can fully worship you and be fed. Is my time in this

region ending in three months, or will you show me some way to return?

I feel no urgency to know right now. You are the faithful one; you will lead me, and I will follow. Praise be to God always, always, always. Milele (forever). Alleluia.

A week later, I wrote in my journal:

March 8, 2005: Well, Father, all this (Bible study lesson) seems to say to my heart, "Wait. Continue serving day by day. You will know what to do when the time comes."

With that thought in mind, I made every effort to put my concerns for the future aside. I returned my focus to the Lord my God and the present task He had set before me. I loved teaching in Tanzania, and I wanted to make the most of every moment I was there.

Pasaka Njema

The angel said to the women, "Then go quickly and tell his disciples: He has risen from the dead and is going ahead of you into Galilee. There you will see him."
—MATTHEW 28:5A, 7

Pasaka Njema—Happy Easter! The bells at the Catholic and Anglican cathedrals rang in the new day, sharing the good news that Jesus had risen. As usual, I attended the Anglican church service. Though the worship songs were rather disappointing, the sermon and communion were good.

Then five of us teachers packed up and drove three hours to Mpwapwa to see a performance at a youth rally. Half of the journey was on painfully bumpy roads, but the gorgeous weather and the scenery along the way made up for the uncomfortable journey. We watched the teens perform and cheered them on, and then we began the long, bumpy trip back to the city.

As we traveled, I remembered the service on the island of Lamu one year ago. I silently conversed with the Lord, hoping the church was growing in faith and strength, that Steve and Jenifer were doing well, and that Lydia had been healed of her tumor. I also prayed for the man who had refused Jesus' gift of salvation, knowing full well that nothing is impossible to our God; I knew that He alone could change that man's fate in the twinkling of an eye.

We teachers had been invited to a friend's house for dinner, so when we arrived back in the city, we headed that direction. The delicious meal and the lively company helped to revive our tired, aching bodies.

I went home pleasantly content with the day. Looking at my new life in Tanzania, I was constantly grateful for the hospitable community that had so readily embraced me in their midst. A few days later, I wrote to my family that I had decided to serve two more years in Tanzania before returning to the U.S.

Within days, the intentions I expressed to my family were disrupted by a second SIL meeting. At the meeting, SIL representatives made it clear that the plans for the move to Dar es Salaam were beginning to fall into place more rapidly than originally anticipated. I seriously wondered what those changes would mean for me personally. I had written in my journal,

> April 18, 2005: Lord, lead on. You have gifted me richly with a family I love and with a heart to serve the lost. Show me how to balance these two loves in my life. May all be done to your glory. Praise be to God.

Possibly Prophetic

Missionary life is a transient lifestyle involving the frequent comings and goings of families and individuals as they come to serve or leave for ministry, furloughs, or personal reasons. We were always saying goodbye to someone. Some would return in three to twelve months, and others would never return to Tanzania. When one young woman was upset about leaving her African home "forever," I wrote her a silly poem to encourage her:

Sarah, Sarah, strong and able,
Sitting at His banquet table,
Pull in close to Him, confide,
Knowing God's your perfect Guide.
He will lead you; He will heal
The memories and the wounds you feel.
You haven't failed! You've done your part
In Kingdom work with all your heart!
You're on His path to learn and grow
And He'll protect you from our Foe,
For God so loves you in His care
That He'll be with you everywhere.
May His love so fill your days
That you'll rise up to sing His praise.
And then look back and thank the Lord
For Tanzania's rich reward!
By then, you'll see He trusted you
To follow Him and listen, too,
For His small whisper in the storm
While He molded your Christlike form.
For He's the One who chose this season;
You can be sure He has His reason.
He promises us the perfect plan,
And He alone is the one who can
Direct your path and make it blessed.
So trust Him, Sarah, with all the rest.
Work through the pain and come up singing,
Knowing your Father is always bringing
Good things into this life of yours,
Gifts supplied by heavenly stores
To enrich your walk with Him alone.
So stand with JOY before His throne.
Alleluia!

April 9, 2005

At the time that I wrote those words, I did not know that within weeks I would be the next person to leave Tanzania "forever."

Visit to Dar es Salaam

Therefore, as God's chosen people, holy and dearly loved, clothe yourselves with compassion, kindness, humility, gentleness and patience. Bear with each other and forgive one another if any of you has a grievance against someone. Forgive as the Lord forgave you. And over all these virtues put on love, which binds them all together in perfect unity.

—Colossians 3:12–14

A few days after the second SIL meeting, I accompanied a family to Dar es Salaam for the weekend. We planned to take a look at the Haven of Peace Academy, commonly known as HOPAC. The parents had informed me that they planned to enroll their two daughters in HOPAC for the following school year. I had agreed to join them while they sought future housing and while they became familiar with the city. I had made it abundantly clear to them that my preference was to remain at the school where I was presently serving, if at all possible, but at their urging I had agreed to at least take a look at the school in Dar es Salaam.

When we arrived in 'Dar,' we checked in to a lovely guesthouse and spent much of the next two days driving around to get familiar with the huge city. Dar es Salaam was the main entry port to East Africa. The population in 2005 was just under three million people. The downtown area was immense. We even found an American "Subway" sandwich outlet. When we went inside to order sandwiches, standing there in line seemed surreal to me—how could we be standing in an American fast-food restaurant in Africa?

In the evenings, we enjoyed visiting with other families on a large roof-top patio. The weather was beautiful, though warm, and the mosquitoes were plentiful. The location of the guesthouse was quiet and peaceful. I thoroughly enjoyed sitting outside with the others.

I had not thought to ask about whether or not I needed to take prophylactics before leaving on the trip, so I had come unprepared to protect myself from the mosquitoes. The rooms had mosquito nets over the beds, but in the evenings the air inside and out was highly populated with the voracious insects.

Visiting the school in Dar confirmed for me that the Lord was not sending me there. The school was beautifully laid out with fine amenities and a solid Christian curriculum, but it was located on multiple small hills with concrete walkways and stairs to reach the buildings. Just completing the tour was painful enough to convince me that I would not survive for long on that campus.

At the end of the tour, our guide informed us that the school had enough teachers for the coming year, but that staff needs often changed during the summer. She offered me an application for their waiting list, but I politely declined it, explaining that the campus would be too difficult for me to maneuver on a regular basis.

Even though they had heard my reason for declining the application, my hosts were grossly disappointed, for they had planned to get a reduced tuition for their daughters by signing me up to teach at the school. They continued to pressure me on the way back to our guesthouse. My declaration that I would definitely not be moving to Dar es Salaam was not well received.

The Beginning of the End

And my God will meet all your needs according to the riches of his glory in Christ Jesus.

—PHILIPPIANS 4:19

The trip back to our hometown was unpleasant, to say the least. On top of the relational discomfort, I was feeling feverish and nauseated. It was a relief to get home to my own little apartment. For several days after my return, I battled intestinal symptoms, feeling generally miserable but trying to self-treat with homeopathic remedies and natural foods. I had read my book, *Where There Is No Doctor,* to try to identify the problem. I had decided I was dealing with another round of intestinal parasites. I limped along with my self-diagnosis and self-treatment for a little over a week.

Then one night, I was suddenly hit with an overpowering wave of extreme weakness. I could barely walk the few steps from my living room to the bedroom. I had a fiery sore throat, a splitting headache, and my neck was painfully stiff. I felt like my head was entrapped in a vice, making it difficult to turn my head in any direction. I crawled into bed and managed to sleep some of the night, though I felt so miserable that I begged the Lord to just take me.

When I awoke in the morning, I was surprised to feel a bit better, so I walked over to school to begin the day as usual. Mr. J and I had been preparing our students for their first SAT exams (British version) and the students were mildly terrified. I did not want to add to their stress by staying home, so I tried to pace myself carefully in spite of not feeling well. Sitting on a tall stool, I had made it through the morning sessions as I read the directions and questions to the students and Mr. J walked around to supervise them.

But when we both went to the teachers' room during the morning break, I knew I was burning up with fever. Another teacher took one look at me and declared, "You look just like my husband, and he is home with malaria." The headmaster overheard the comment from the next room. He came to check on me, and he immediately asked an office worker to drive me to "the lab."

The city had no medical facilities or doctors, but there was one small lab where malaria tests were performed regularly. My companion knew the way and drove me there directly. The lab technician took my blood sample and asked us to wait while she ran the test. When she came back out, she simply said, "Pole sana" (so sorry) as she handed the results to my companion. The diagnosis was cerebral malaria and anemia.

I still remember the lab technician's explanation of the results. She told us that if the blood test showed even one red blood cell was infected with malaria parasites, I should begin malaria meds at once. My test results showed fifty per two hundred units were infected, indicating a serious case—that ratio meant 25% of my red blood cells were infected. She said the level of infection indicated that I had probably had malaria for seven to ten days.

There were several types of malaria in Africa, but cerebral malaria was considered the worst, usually ending in death. But I did not know that fact; I had never even heard of cerebral malaria before that day. Perhaps it was a grace that I knew so little about the disease.

The lab technician gave my companion a piece of paper with two words written on it, and she told us to pick up the medication as soon as possible. In the African nations where I had lived, no prescriptions were necessary for buying medications. Customers simply walked into a pharmacy and requested whatever medication they desired.

My companion drove us to a nearby pharmacy, where she paid for a packet of Cloartem and a bottle of liquid iron. Because I was a "rich" American, I could afford the medication, costing the equivalent of $5.00 American money.

Little did I know that the Cloartem would make me even sicker than I already was. Though I had been quite limp and unresponsive before taking the drug, my mental status was about to change quite rapidly. After I took the first dose, I was thrown into a chemically-induced panic attack which thoroughly terrified me. Instead of being too sick to care whether I lived or died, I was suddenly frantic to get home to see my family. I suspected that dying would have been easier, but I desperately begged God to let me live.

We had only four more weeks of school, and I seriously wanted to finish the school year with Mr. J and our students. I tried hard to rest and heal in my own strength, but I was greatly concerned about the extra work created by the SAT exams. Though I could not go to school, I wanted to do what I could to support my teaching partner, so I forced myself to spend every ounce of my energy on scoring the exams.

In the spirit of loving community, my fellow missionaries brought me a home-cooked meal each afternoon. On one occasion, a friend offered to pick up my favorite dinner at the Indian restaurant. Though I had specifically requested a mild dish on the phone, the food was so spicy that it burned my mouth and throat. I ate it with high hopes that the spices would kill off the disease within me. Sadly, I did not yet fully understand how malaria attacks the body.

I continued taking the Cloartem and liquid iron with high hopes for recovery. But on top of everything else, I began to manifest symptoms of Chronic Fatigue. I had had the disease twice in my forties, so I recognized the symptoms all too clearly. I guessed the Chronic Fatigue was why I felt so awful because I knew the Cloartem was supposed to have killed the malaria infection within a few days. I prayed for God's grace to heal the severe exhaustion and weakness that I was experiencing.

And then a dear friend came to visit me at the apartment. She told me point-blank that if I did not get to Nairobi very soon, I would surely die. She told me she had lived through a similar attack some years earlier, and by trying to stick it out in-country, her health had been seriously impacted long-term. It had taken her three years to recover. She warned me that if I did not want long-term health issues, I must leave Tanzania as soon as possible.

I finally came to my senses; I contacted MAF and booked a seat on the next flight to Nairobi.

Back to Nairobi

Do not fear, for I have redeemed you;
I have summoned you by name; you are mine.
When you pass through the waters,
I will be with you;
and when you pass through the rivers,
they will not sweep over you.
When you walk through the fire,
you will not be burned;
the flames will not set you ablaze.
For I am the Lord your God,
the Holy One of Israel, your Savior.

—ISAIAH 43:1B–3A

The next two weeks were a nightmare; I had never been so sick in my life. I had to wait a few days for the next MAF flight to Nairobi, allowing me time to organize my things and pack a suitcase while also doing the best I could to finish scoring the students' SAT exams. I felt horrible about deserting my teaching partner, but we both knew I had no choice.

In spite of the seriousness of my situation, I still hoped to regain full health in time to return to Tanzania for the following school year. Because the airplane had minimal space for luggage, I felt perfectly comfortable leaving all my teaching materials and most of my clothing behind, figuring I would be back in two months.

Riding in a small plane to Nairobi was not as exciting as usual because I was too sick to enjoy it in the least. My fellow passengers were a family of three headed for Nairobi hospital. The parents were escorting their young son who had broken his arm and was scheduled for emergency surgery. The pilot and the parents were totally focused on the child's pain and discomfort, so I was basically on my own regarding the required steps of weighing me and my suitcase, dragging it onboard, and boarding and leaving the plane unassisted.

As soon as we landed at the airport, the pilot and the family disappeared, leaving me standing there alone on the tarmac. I pulled out my cell phone and called a taxi. When he arrived, I asked him to drive me to Dr. Chunge's clinic. Dr. Chunge was a man known to be the top tropical disease expert in Nairobi. I had had his contact information since 2002 when the school administrators had distributed it during orientation. In God's perfect grace, I had always kept the doctor's business card in my wallet.

When I entered the clinic, Dr. Chunge's staff immediately ran various lab tests, and then he met with me personally to explain the results. Not only was I recovering from cerebral malaria and anemia, but I also had bilharzia (known as schistosomiasis in the U.S.) and giardia.

Dr. Chunge further explained that testing for malaria often revealed the presence of other diseases that had been hiding in the patient's body for some time. He suspected I had had bilharzia since serving in Niger. He gave me medications for the two newly-diagnosed diseases and advised me to discontinue the liquid iron at once to avoid possible iron poisoning; he felt the dosage I had been given was seriously dangerous. The medication he gave me for bilharzia was called Biltricide, but a better name for it would have been 'suicide.'

When I thanked the doctor for his help, he urged me, "Do not leave Africa. We know how to care for you in this country, but in America you will not find doctors who know how to successfully treat most African diseases. Stay in Nairobi and come back to my clinic if you need further assistance."

I explained to him that I had already bought a ticket to go home for a family wedding, but that I planned to return to Africa at the end of the summer. I promised that if I had any problems, I would return to confer with him before flying back to Tanzania.

After I had finished at the clinic, the taxi driver drove me to a dear friend's apartment. I had contacted her in advance to tell her of my plight, and she had graciously invited me to recover at her home. When I arrived at her apartment, we spoke briefly, she showed me all the enticing healthy food she had prepared, we prayed together, and she promptly left for work.

I was so relieved to be in a clean, safe environment, hosted by a compassionate woman whom I had met in California when she was on furlough some years ago. I took the Biltricide and climbed into a cozy bed, snuggling into the comforter and soon falling fast asleep. However, I awoke in the night doubled over with extreme abdominal pain. I honestly did not expect to survive the night, but I was in too much pain to try to do anything about it.

To my surprise, I survived the night. The next morning, I began the long, painful process toward recovery, inching along, one tiny step at a time. By the grace of God, and due to my friend's compassionate care, I slowly improved a little each day.

At the appointed time, I climbed on a plane and came home to my family in California—sick, weak, and immeasurably grateful that God had answered my prayer!

CHAPTER SIX

DISCIPLESHIP DETOUR
(MAY 2005-MAY 2007)

|||||||||||||||||||

Homecoming

The Lord will keep you from all harm—
he will watch over your life;
the Lord will watch over your coming and going
both now and forevermore.

—PSALM 121:7–8

I arrived back in California several weeks before the date of the family wedding. My homecoming was a sweet time of reunion with family and friends, our days filled with hugs, laughter, and the gift of just being together. We also mutually expressed our joy and relief that I was back on American soil, safe and sound. Thank you, Lord!

Feeling the crisis had passed and that our focus should be on the wedding, I told my family very little about the malaria treatment and the nightmarish side effects. Instead, I jumped in to help with wedding preparations as best I could with minimal energy. The next weeks flew by as we all prepared for the big day.

The family wedding was another joyous day of reconnecting with many of my loved ones. I was delighted to have a reason to fully focus on something totally unrelated to my recent health scare. Though I was still unwell, I honestly believed that I would attain full recovery by the end of the summer.

Return to American Worship

Ascribe to the Lord the glory due his name;
worship the Lord in the splendor of his holiness.
—PSALM 29:2

After becoming accustomed to worshiping African-style, returning to an American church was a definite adjustment. For starts, most of the African congregations I had attended consisted of forty to fifty worshipers, but I returned to an American church that served a total of 1200-1500 people in three separate services each Sunday.

When I had been commissioned to serve as a missionary, that same church had met in a small sanctuary serving 150–200 people each week. But while I was absent, the church had drastically changed in identity and size. A massive new building had been constructed on the edge of town, and the previous church buildings had been sold.

Instead of a small sanctuary with stained glass windows all around us, now the services were conducted in a huge multi-purpose room surrounded by floor-to-ceiling windows with heavy curtains pulled back. There was a full-sized stage with beautiful thick curtains and elaborate lighting, a large worship band with electric instruments, an impressive sound system, and two huge projector screens where the song verses were displayed. I was overwhelmed by the magnitude of the new surroundings.

I was also overwhelmed by the number of people in attendance. While I was overseas, my home church had adopted a "seeker-friendly" outreach program specifically designed to extend the church's membership and services to the community. The program had been highly successful, but for me as a returning member, the sense of intimacy and community had been lost. When I attended Sunday morning services, I was one face among hundreds, a complete stranger to most of the people around me.

Oddly enough, I also had difficulty readjusting to a congregation that was primarily white worshipers. I was amused to realize that my eyes and brain had unconsciously adapted to seeing darker skin colors as normal, so now the majority of my American peers looked pale and unhealthy to me.

After living and working with people who had had so little and were content with the little that they had, I was uneasy returning to a materially rich culture. I was acutely uncomfortable with the topics that seemed to dominate conversations during fellowship times, or even occasionally during the sermons. I could no longer relate to caring about the newest fashions, the latest model of cars, the longing for a bigger house, or the drive to climb the social or professional ladder of success. I quickly realized that returning to my home culture was just as difficult as entering a new culture had been in 2001.

It took me a while, but I eventually reconnected with a number of the people who had known me in pre-Africa days. The old Bible study group still existed, and when I was well enough to attend, I was blessed by the fellowship and the stimulating lessons. I also extended my participation to a second church that was smaller and closer to my home.

Before I had left for Africa, I had seen the signs indicating a shift was coming in my home church's overall focus. A few friends who were aware of my concerns had invited me to visit their smaller church, and when I did, I found a place where I felt I could more effectively grow and worship. Consequently, each summer when I had come home on furlough, I had routinely attended both churches every Sunday.

I was forever grateful to the large church for sending me to the mission field, but I was also relieved to worship in a more family-like setting where I did not feel like a total stranger. In 2003, to my surprise and delight, the smaller church had voluntarily begun supporting me, both in finances and in prayer. I was truly blessed to have two church families cheering me on.

When I returned to California in 2005 for my fifth summer furlough, I was faced with only one drawback in both churches: I needed to relearn a worship style that better fit the expectations in an American congregation. I had to consciously readjust my actions to match those of the worshipers around me by stifling the occasional temptation to dance to the worship songs. Internally, I was often dancing, but externally I maintained a stance of quiet reverence more familiar to those around me.

I remembered the Lord's exhortation expressed by Paul that "everything should be done in a fitting and orderly way" (1 Corinthians 14:40). I recognized, too, that in curbing my outward actions, the Lord was chiseling away at my willingness to honor Him in all circumstances. He was teaching me the vital importance of always waiting on Him.

The Desert Years

*I will lead her into the wilderness
and speak tenderly to her.*

—HOSEA 2:14

As the days swiftly passed, my physical status did not change. I continued to battle debilitating hot flashes, extreme exhaustion, and daily nausea, not to mention the ongoing insomnia and panic attacks.

When I had first arrived back on American soil, Wycliffe had assigned a personnel advisor to monitor my progress toward regaining full health. According to Wycliffe, his primary role was to encourage me during the healing process, but he was not particularly gifted at dispensing hope. In fact, he suggested several times that I should seriously consider giving up my Wycliffe membership. He called me often to ask what steps I had taken to improve my health, and then he would ask what progress I had seen as a result of those steps. From his tone and comments, I was fully aware that he was seldom pleased with my replies.

When I first returned to Davis, I had been thoroughly examined by my primary care physician, who honestly admitted that she had little or no knowledge of malaria or its treatment. Nonetheless, she encouraged me to do whatever I could to follow general recommendations for any normal recovery process.

In seeking more supportive input, I had hired a professional nutritionist. In contrast to my doctor, the nutritionist was extremely knowledgeable about the disease. She immediately recommended various supplements and a healthy diet with specific foods to naturally improve my iron level, recovery process, and immunity system. She gave me the specific tools I needed to feel actively engaged in the process of recovery.

I also spent hours searching the internet for helpful information, and I bought every book I could find that might have reasonable solutions for my situation. Yet, in spite of all my efforts during the next two months, I was aware that my physical status was not much better than when I had first left Africa. I began to recognize the possibility that I might have to extend my original goal of returning to Tanzania in late August or early September to a slightly later date.

In mid-August, my personnel advisor informed me that Wycliffe had decided I needed to be medically evaluated before returning to Africa. He informed me I was required to meet with the tropical disease expert who was serving at the Wycliffe linguistic center near Dallas. I booked a ticket, packed a suitcase, and headed for Texas.

But from then on, things did not go as I had hoped or envisioned. After three days of multiple medical tests and exams, I was diagnosed with CFIDS (Chronic Fatigue and Immune Deficiency Syndrome), and I was assigned to a mandatory Medical Leave for one to two years, an assignment I viewed as a painful sentence.

Flying back to California, I was basically in a state of shock as I tried to absorb the doctor's final words. I did not want to believe I could be stuck in limbo for an extended period of time. When I told my two dearest friends of my unwelcome news, they made every effort to comfort and encourage me as I painfully adjusted to the reality of the mandate.

Wycliffe's decision left me with a handful of tough realities, starting with my need for long-term housing. For the past two months, I had been graciously hosted by several different church families, but with my unexpected change in status, I realized I would have to find somewhere more permanent to live.

Though I still owned a house in Davis, that house was not available for my use. Unfortunately, before I had gone to Texas, the woman who had been renting it for several years had already signed a one-year renewal contract. My rental manager was insistent that I could not legally break the signed agreement, regardless of the change in my own personal circumstances. With his words ringing in my ears, I was forced to seek and find an apartment to rent for the next twelve months.

Davis was and is a university town, so the availability of apartments was widespread. I chose one that was not far from my house and was located in the part of town with which I was most familiar. It was also a fair distance from the university campus, so I assumed most of my neighbors would be established Davis residents.

Unfortunately, though the apartment complex had seemed quiet and inviting when I visited, I soon discovered that almost all of my neighbors were young college students who seemed more interested in partying than in studying. The noise level was often high, both day and night, and I had lost my ability to sleep through almost anything, or, perhaps more accurately, I had lost my ability to sleep much at all.

My personnel advisor was directed to help me find solutions for any financial short-falls that might occur during my extended presence in the U.S.; evidently, Wycliffe was aware of a certain pattern that was common when a missionary came home ill. Even though my financial supporters knew I was recovering from a serious bout with malaria, I was quite surprised when several of them decided to discontinue their monthly financial support. By the end of the summer, my Wycliffe account balance had dropped significantly. That change could have been a serious problem, but in God's perfect timing, I had reached the age to begin receiving a long-awaited pension. Thank you, Lord; Jesus to the rescue!

God's Grace

Three times I pleaded with the Lord to take it away from me. But he said to me, "My grace is sufficient for you, for my power is made perfect in weakness."
—2 CORINTHIANS 12:8

Over the next ten months, I battled daily nausea, weakness, exhaustion, insomnia, and deep grief at the loss of a ministry I had loved, not to mention the stark isolation and depression of chronic illness. I was especially thankful for two older women who faithfully came to visit and pray with me each week, and for the family members and friends who had always supported me in the good times and the bad. Their love and compassion kept me sane.

Tragically, I also continued to experience frequent panic attacks. The internal shakiness had started in Tanzania when I had first ingested the Cloartem, but the symptoms had continued long after I had finished the prescribed medication. A fellow teacher in Niger had experienced similar trauma when she took Larium, a malaria prophylactic, so I suspected that Cloartem contained some of the same chemical ingredients. I knew from her letters that she had eventually broken free of the side effects, so I hoped and prayed that I would, too, God willing.

When the panic attacks would hit me for no apparent reason, I learned to immediately pray or recite Scripture aloud, and then to focus my attention on solving Sudoku puzzles, doing Bible study, reading a book, or doing anything else I could think of that would take my mind off the physical shakiness of my body. In the process of distracting myself, the shakiness would soon cease and I would be at peace again for a while. The cycle repeated itself several times a day.

Because I viewed the attacks primarily as a spiritual battle, their frequent occurrences regularly reminded me that the only lasting peace I could expect would be from the Lord. I grew evermore aware and dependent upon His constant presence while His Word consistently sustained me. The following are just a few of the excerpts from my journal during that season:

- Turn to me and be gracious to me, for I am lonely and afflicted (Psalm 25:14-15).
- It's a battle to stay focused on You here—it's easy in Tanzania! Teach me Your way, O Lord; lead me in a straight path because of my oppressors (Psalm 27:11).
- My times are in your hands! The Lord preserves the faithful! BE STRONG AND TAKE HEART, ALL YOU WHO HOPE IN THE LORD (Psalm 31:15, 23-24).
- I will not die but live, and will proclaim what the Lord has done. The Lord has chastened me severely, but he has not given me over to death (Psalm 118:17-18).
- I wait for the Lord, my soul waits, and in his word, I put my hope! (Psalm 130:5).
- The Lord will fulfill his purpose for me; your love, O Lord, endures forever—do not abandon the works of your hands (Psalm 138:8).
- I remember the days of long ago; I meditate on all your works and consider what your hands have done ... my soul thirsts for you ... show me the way ... rescue me ... teach me to do your will, for you are my God (Psalm 143).

- Lord, the offering I bring You is my brokenness, my failures, my shortcomings, my unworthiness and, in exchange, You give me Your love. Thank you! Sing alleluia to the King!
- David said to his son, Solomon, "Be strong and courageous, and do the work. Do not be afraid or discouraged, for the Lord God, my God, is with you. He will not fail you or forsake you until all the work for the service of the temple of the Lord is finished" (1 Chronicles 28:20). Lord, help me do the 'work' You have for me—resting and healing when I'd rather be active.

His Loving Care

A friend loves at all times,
and a brother is born for a time of adversity.
—PROVERBS 17:17

I hasten to emphasize that my life was not all darkness. In God's gentle kindness, He chose that particular time to gift me with a treasure I could never have sought. At the larger church, I was surprised to meet several Ugandan women who regularly attended the services. We immediately became the best of friends. They were excited to meet someone who had been to their home country, who spoke and understood some Kiswahili, and who loved African foods, and I was excited to find someone who could relate to my experiences in Africa.

My new friends, my sisters in Christ and in shared experiences, readily plied me with chapati, Sukuma wiki, and African stew, and they took me with them to several Ugandan gatherings that met in the area. Because of my illness and lack of energy, we did not see one another often, but a rich sisterhood developed that has continued for decades.

Serving in the Quiet Moments

In spite, or maybe because, of the daily struggles, I spent hours and hours reading the Word of God and snuggling in to conversational prayer with Him alone. I also consumed an unbelievable number of Christian books, both fiction and nonfiction. I was constantly writing in my journal, processing the most recent Scripture or author's message that I had read. Being homebound most of my days, I had more than enough time to allow my faith to grow in the season the Lord had ordained.

Our God is gracious; He knows our every need. While I was growing spiritually through constant study, I still had a need to be needed, a desire to serve in some tangible way. In His infinite grace, the Lord gave me a subtle ministry that required very little energy on my part: He allowed me to minister to the women around me through listening, encouraging, and praying for them. My physical confinement made me readily available to others, so my days were often marked with unexpected encounters, or maybe they were divine appointments.

Now in their twenties, several of the girls who had been in the 1990's youth group sought me out for private one-on-one mentoring, and several older women often called me for a lengthy phone conversation followed by prayer.

And then there was my dear neighbor who had been one of my prayer supporters overseas. When she discovered that I lived near her apartment, she reached out for the fellowship she had been so desperately missing for decades. She was a special needs adult who grappled with mental and social issues, making it difficult for her to feel comfortable in any group situation. But I was not bothered by her strange behavior, and she knew it. She often showed up at my door unannounced, and we became like sisters. I was pleased that the Lord could use me to offer her a friendship that continues to this day.

I was also blessed with another friendship that lasted for only a matter of months. Shortly after moving in to my apartment, I had called the church office to ask if they knew of a homebound woman who would like an occasional visitor. The church secretary gave me the phone number of an elderly woman who was in a rehabilitation center nearby. Eager to encourage her, I called and set up an appointment for our first meeting.

But our God has a sense of humor—she was the one who encouraged me! Each time I went to visit, she would ask me to push her wheelchair from room to room so that she could chat and pray with her rehab neighbors. She was an amazing woman, filled with joy and the love of the Lord. I was truly sad to lose her cheerful companionship when she died unexpectedly, but I thanked God for a memorial service that truly glorified His name and recognized His servant's faithfulness. I prayed, too, that my friend's incredible witness would eventually draw her lukewarm daughter into wholehearted devotion to the Lord.

Flickers of Hope

But the eyes of the Lord are on those who fear him,
on those whose hope is in his unfailing love.

—PSALM 33:18

After twelve long months, I began to experience moments of feeling a little better. The moments began to increase in frequency, and gradually I began to regain some semblance of normal health, though sleeping was still a major hurdle. In September, 2006, I was delighted to move back into my own house in a quiet, peaceful neighborhood. Thank you, Lord! Things were looking up.

Around that same time, the larger church invited me to be one of the speakers at their annual women's retreat. I was thrilled! I loved writing and sharing about Jesus, and the preparation process kept me pleasantly engaged for an extended period of time.

The main speaker had chosen the theme of "The Woman with the Alabaster Jar" (Matthew 26:7, Mark 14:3, and Luke 7:37). She used all three biblical references to challenge us to demonstrate our love for Jesus, in spite of any social or personal repercussions that could hold us back. The speaker presented her message in four sessions, and she asked me to give my personal testimony in between two of those sessions. Then she used my life experiences to demonstrate God's faithfulness when we dare to step out in faith.

The weekend was physically draining but spiritually and emotionally uplifting as the Lord gave me the ability to share my testimony with strength and great joy. Speaking of His faithful history in my life had encouraged not only the audience, but had also encouraged me by reminding me of His everlasting love and care. Truly, our heavenly Father never wastes a thing (Romans 8:28).

Tough News from Africa

This is what the Lord says: "When (the years of exile) are completed, I will come to you and fulfill my good promise to bring you back to this place. For I know the plans I have for you," declares the Lord, "plans to prosper you and not to harm you, plans to give you hope and a future."

—JEREMIAH 29:10–11

During my two-year confinement, I had often dreamed of going back to teach in Tanzania to reconnect with all my previous students, especially with Afzal. I longed to hear of their progress, and to know that he was going forward in his faith. I had stayed in contact with the school through occasional emails, but when I received one from them after several months of silence, their news rocked my world.

The email informed me that on Good Friday in April, 2006, Afzal had died of malarial complications. That same day, his Muslim father had gone to the Christian church during the afternoon service to quietly request speaking with someone from the school. When the headmaster came to speak with him, Afzal's father invited all the teachers to come to the funeral service for his son that same afternoon.

The teachers honored his request by following him to the funeral site where they joined Afzal's family in their grief. At the meal following the funeral, Afzal's father told the headmaster, "I know it is no accident that my son died on a Christian holiday."

When the school wrote to tell me of Afzal's death and his father's comment, I was deeply grieved to think his life had been snuffed out so young, and to realize I would not see him again on this earth. It seemed so unfair that I had survived that same terrible disease and his life had been taken. But I also thanked God for the opportunity He had given me to love and minister to that boy and to witness the dynamic change in his countenance during the few months that I had known him.

Instead of dying alone and depressed, he had died with the joy of the Lord in his heart and with a school full of friends who had learned to love him as he was. I also rejoiced at his father's subtle recognition of Afzal's faith, and I prayed that Afzal's witness to his family would bring about their salvation as well. Our God is mighty; He can even touch the lives of those who have only brushed shoulders with His people.

Ocean Baptism

Peter replied, "Repent and be baptized, every one of you, in the name of Jesus Christ for the forgiveness of your sins. And you will receive the gift of the Holy Spirit."

—ACTS 2:38

One evidence of God's amazing grace for me during that difficult season was the treasured fulfillment of a longstanding desire: on September 4, 2006, I was baptized in the Pacific Ocean!

Years before I had joined Wycliffe, I had wanted to be baptized by immersion to confirm as an adult what had been done for me as a child. As my faith had grown over time, my full understanding of the gift and purpose of baptism had also grown. I remembered well when I was sprinkled with water and welcomed into the family of God as a child, but as an adult I wanted to publicly acknowledge my submission and gratitude for all He had done for me throughout my life. In my eyes, submitting to immersion would be a confirmation of the faith He had planted in my heart when I was only a child.

In the 1990's, I had been unsuccessful in finding a pastor who was willing to baptize me in California's cold, rough waters. Then when I was in Mombasa where the waters were actually warm, I had wanted to be baptized in the Indian Ocean, but again I was unsuccessful in bringing that hope to fruition. Now that I had returned to California, a notice in the larger church's weekly bulletin had reignited that desire in my heart.

When I read there would soon be a baptism ceremony in a nearby lake, I requested to be included among those who would be baptized. But the pastor was horrified at my request; he was convinced that since I was serving as a missionary, to be baptized as an adult would be misunderstood by observers as negating all the Lord had done for me in my past fifty-six years of faith. I heartily disagreed with his perspective, but recognized he had the final say as the pastor of the church.

Shortly thereafter, I asked the pastor of the smaller church if he would perform the baptism, and he readily agreed. The following week during service, he announced that a date had been set to baptize me in the ocean, and that he was extending an open invitation to anyone else who would like to join me. Within days, my dear friends' two sons and their grandson had decided to join me in the sacrament of baptism.

One Sunday morning, twenty-eight members of the church family traveled with me to Point Reyes National Park, hiked down to the beach, and shared a public baptism ceremony in the sight of other beach-goers. We ended the celebration with an agape feast picnic on the sand.

I am embarrassed to share an amusing moment that occurred during the baptism itself. After the pastor had lowered me into the water and raised me back up, the two of us were hit from behind by a large, forceful wave. Because of my foot disability, I could not hold my balance and when I went down, I took the pastor with me. When we both came up sputtering, he told me I was the only person he had ever baptized who had been double-dunked!

Not only was I blessed by a dream come true, but I was further blessed to share it with special friends, and to know that the Lord was using our boldness in mighty ways. The strangers around us were exposed to the Scripture readings, the songs, the pastor's explanation of the reasons for baptism, and the act of watching five individuals go into the icy ocean to publicly declare their devotion to the Lord. Yes, the water was cold, but the day could not have been more perfect. Sing alleluia to the King!

Saying Goodbye to Africa

Though the fig tree does not bud
and there are no grapes on the vines,
though the olive crop fails
and the fields produce no food,
though there are no sheep in the pen
and no cattle in the stalls,
yet I will rejoice in the Lord,
I will be joyful in God my Savior.
—HABAKKUK 3:17–18

I spent two full years actively working toward official release from Medical Leave. Near the end of the second year, the panic attacks slowly disappeared and then finally, at the end of what seemed like an eternity of waiting, my personnel advisor informed me that I could begin preparing to return to active duty. I was thrilled to receive that news, but to my great disappointment, he also informed me that Wycliffe had decided I would not be allowed to return to Africa; in fact, I would not be assigned to any location overseas.

Needless to say, I had been devastated by the news of Afzal's death, but in some strange way, that news may have helped me to begin letting go of my determination to return to Africa while my own health was still fragile. I continued working toward full wellness, but I also finally accepted that only the Lord knew where I would serve in the future.

Season of Growth

I will instruct you and teach you in the way you should go;
I will counsel you with my loving eye on you.
—PSALM 32:8

My long season of physical illness had been emotionally painful, but the time had not been wasted. God had performed a deep work in my heart. He had sustained me, day by day, inch by inch, and He had never left me or forsaken me.

He had given me two years to be actively involved in coming alongside my unbelieving family members, encouraging and supporting them through their own joys and struggles and living my faith under their watchful eyes.

The Lord had taught me to truly trust His choices and to draw ever closer to Him. As I changed my focus from my problems to His majesty, my overall outlook improved and, like Job, when I became more involved in praying for others, God answered my prayers as well.

I thanked God that I was well enough to start taking baby steps forward. Finally, after twenty-four months of waiting, I was free to begin searching for a new position with Wycliffe Bible Translators.

Job Search

Stating that I would not be allowed to serve overseas definitely clarified my choices for future service with Wycliffe. My only remaining option was to find an assignment on or attached to the North American continent. Consequently, there were only three possibilities: Mexico, Texas, and North Carolina

First, I contacted our Mexico base to ask about possible openings in Oaxaca, but the Human Resources department replied they were not in need of any more missionaries. That left Texas and North Carolina as my only options.

The Texas center was and is the home of what was known as GIAL, Graduate Institute of Applied Linguistics, more recently renamed Dallas International University. The sole purpose of GIAL's graduate and undergraduate programs was to educate students interested in linguistics and language development, most of whom were planning to serve as overseas missionaries. I had no training in linguistics, so it was clear that Texas was not the answer.

That left North Carolina, the home of JAARS, where I had completed my initial training for overseas placement. From the minimal exposure I had had there, I knew I loved the international environment, so I hoped there would be a good fit for my particular skills. I contacted the Human Resources department to let them know of my interest and availability.

When the personnel director contacted me, we began a long conversation that continued through emails and phone calls, covering my history, interests, and desire to continue serving. When I mentioned missing Africa, he shared that he, too, had served in Kenya, and that he had been forced home by health issues, so he totally understood my grief. But he emphasized that we had both been called to missions, not to Africa, and that our job was to serve wherever God led us in any given season.

Together, we spent several weeks researching various job possibilities, and then he invited me to join his staff in the Human Resources department. The job he described did not sound ideal to me, but while I was still in the process of regaining full health and strength, it sounded like a good start. I was happy to accept his invitation.

Before I could begin my new assignment, I needed to rebuild my financial and prayer support teams to meet 100% of Wycliffe's requirements. As I had done before, I began making presentations at church services and small groups to share the details of my new assignment and to invite the listeners to come along as supporters. I loved sharing what God was doing! Once again, the Lord was faithful to touch the hearts of those He was calling to walk with me in accomplishing His work. In only six months' time, I was ready to go.

I did not miss God's sense of humor in my being assigned to JAARS. In my own strength, my plan had been to teach in Africa for ten to fifteen years, and then I would return to Waxhaw when I was too old to serve overseas. But in fact, I had served in Africa for a little less than five years, and now I was headed back to JAARS. Clearly, the Lord had a different timetable than the one I had independently created!

Waxhaw, North Carolina
June 2007-September 2015

PHOTOS: International flags, translated Bibles, and missionary kids

CHAPTER SEVEN

JAARS, INC.
(JUNE 2007-SEPTEMBER 2015)

|||||||||||||||||||

What is JAARS?

JAARS, Inc. (originally known as Jungle Aviation and Radio Services) is the sister organization that was created by Cameron Townsend, Wycliffe Bible Translators' and SIL's founder, to provide the necessary support services to keep translators on the field. The title was officially shortened to JAARS, Inc. when the technologies advanced and the services offered were extended.

JAARS was and is committed to supporting Bible translation through training new members; servicing planes and communications systems for remote areas; providing optimal air, ground or water transportation for remote areas; and creating the latest computer and media programs available to produce gospel materials for Bibleless people groups throughout the world. The JAARS Youth department is also committed to raising the next generation of missionaries. All members and volunteers are committed to prayer and service as vital tools for furthering the kingdom of God.

The JAARS campus is located near the town of Waxhaw, North Carolina, about an hour south of Charlotte. The campus was originally about 250 acres, but it has grown to more than 550 acres of gorgeous countryside with a man-made lake and a private air strip. When I lived there, the buildings on campus included:

- The *Townsend building,* which housed an attractive reception area, tour room, auditorium, dining room, and a popular gift shop, along with offices for marketing, accounting, partnership development, and human resources
- The *Alphabet Museum* and the *Cardenas Museum,* where the public could learn about the history of the written language and Wycliffe Bible Translators' beginnings
- The *Housing* and *Housekeeping* departments, which provided services for both missionaries and volunteers
- The *IT/Language and Translation, Vernacular Media,* and *Creative Services* departments and the *JAARS Library*
- The *Aviation, Maritime Services,* and *Land Transportation* departments
- The *Trucking* department, which transported missionary families' household goods anywhere within the United States
- The *International Shipping* department, where the team collected, packed, and shipped essential supplies to Wycliffe missionaries all over the world
- The *Auto Shop* and *Construction and Maintenance* department
- The *Boutique,* where free clothing was available for all missionaries and volunteers
- The *Health Clinic, Counseling Center,* JAARS *Post Office, and JAARS Preschool*
- And the *Youth and Family Ministries* department, which included a large clubhouse, an outdoor pool, and a children's playground.

JAARS tours were available Monday through Friday, both for walk-ins and for large groups who made reservations in advance. Six times a year, JAARS invited the public to join them for JAARS Days when every department offered informative presentations. The Aviation department also sold tickets for small plane and helicopter rides. Each JAARS Day had a different theme to emphasize the many services JAARS offered to support Bible translation. JAARS Days usually hosted a crowd of several hundred people, some flying in from exceptionally far distances to attend.

In the summertime, JAARS welcomed volunteer church groups who came to learn about missionary work while serving in various support roles, such as refurbishing apartments, painting houses, or clearing brush from the runway edges. Meanwhile, church youth groups could sign up to come stay at the rustic outdoors camp for a week while they, too, learned about missions and actively served in some group capacity.

At Christmastime, an extensive staff of volunteers presented Passport Christmas, converting the auditorium into an imaginary airplane and 'flying' children to several passport countries to learn about the cultures and the translation work being done there. Each year, three or four different countries were highlighted. The children were divided into small color groups to travel from country to country. The volunteers wore traditional clothing for the countries they represented.

At the beginning of the day, the children were issued passports to fill with entry and exit stamps. As they traveled, they sampled foods, music, and games from each country. They ended the day with the flight home on the big plane and a final presentation of the gospel message. Many children heard about Jesus for the first time, some gave their hearts to Him, and others committed their lives to mission work in the future. Many of the parents, too, were positively impacted by learning about JAARS' outreach to the nations, and about Jesus Christ.

Seasonal Splendor

Then God said, "Let the land produce vegetation: seed-bearing plants and trees on the land that bear fruit with seed in it, according to their various kinds." And it was so ... And God saw that it was good.

—GENESIS 1:11–12

I had never lived back East before, so I was especially impressed by the personality of the seasons and the dramatic change in colors throughout the year. The scenery around me was truly magnificent. Much of the year, there were trees of every possible hue all growing together along the roads. I had never before seen so many shades of green.

Summers reminded me of the wet seasons in Africa because of the hot, humid days. Autumn took my breath away with the variety of vibrant colors on the trees; I had had no idea that trees could exhibit so many colors of the rainbow. Winter was marked by the contrast of bare and evergreen trees and the beauty of freshly fallen snow, which crept in a time or two each year. I was not fond of the cold in winter, but it was quite survivable when I was snuggled in to my cozy little apartment. And finally, the spring completed the visual splendor with an array of new greens on the trees and a burst of pastel blossoms everywhere.

My apartment was within walking distance of the picturesque lake. In fact, I was within walking distance of most of the buildings on the campus. But I was not within walking distance of any grocery stores! The nearest shopping area was about thirty minutes away. The JAARS campus was peacefully nestled into a beautiful section of countryside way out in the middle of nowhere.

Culture Shock Again?

Sometimes, I joked with my supporters that I had served in two foreign countries: Africa and North Carolina! The culture of the southern states was definitely different than the California lifestyle familiar to me. Growing up, I had had certain imaginings about life in the South, but moving there, I found my fantasy was a little off. I had not exactly entered the pages of *Gone with the Wind*, but the modern-day version was close enough to suit me. I loved the southern accents and gracious hospitality, the 'sweet tea,' hush puppies, and grits, while I was simultaneously stunned by the volume of fried foods regularly consumed by local residents.

Living on the Bible Belt was a stark contrast to living in an ultra-liberal state. I was amazed at the number of public billboards with Bible verses or Christian messages openly displayed. Furthermore, from all appearances, I was relieved that there seemed to be no major racial hostility among residents, at least in the Waxhaw vicinity. Overall, the atmosphere of friendliness and cordiality reminded me of bygone days—as far as the social attitudes, I felt like I had reentered the 1950's.

JAARS Assignments

Whatever you do, work at it with all your heart, as working for the Lord, not for men, since you know that you will receive an inheritance from the Lord as a reward. It is the Lord Christ you are serving.

—COLOSSIANS 3:23–24

Over a period of eight years, I served in three different departments. When I first arrived, I was assigned to be a Volunteer Coordinator in the Human Resources department. My job was primarily to "meet and greet, encourage and pray." With new volunteers arriving all the time, it was my job to conduct personal interviews to determine the individuals' skills and interests, and then to begin the long process of joining with them to find the job the Lord had specifically put aside just for them.

I was supplied with a huge binder that contained descriptions of all the open positions available in each JAARS department. The binder was frequently updated and I was expected to keep abreast of the constantly changing needs. When I found a possible fit for a new volunteer, I would call the appropriate department head and report back to the volunteer if an invitation was extended. Then the volunteer would go visit the department to see if he or she was interested in accepting the invitation. When a match was successfully accomplished, I would prepare the required paperwork and send it with the volunteer to begin service in his or her new role.

Most of our volunteers were retired persons looking for a way to serve the Lord in their later years. Many of them came with helpful skills that were vital to our daily operations: retired IT experts, engineers, airplane or auto mechanics, receptionists, store managers, preschool teachers, homemakers, accounting experts—the list was endless. I loved meeting with new volunteers who were eager to discover their role at JAARS, and I always loved praying with them as well.

But other than the social interactions, I was not particularly excited about my new job. Though I was glad to be back on active duty, I felt that most of my particular skills were not being utilized in the Human Resources department.

I was comforted by the fact that at least my presence was supporting Bible translation. I remembered well the humble servants I had met overseas who were willing to perform whatever task was necessary to bring the Word of God to the nations, and I prayerfully sought to embrace a similar attitude. I was still coping with major insomnia and chronic fatigue, so my daily prayer was that the Lord would bless me with contentment and the strength to serve as best I could. I had written in my journal:

June, 2007: Lord, as I stare at a painting of you with your arms outstretched, beckoning me, I hear, "My daughter, give me everything." You are teaching me to stop, rest, listen, wait, meditate, research, grow, change, and to let go! Help me to absorb the lessons.

I give you my body, mind, spirit and emotions. I give you my aches, pains, symptoms, and concerns. I give you my family, friends, and enemies. I give you my hopes, dreams, expectations, disappointments, unhealed spots, and struggles. I give you my short-comings, obsessions and compulsions. I give you my weariness, nausea, confusion, and concerns for the 'right' diet and exercise. I give you my time, schedule, and desire to be productive.

I give you my job and attitudes about it. I give you my physical surroundings. I give you my grief and longing for Africa. I give you my goofy foot and physical limitations. I give you my fears—all of them. I give you my sins: pride, criticism, judgment, rebellion, fear, worry, and perfectionism. I give you my thoughts, words, and actions. I give you my joys, enthusiasm, and personality.

Lord, I give you my past, present and future. I give you my physical needs and desires. I give you 'my' spiritual gifts and the use of them. I give you my fears, laughter, anger, and frustrations. I give you all my responses. I give you my life, health, intellect, and talents. I give you 'my' money. I give you my potential.

> I give you my exhaustion and grumpiness, my ups and downs.
>
> Lord, I give you all that I am, all that I possess. Lord, use me as you will. Direct my paths!

There were two other volunteer coordinators who had been serving with JAARS for some years. Together, the three of us met weekly with the personnel director to divide up the jobs for the week. Before long, I noticed a pattern of frequent misunderstandings regarding the director's instructions to the three of us, so I began taking meeting notes in shorthand. Then each week, I emailed the transcribed minutes to my boss and the other two volunteer coordinators, asking them to correct me on any misinformation. The minutes effectively ended the misunderstandings and allowed us to proceed forward as a more cohesive team.

Still, I struggled with my own limitations. Even though I was actively working toward full energy, I often felt like I was not contributing enough to the team. I had written in my journal:

> July 2, 2007: Proverbs 3:5-6, Trust in the Lord with all your heart and do not rely on your own insight; acknowledge him in all things and he will make your paths straight. And verses 7-8: Do not be wise in your own eyes; fear the Lord and shun evil. This will bring health to your body and nourishment to your bones.

> August 4, 2007: Help me, Father, to give up my fears of failure and not doing enough. Help me to learn to rest!

Little did I know that the Lord would use my shorthand ability to move me into a new position. Unbeknownst to the rest of us, for some time my boss had been in the process of creating a new department at JAARS. Fifteen months after stepping in to my position at Human Resources, the director met with me privately to thank me for writing the minutes and to tell me that he wanted me to move with him to a new department.

He informed me that he wanted me to serve as the communications coordinator for the newly formed Business Services Team, a team of seven

IT experts who would be creating advanced computer programs not only for JAARS but for the IT experts serving Wycliffe translators throughout the world.

I was more than a little surprised, but agreed to make the move. On my new team, my primary role would be to attend long, technical meetings, take notes, and write endless reports for various IT projects, and then to email the reports to our team and to other JAARS departments involved in implementing the plans.

Once again, the job description did not seem to fit my particular skills (other than shorthand), but in prayer, I sensed the Lord was prompting me to make the change. I felt He was challenging me to accept that the best way for me to support Bible translation might not look like what I would choose. Would I trust Him? Yes, Lord; I will trust You.

Initially, I was overwhelmed by working with an all-men's team of experts who spoke a technical language I did not understand, and who communicated with one another in what seemed to me to be an overly aggressive manner. I was definitely intimidated by the way two of them would speak directly to me.

In God's perfect grace, He blessed me with one team member who noticed my discomfort. He privately asked me why I appeared to be distressed at some of the meetings. When he understood the reasons for my uneasiness, he educated me on some of the key technical terms and on "the ways of men." He assured me that in a business meeting, men often speak more aggressively toward one another than women do. He pointed out that their communication style was not meant to be offensive to me or to each other. I greatly appreciated his kindness and his camaraderie as I settled in to my new role.

I also appreciated that he asked the two men to curb their communication style in the presence of women, a suggestion that was well received and implemented. As the size of the team grew, a few more women joined the team, and the meetings naturally evolved into more acceptable coed communications. Before long, we became a close-knit team, even sharing frequent social events that included spouses and children. Within months, I thoroughly enjoyed every member of our team, and I happily survived the long, technical meetings.

Longing for Home

*Then he said to them all: "Whoever wants to be my disciple must
deny themselves and take up their cross daily and follow me."*
—LUKE 9:23

I had been living in Waxhaw for three years when I went through a season
of desperately missing my family. Though my sons continued to support
my choice to serve with Wycliffe, other family members were insistent that
I "belonged" in California. When I would visit, those individuals would
consistently pressure me to quit my job and move back to California. And
yet, my heart did not confirm that the time had come for me to move.
While wrestling with this issue, I wrote the article shown below, titled
"Home":

> Like every Christian, I know that heaven is my true
> home: no tears, no pain, no illness; streets of gold, river
> of life, constant fellowship with God. Amazing grace! Yet
> knowing of heaven, I am in no great hurry to get there,
> and in the meantime, I wrestle with my feelings about
> home here on earth.
>
> It is said that "home is where the heart is," but for
> me, that description only complicates matters. I seem to
> be caught between two homes. My heart longs to be with
> my family in California, while it also longs to serve God
> the Father wherever He so chooses here on earth. These
> passions for family and God have long battled within my
> very soul.
>
> When I lived in Africa, the greatest trial for me was
> missing my family. When I came home to visit family,
> the greatest trial was missing the people I loved in Africa.
> For many missionaries, this ongoing tension between the
> familial desires of the heart and the heavenly desires of the
> soul is well known.
>
> When I came back to the U.S. with malaria, I was not
> given the choice of returning to Africa, but my dichotomy

of feelings did not end. As a follower of Jesus Christ, I remained caught between two major biblical principles: one is that of treasuring the gift of family, and the other is that of sacrificing all to follow Christ.

How do I fit together "Honor your father and mother that life will go well with you" and "Children are a gift from God," with "Leave your father and mother and follow me?" (Exodus 20:12, Psalm 127:3, Mark 10:29). Should I cling to the promise of eternal reward for denying all for Christ, or should I cling to my own desire to be personally involved in, and maybe even witnessing to, my own family?

I am so aware of God's many blessings in my life. He gave me a wonderful childhood. Later, He gave me two beautiful sons, rescued me from a horrendous car accident, gave me new joy and purpose in missions service, and saved my life from malaria and cancer. He has made Himself known to me on a daily basis for as long as I can remember. So how could I turn my back on going where He sends me?

I am daily surrounded by evidence of God's majestic love in the beauty of the world around us, the joy of a call on my life, and the gift of rich friendships. Yet simultaneously, I have long wrestled with the continual pull between a ministry I love and the separation from my family.

I thank God for dependable phone lines, a postal system, and emails. But I am even more thankful for the greatest connection of all—the gift of prayer! When I cannot be with my loved ones, I am confident that my Father in heaven always is. And when I am concerned about them or missing them, all I have to do is discuss it with Him. I have chosen to entrust my family's well-being to the Father of all, and to recognize that He loves them even more than I do.

Lord God Almighty, my home is with You. Hold my family members in the palm of Your hand, today and always, whether we are near or far from one another. May I fully entrust them to You and follow in obedience to Your call, wherever that call may take me. In Jesus' name, Amen.

My Third Job Assignment

Send me your light and your faithful care, let them lead me.
—Psalm 43:3

Somehow, writing that article helped me to accept the peace of knowing I was exactly where I was supposed to be. Shortly thereafter, the Lord confirmed that knowledge and rewarded me for my willingness to put Him first. My third job assignment began to unfold in a way that only He could have orchestrated.

Each Tuesday morning, the six hundred people working at JAARS would come together for worship, prayer, and an informative presentation on a specific translation project or an aspect of JAARS operations. About a year after I had arrived at JAARS, the Youth and Family Ministries department gave a presentation. When the youth director made a plea for more volunteers to help with the teens each week, I sensed the Lord's prompting to volunteer.

With my heart in my throat, I spoke with the youth director briefly after the meeting, and I agreed to attend the next Thursday night meeting. That commitment would continue for the duration of my time at JAARS. The commitment began as a voluntary agreement, but in God's time, my involvement with the youth team would become an official position.

The first few weeks at youth group, I felt out of place in a room full of rowdy teenagers, but with the passage of time, my discomfort disappeared. I was richly blessed to discover that the majority of those present were 'MKs,' missionary kids who had served with their families all over the world. Their knowledge of worldviews was far beyond the average American high school student. Many of them had lived overseas most of their lives, and they had returned to the U.S. either for a one-year furlough or to begin attending an American high school.

The transplanted teens often found acclimating to American life an unpleasant adjustment. I certainly related to their discomfort. I, too, was still trying to readjust to the American culture, and I had been home for three years! Living in Africa had permanently changed my worldview. Like these teens, I saw American culture as primarily materialistic and self-seeking with little awareness or concern for the poorer people of the world. After living in a culture where the focus was on community, the teens found it difficult to return to a society focused on individuality.

I soon realized that the Lord might be calling me to minister to these 'TCKs' because of our shared experiences. TCKs, Third Culture Kids, had been given that nickname because of their life experiences which separated them from exclusively identifying with either their home culture or their adopted culture. Instead of feeling they truly belonged to either group, these teens had unintentionally become a unique third culture of individuals who drew their identity from a unique combination of social nuances experienced in their two worlds.

The youth group also welcomed local teens whose families lived on or near the JAARS campus. The local teens endured the constant turnover of forever-traveling peers as families repeated the cycle of two to three years on the field and one year home on furlough. A common complaint among all of the students was that they were frustrated with developing and losing friendships so often because of the missionary families' transient lifestyle.

Weekly youth group meetings included a time of hanging out with friends, a time of group worship, and then a time of listening to a Bible-based lesson designed to encourage and challenge their growth as Christian believers. After the lesson was completed, the students were welcome to remain for a while to discuss the lesson with one of the youth leaders or to simply hang out with their friends.

The teens were also involved in periodic community service projects, picnics, pool days, an annual summer camp-out, and an annual summer mission trip to some faraway land. All activities were designed to further build their sense of community, their identity as Christians, and their devotion to God.

After a few months of looking on, I met with the youth director and voiced my desire to share in teaching the weekly lessons. He welcomed my willingness, and for the next several years, I presented a lesson every six weeks. He also asked me to privately mentor at least one girl per year, another assignment I happily accepted. In their twenties now, several of the girls I mentored from 2008 to 2015 have continued to stay in contact with me by phone or written communications. What started as mentoring relationships has turned into precious long-term friendships.

After I had volunteered with the youth team for three years, the youth director asked me if I would be willing to change my official assignment from the Business Services Team to the Youth and Family Ministries team. The invitation was sorely tempting, but I knew I was needed for the production of weekly business reports. We discussed a few possible solutions and prayed together, and then I asked him to speak directly with my present boss about his invitation.

When they met together, the two men came up with a plan: they decided I would be serving in each department 50% of the time, a solution that suited me just fine. Split positions were common at JAARS: I continued to serve as the communications coordinator for the business team, and I began serving as the prayer and activities coordinator for the youth team.

I continued teaching a lesson every six weeks, but from then on, I also started sharing the responsibilities for keeping records, creating power-point presentations, leading prayer meetings, and organizing the various youth activities. My plate and my heart were full, and Thursday nights were my favorite time of the week!

Over the next few years, the Business Services Team grew in numbers and responsibilities. At one point, I realized that on the business side I was trying to fit a full-time workload into half-time hours while not short-changing the youth department. My perfectionism was getting the better of me. Eventually, I made the difficult decision to quit BST and serve full-time with the youth team.

Five years after arriving at JAARS, I was finally serving full-time in a role that more closely matched my skills and my heart's desire. I loved working with the teens and being included in their daily lives. Many of them sought me out for one-on-one conversations or for participation in their school activities, such as sports events and theatrical presentations.

Though I still had to pace my energies carefully, I was delighted to be closely involved with young, growing believers who would be positively affecting future generations through mission work or other worthy occupations.

Each of my assignments at JAARS had served God's purpose for the season He had chosen, but my personal favorite was working full-time with amazing young people at the youth center. In that role, I was able to incorporate my organizational skills, teaching skills, and passion for corporate prayer, working side-by-side with both the students and their parents. The Lord had given me back the joy I had embraced in teaching overseas. In His time and way, the "years the locusts had eaten" (Joel 2:25) had been lovingly replaced.

Cameroon

May 10-June 20, 2011

CHAPTER EIGHT

CAMEROON, WEST AFRICA
(MAY 11-JUNE 20, 2011)

IIIIIIIIIIIIIIIIII

Holy Spirit Message

Take delight in the Lord,
and he will give you the desires of your heart.

—PSALM 37:4

Sometimes, the Lord moves in ways we cannot foresee, and sometimes He catches us completely by surprise. For three years, I had been delighting in my volunteer work with the JAARS Youth team. I loved spending time with the teens on Thursday nights and I was happily engaged in mentoring two of the girls: Jamari was a junior and Elizabeth Joy was a sophomore. I usually mentored them separately, but occasionally the three of us got together for a joint adventure.

Twice a year, I had hosted a girls' tea at my tiny apartment, and at the end of each school year, I had invited all the senior girls to dress up and join me for an ice cream social at a favorite restaurant in town, finishing the evening with a group prayer time at my apartment. In the summers, I invited all the college girls who had returned home to get together at my apartment for a time of reconnecting and praying for one another. But of all the activities with the teens, my favorite was mentoring the two girls, one-on-one.

During one of our meetings in February, 2010, Elizabeth was very upset. She told me that her family was going to Africa for the following school year, and she was not happy about this shocking change in plans.

Her news surprised and seriously concerned me. I knew her parents had served in the Philippines until she was two, but her mother was diagnosed with cancer and they had returned to the U.S. for her treatment. Five years later, her mother had died, and two years after that, her father had remarried a recent widow who became stepmother to Elizabeth and her two older sisters. Together, the couple had planned to remain in the U.S. until all three daughters, ages thirteen, eleven, and nine, graduated from high school.

However, a few years later, the chance to serve short-term in Papua New Guinea had arisen. When her father asked the girls if they were willing to move, the oldest had said no, so their family remained in Waxhaw. Now another opportunity had arisen: her father had been invited to fill in for a furloughing pilot for one year in a small town in West Africa. Though the first two daughters had graduated, Elizabeth had two more years of high school to go.

When her father told her about the offer, he explained carefully that if they accepted it, he and his wife would live in Banso while she would be living in a different city several hours away by land or helicopter. If they went to Cameroon, Elizabeth would live in a hostel with other missionary kids while attending a school nearby.

After the three of them thoroughly discussed the possibilities and prayed together, Elizabeth decided she was willing to give up her junior year in Waxhaw to make the move to Cameroon. She did not want to disappoint her father, but she was devastated at the possibility of being away from her friends for a whole year. Furthermore, she was terrified at the thought of living in Africa; she knew absolutely nothing about Cameroon or any other African nation.

I could not help her with her grief regarding separation from her friends, but I could help her with learning about Africa. I researched Cameroon, collected photos and maps, and gathered some of my photo albums from Africa days. Living on a missionary base, I was also able to find several other students whose families had lived in Cameroon in the past.

For the next several months, when we met for mentoring, Elizabeth and I spent most of our time talking about Cameroon and meeting with other students who had lived there. As she learned about Cameroon and the school, she became excited about the adventure that lay ahead of her. It helped, too, that two of her friends had promised to go visit her in Cameroon during their Christmas break. Naturally, even though she was excited about exploring a new world, she also experienced bouts of intense apprehension as she thought about having to make new friends, go to a strange school, and live so far from all that was familiar.

One day when I was praying for the Lord to encourage her, the Holy Spirit whispered to my heart, "You could go to Cameroon." I was startled by the thought, but the idea stuck with me all morning. During that day's prayer time at the youth department, I shared what I had heard in prayer. Both youth leaders immediately encouraged me to follow the Lord's lead. To my surprise and delight, I began to research the possibility of returning to Africa. It had been almost six years since I had left Tanzania.

Preparations and Concerns

May your hand be ready to help me,
for I have chosen your precepts.
—PSALM 119:173

It was obvious the Lord had gone before me. When I contacted Wycliffe, they were open to my serving in a short-term assignment overseas, and when I contacted the school in Cameroon, the principal told me she could definitely use another teacher to administer the end-of-the year SAT testing for the sophomore class. She invited me to join the school staff for the last five weeks of school. Was it a coincidence or a God-incident that I was asked to administer SAT exams? That was exactly what I had been doing before I left Tanzania! How many of those little parallels do we notice as the Lord directs our lives?

I was thrilled to be invited to come. When I offered to buy and hand-carry any school supplies they might need, the principal gladly sent me a long list of requested supplies. When I started purchasing them, I finally began to realize that I was actually going back to Africa!

Over the next months, I continued to prepare Elizabeth for the big life-change ahead of her while I also began the extensive process of preparing to join her there in the Spring: writing to my prayer team to seek the Lord's confirmation and provision, completing official paperwork to be temporarily released from JAARS and assigned to Cameroon, completing the necessary vaccinations, renewing my passport, flying to California in January to spend two weeks visiting churches and small groups to raise prayer and financial support for the trip, and spending time with my family members to assure them of my love and concerns for them as I dared to return to Africa.

My health was still often unpredictable, especially when I had to periodically undergo parasite treatments. I still battled the frequent reemergence of Bilharzia within my body, and when I ingested the strong, toxic medications, they usually made me very sick. In one of the church presentations in California, I had openly shared that returning to Africa was a little scary because of the threats of disease.

One man, a pastor from Uganda, had stood up to speak words of encouragement to me, ending with the declaration, "You will be well!" I received his words as a prophetic encouragement from the Lord, and I thanked Him for giving me a promise to savor. A month later when I wrote to my prayer team to ask for the Lord's hand on my health, that same man called me from California and again spoke words of encouragement, reminding me to cling to his earlier prophecy.

His words, the prayers and encouragement of my church family, and the Holy Spirit's daily illumination of the Scriptures I read gave me the motivation to keep going forward. Yet, like the girl I was mentoring, I still had moments of uneasiness. I had written in my journal:

> March 6, 2011: Thank you, Lord for Your amazing grace! At church this morning, I confessed in prayer that I'm terrified of going to Cameroon—I just don't want to get that sick again! And while I prayed, You

gave Joe a vision of my walking on a path with a light about twenty feet ahead of me, a path hedged in on the sides & top by thick hedges. He said the only way to go was forward a little at a time. Thanks, Lord—You have me hedged in by Your protection; the Scripture that comes to mind is Psalm 139, and as I read it, I am bathed in the awareness that You know me & love me completely.

But concern for my health was not the only obstacle in my pathway. I was also apprehensive regarding my aging mother's well-being. My sister lived within driving distance of Mom, but she often went on long trips. Who would be there for Mom while I was in Africa? I presented my concerns to the Lord:

March 21, 2011: Lord, Lord, Lord, I am desperate for You. I woke up singing, "I have decided to follow Jesus—no turning back." Is that Your answer to me as I struggle with feeling sick & worrying about my mom? She fell again! Oh Lord, how do I go to Cameroon for six weeks when her health is so precarious? Is this Your test or my foolishness? Help me sort it out to Your glory. Diane (my prayer partner) says, "Go," the Ugandan pastor says "Go," my heart says, "Let your yes be yes." I have the ticket & the official invitation. Lord, direct my steps! Direct them to Your glory. (Later in the day, I kept hearing, "TRUST ME.")

After discussing my concerns and praying with Diane on the phone, I called my sister and told her of my anxiety regarding Mom's well-being in my absence. To my relief, my sister told me that she would return from Europe the day before I left for Cameroon. She urged me to go to Africa and promised to stay in California until I returned to North Carolina. Her promise lifted a weight off my mind; thank you, Lord.

Over the next months, when I periodically wrestled with my concerns about health and family matters, the Lord consistently encouraged me through His Word and His people. Meanwhile, the time came for Elizabeth and her family to leave for Cameroon.

Brave Young Girl Steps Out into the World

You have searched me, Lord,
and you know me.
You know when I sit and when I rise;
you perceive my thoughts from afar.
You discern my going out and my lying down;
you are familiar with all my ways.
Before a word is on my tongue
you, Lord, know it completely.

—Psalm 139:1–4

In late July, all the students at the youth group laid hands on Elizabeth and prayed for her and her family, and then they left for Cameroon. Her parents got her settled in her new housing, attended the orientation day to meet her teachers, and then headed upcountry to begin his exciting new job. Suddenly, Elizabeth found herself surrounded by strangers who lovingly welcomed her into the school community.

Elizabeth and I had promised to stay in contact by emails and Skype, so I was well aware of her daily challenges and her response to them. Though she fell in love with Cameroon in the first few weeks, she also dealt with a host of tough adjustments: a drastically different culture, hot, dusty weather and pollution, living with house parents and eight other 'siblings' (male and female), sharing her bedroom space with three other girls, coping with a demanding academic program, learning a new language (French), and finding her place in a new school environment.

Sadly, a few months after she arrived, she learned that her two friends back home would not be able to join her as promised. For personal family reasons, both of them had had to give up their dreams, causing great anguish on both sides of the world.

I was fully aware of her disappointment. I was also aware that she was feeling quite lonely and abandoned, even though she had made lots of new friends at the school. She often contacted me in the low moments to share her misery and frustrations, and I frequently sent online photos and news about JAARS activities to help her know that she was loved and her friends had not forgotten her.

The next time I talked with Elizabeth on Skype, I asked her, "What's your favorite Mexican food?" (I knew she loved Mexican food). When she described a chicken burrito from her favorite restaurant, I informed her that I would bring her one in person in May. At first, she thought I was joking, but when she realized that I was serious, she was so happy! My news gave her something to look forward to in the months ahead.

Meanwhile, my own struggles with health and family matters continued. Coincidentally, in God's perfect way, that year I was asked to carry a newly-published Bible in JAARS' annual translation celebration. To my delight, I was given a Bible translated for a tribe in Cameroon. What a moving experience to carry that Bible in the procession and to hold it in my hands while we prayed as a community that the Lord would speak to those in Cameroon through His Word in their native tongue. I could see that the Lord was already planting His love for the Cameroonian people in my heart, and He was challenging me to focus more on what He was doing than on my own concerns. Again and again, He quietly whispered to my soul that I could entrust my family members to His loving care.

As I continued the long process of preparation and the struggle to regain some semblance of reasonable health, Elizabeth and I communicated often, sharing our daily lives and the lessons we were learning from the Lord. She had attended a public school all her life, so being immersed in a Christian environment was a new and exciting experience. I relished in sharing her new insights and seeking out answers to her questions. Even though we were miles apart, we basically continued our mentoring relationship online. When she was discouraged, I sought to lift her spirits, and when I was discouraged, she challenged me to trust God and keep moving forward. Out of the mouths of babes!

Ten months after she had left the U.S., my turn to join her finally arrived. My health was not ideal, but it was certainly better than it had been a few months earlier. In faith, I climbed on an airplane with my suitcase filled with personal items and one huge shipping carton carefully packed with school supplies. Thankfully, the youth leader had accompanied me to the airport to help me get checked in with the oversized carton. I waved goodbye to North Carolina and settled in for the long flight to Cameroon, West Africa.

Welcome and Unwelcome

If it is possible, as far as it depends on you, live at peace with everyone.

—Romans 12:18

Our God is gracious! Years after I had let go of any hope of returning to Africa, He gave me a chance to go back for a brief visit. He also provided the closure I had missed in my previous untimely exit.

From the moment the plane arrived on Cameroonian soil, I felt at home again. The sounds, smells and sights were all familiar, and the sense of God's presence was strong. He blessed me with six amazing weeks tucked carefully under His wing—and I was healthy! Praise God! The Ugandan pastor's prophecy proved true.

The city's population in 2011 was close to two and a half million people. The weather was usually hot, dry, and dusty, though there were intermittent spurts of rain almost daily. However, the ground never stayed wet for long, and the air was always polluted with thick car exhaust and smoke. I could even taste the pollution in the air.

When I exited the airport, I was joyfully greeted by Elizabeth, her boyfriend, and his mother. She and I hugged and laughed and talked nonstop as we piled into a van to begin the long trip to my apartment. As promised, I had taken a chicken burrito to Elizabeth by freezing it for several days and then placing it in a Styrofoam container deep in a crate of school supplies. Though thawed, it was still cold when I arrived in Cameroon, and Elizabeth was delighted with her feast.

The apartment where I would be living was within city limits. When we arrived at the gate, I was escorted to the three-story concrete building inside the guarded compound. Our apartment was on the second floor. I say "our" because I was housed with another teacher, Emma, who had been there all year long. She was young and set in her ways, and she made it abundantly clear that she preferred to live alone. However, because she was the only teacher with an empty bedroom, SIL had not given her a choice.

Really, Lord? I had had a similar experience in Niger! Once again, I found myself blatantly unwelcome. For the next six weeks, I did all that I could to be a peacemaker, but she was not exactly responsive. Sadly, I would soon discover that her cool reception was only the beginning of many such responses, but first the Lord gave me a little gift.

The apartment was very large by African standards. We had a spacious living room, a large kitchen area with a full-sized kitchen table, and two bedrooms and bathrooms. Emma's master bedroom was at one end of the apartment and my smaller bedroom was at the other end. There was a small bathroom conveniently located just outside my bedroom door. We both had a perfect view of the entire city through the large picture windows along the back side of the apartment. In fact, I could even see the city from the small window in my shower!

The school officials had advised me to spend a few days at the apartment before jumping in to actively working at the school. Consequently, the next morning I was blessed to meet Doris, our house-girl, when she came to bring us groceries and clean the apartment. She and I became the best of friends that first day. She shared that she was married with three children, but her husband regularly disappeared for months at a time. Consequently, she had been left to raise and provide for their family on her own. But she knew the Lord, and she trusted in His protection and provision.

I shared with her that I, too, was a single parent who had known the devastation of abandonment and the relational challenges of a difficult marriage, so I could readily sympathize with her trials. We talked a lot that first day, and we earnestly prayed for one another and our families. Thereafter, whenever she came by on her weekly visit, we reconnected and prayed when we had the freedom to do so. My housemate saw Doris as only a servant, but I saw her as a friend, so the two of us could interact with one another more comfortably only when Emma was not at home. I was thankful that the Lord had given me a Cameroonian friend as soon as I had arrived, and little did I know how valuable her friendship would be to me.

Teaching in Cameroon

Rejoice in the Lord always. I will say it again: Rejoice! Let
your gentleness be evident to all. The Lord is near. Do not be
anxious about anything, but in every situation, by prayer and
petition, with thanksgiving, present your requests to God. And
the peace of God, which transcends all understanding, will
guard your hearts and your minds in Christ Jesus.

—PHILIPPIANS 4:4–7

After a few days' recovery from jetlag, the interim principal drove me to the school to meet the other teachers and tour the campus. It was then that I learned the principal who had invited me to come was on furlough. When the interim principal introduced me in the workroom, the response was noticeably cool; the other teachers barely looked up from their work. However, I could see that they were tired and focused on finishing their preparations for the day. Having been a teacher in the U.S. for many years, I remembered well the rising stress on teachers as the close of the school year approached, so I tried not to take their disinterest personally.

When the teachers learned that I had brought school supplies and lots of M & M's (not available in Cameroon), their response was a bit more positive, but they were obviously in no mood for chatting. It seems the principal had neglected to tell anyone but the interim principal that I would be arriving, and she had not chosen to share that information with the others. Consequently, my sudden appearance was received more as an unexpected interruption than as a reinforcement for end-of-year activities.

After a brief introduction, the interim principal suggested that I tour the campus on my own because she was too busy to escort me. She said she had plenty of work to do in her office. With that comment, she left me standing there in the teacher's lounge. Her unwillingness to take the time to accompany me confirmed my feeling of being more than a little unwelcome. I quietly exited and began my self-tour.

The campus was gorgeous! The two-story buildings were spread out over a large open area along the edge of the rain forest, creating a huge circle around the grassy section in the middle. There were splashes of color provided by a few tropical flowers planted near the buildings. The grounds gradually sloped downward from the parking lot to the far end of the campus.

While strolling from building to building, I took multiple photos to later share with the JAARS youth and Elizabeth's friends back home. The assistant librarian (a Cameroonian man) was very friendly, and while I was in the library, I unexpectedly met up with Elizabeth and three of her new friends. I took more photos for the kids at home and was relieved to briefly converse with a few individuals who were actually glad I had come.

At lunchtime, I joined Elizabeth and her friends at one of the tables in the outdoor lunch pavilion. She was excited to introduce me to her classmates as she announced that I was her mentor and had brought her a burrito! That first day, I enjoyed eating my lunch while listening to the teens' jovial bantering around the table. Thereafter, we seldom saw each other during the school days for more than a few moments, both because our schedules were vastly different and because I did not want to intrude on her school day interactions.

However, her hostel was within walking distance of my apartment, so we were able to make plans to meet after school and on weekends fairly often. She was glad to have me near enough to help her process many of her daily struggles. Entering a new culture, living away from parents for the first time, falling in love, and adjusting to the high academic and spiritual expectations of a Christian school can take a toll on a young girl's heart. The Lord gave us rich times to spend together, and I would dare to say that we both grew monumentally in our faith during those weeks.

I began administering the SAT tests the following day. During the first exam, the Lord directed me to walk from student to student, not only supervising their work but praying for each individual as I passed. As a result, I quickly learned their names (posted on the tables) and developed a love for each one. We spent each morning together, chipping away at the pile of exams to be completed. The exams were long and exhausting for the students, giving me plenty of time to pray for them and ample reason to encourage them whenever I could. I tried to set a light-hearted atmosphere by coming up with silly ways to read the identical directions that were required to be read before each section.

Each day during my lunch break, I started my afternoons with a prayer walk around the perimeter of the school grounds. Then I served in whatever assignment I was given for a particular day: preparing materials for the teachers, counting and storing books for the summer, correcting papers, cleaning and organizing supplies—whatever was needed.

Once or twice a week, with the teacher's permission, I attended Elizabeth's Bible class, as she had requested. Elizabeth was anxious for me to share in the lessons she was learning, and I was pleased to see the quality of biblical education she was receiving. I sat quietly observing from the back row while her teacher presented the day's lesson and the students discussed its content.

Seeing each other in a classroom setting was definitely a new experience for both Elizabeth and me. I had warned her in advance that she would need to respect me as a teacher in the classroom rather than interacting with me as a friend, and she readily complied. I thoroughly enjoyed the opportunity to get to know some of her classmates and to see them interacting with each other and the Bible.

I also attended the sacred dance club with her. She had never been involved in dancing before, but one of her new friends had convinced her to give it a try. She knew that I had a great interest and background in dance, so she invited me to come along. It was so much fun to watch her and the other girls practicing their dances for an upcoming performance, and to share in the discussions about the value of sacred dance in prompting corporate worship. A bonus for me was that the dance teacher openly welcomed me as a fellow dancer. Thank you, Lord, for a friendly face!

Ironically, Elizabeth's small group leader was my housemate, Emma, who showed a much kinder side of her personality in the presence of the students. Each week, five or six girls met with Emma to just hang out and share whatever was on their minds. Then they would end their time together with a brief corporate prayer.

Two and a half weeks after I arrived at the school, one of the teachers had a family emergency and flew home late that same night. The next day, which happened to be a Saturday, I was casually informed that I would be teaching sophomore and junior English classes the following week—surprise! Once again, I was reminded that missionaries need to remain flexible in expecting the unexpected. The lesson plans were provided and the students readily adapted to the change of plans.

Missionary kids are used to constant change, so they were unphased by the switch in teachers.

I was thankful that I already knew all the sophomores, and I enjoyed the chance to meet a few more of Elizabeth's classmates. Thankfully, Elizabeth was not in my classes, so we did not have to scale that hurdle! Because it was the last week of instruction before finals, the lessons were especially creative and interactive, making it easy and fun for me to step in and teach.

Life Comes with Challenges

In this world you will have trouble. But take heart! I have overcome the world.

—JOHN 16:33

While being back in Africa and a classroom setting filled my heart with joy, I also had my share of physical challenges along the way. I had written in my journal:

> May 13, 2011: This is the day the Lord has made. I shall rejoice & be glad in it! Lord, I am dependent upon You—I have my first mosquito bites. I pray the prayer of Malta, that anything that could harm me is made harmless by You. Lord, cover me with Your full armor in this land of disease.

With that prayer in mind, I put my concerns into the Lord's lap and refocused on the daily responsibilities laid before me.

Around the same time, I began to experience major asthmatic symptoms, making it necessary to find immediate relief. I had not experienced any asthma attacks in the U.S. for several years, so I had brought a facemask but had not thought to bring an inhaler with me.

I contacted a missionary nurse who told me where to find a local pharmacy. Then Elizabeth, her boyfriend, and his mother accompanied me in a taxi to find the pharmacy. The trip downtown was extremely difficult for me, even though I kept a heavy sweater tightly pressed over my nose and mouth. When we arrived at the pharmacy, her boyfriend's mother told the pharmacist in fluent French exactly what I needed, and he readily produced it. Then we were off to repeat the miserable ride home.

From then on, I wore a face mask to ride in the van to and from school, and I used the inhaler as needed. The school itself was far enough out of the city limits that the air was clean and fresh, so the mask was not needed during the day. Thank you, Lord!

Of course, I had expected to deal with mobility challenges because of my funky foot, but that problem, too, was resolving itself in a most unexpected manner. Though I was initially coping with severe pain in both feet because of walking on concrete, by the third week, I realized I was walking with little or no pain. I had written in my journal:

> May 28, 2011: God, I love You so much! And I thank You for the daily miracle of health & breath. I've been here almost three weeks & I'm doing well. Thank you for the special treat of an evening of sacred dance (with Elizabeth's dance teacher and a few other adult women). The focus was "Worship & Motion."
>
> I lift up my sons & mom to Your gentle care, & I lift up my dear friend, Diane. Lord, this time in Africa is such a gift! And, of course, I lift up Elizabeth as she struggles with relational challenges, & I lift up all the JAARS kids as they prepare for graduation.

The only other problem that plagued me was not a physical one, but a relational one—it was that of coping with the unfriendly attitudes still being exhibited by most of the teachers. I was thankful for the few who were friendly, such as the sacred dance teacher and the French teacher whose desk was next to mine in the teacher's workroom. Yet the repeated occurrence of being totally ignored or treated rudely when I sought to make simple conversation definitely weighed me down. I had written in my journal:

<u>May 19, 2011</u>: From *Following Jesus (book)*: "Jesus wants us to be humble servants instead of seeking popularity, prestige & security." Thanks, Lord—what a perfectly timed confirmation! I've been feeling pretty invisible & devalued at the school & You've been impressing on me to just quietly serve without personal expectations. Use me, Father, to minister Your love & encouragement to the students, & help me to relinquish my own expectations. May my time at the school be to Your glory.

Cameroonian Worship

Praise the Lord.
How good it is to sing praises to our God,
how pleasant and fitting to praise him!
Praise the Lord.
Sing to the Lord a new song,
his praise in the assembly of his faithful people.
—PSALMS 147:1 AND 149:1

The first week in Cameroon, I went to Elizabeth's church; she and the other hostel students were driven to a church service in a nearby hotel auditorium. The service was 100% American—a nice service, but none of the African flavor I had hoped for.

The second week and thereafter, I went to a Cameroonian church that was within walking distance of our apartment. What a difference! The wide-open church building had a roof supported by 4 x 4 columns and partial walls about three feet tall, allowing the breeze to pass through the congregation. There were simple wooden benches and dirt floors. I would guess there were seventy to ninety worshipers each week, all of them friendly and welcoming, and all of them in beautiful traditional African clothing.

I was amazed that a Cameroonian woman led the worship songs in high heels! She was extremely lively, in constant motion, almost dancing as she drew us into praise and worship with her animated style of leadership.

I cannot imagine how she kept her footing on the uneven dirt floor, but she made it look easy. The sermons, presented in French and English, were Bible-based, and the prayers were passionate. I had found my 'home' for worship in Cameroon.

Spring Concert

He (Jacob) had a dream in which he saw a stairway resting on the earth, with its top reaching to heaven, and the angels of God were ascending and descending on it.

—GENESIS 28:12

When I went to Cameroon, I had consciously had two major goals in mind: support and encourage the girl I had been mentoring, and offer end-of-the-year assistance to the other teachers. But the Lord had had much bigger plans in store for me: He had brought me into another major season for spiritually stretching lessons and experiences.

The students had prepared for months to produce an evening of musical treasures. All of their parents and siblings were invited to come, but Elizabeth's parents had decided not to fly in from Banso. Consequently, I was the only person present who was specifically attending to cheer her on, or so I thought.

The evening had started with the orchestra's performance, and then the various choirs followed. All of the performances had been magnificent and inspiring. Lastly, a dance number was performed by the sacred dance choir. As a praise song was played in the background, seven or eight girls entered down the two aisles, spreading out on the stage with their colorful flags. Each girl danced barefoot wearing a black skirt and a different colored T-shirt. The flags were equally unique in various colors, completing the illusion of a rainbow.

As they began to dance, I was enthralled by the beauty of their dancing and the perfect incorporation of the praise song. I thanked God for the opportunity to witness Elizabeth's dancing before the Lord and her peers, and I was rejoicing at her willingness to boldly step out of her comfort zone. It was then that I realized I was not the only one cheering for her.

As I began clicking countless photos, I suddenly had the sense that the roof directly above and behind me had opened up and Elizabeth's mother was watching from heaven, rejoicing that her daughter was thriving in a difficult season. The sense of her joyful presence was so strong that I was overwhelmed by the feeling, frozen in place and unable to continue taking pictures.

Elizabeth and the others continued to dance as I tried to absorb what was happening in that room, both in front of me and directly behind and above me. I was overcome by a strong sense of the Holy Spirit's powerful presence.

The concert ended with the dance number, and then Elizabeth came rushing over to me and gave me a big hug, saying, "Thank you for being here! I love you!" When she threw her arms around me, I experienced what felt like an electric shock go through my whole body. I was speechless (a rarity)!

In her excitement, she hugged me three more times and repeated her gratitude. The same thing happened each time—a jolt of energy passed between her body and mine, but she seemed unaware of it. She ran out with her friends to go get refreshments, and I stood there trying to figure out what had just happened. Eventually, I joined the rest of the crowd in the other room, but I could not shake off my sense of wonder and awe. When I got home, I wrote in my journal:

> May 19, 2011: Elizabeth danced! Lord, thank you for bringing me to her school to be there for her tonight— someone who loves her to cheer her on! And help me sort out the powerful emotional response I had as the thought came to mind that Elizabeth's mom was cheering her on from heaven. I am aware of the deep privilege it was to be there to speak words of encouragement. It was a victory dance—spiritual warfare—it was Elizabeth daring to give her all, no matter what. And I'm so proud of her! I'm blown away by the love You've given me for this girl. Show me how best to minister to her, what to share & what not to share—only You know.

That night when I crawled into bed, I lay awake for hours, asking God what had happened and what it meant. I kept reliving the memory of the roof opening up and of the powerful jolts that had passed between Elizabeth and me. I kept asking the Lord what I was supposed to do with what I had witnessed. I kept hearing, "Tell her." I argued that she might think I was imagining things, or that my words might upset her. But each time, I heard the Lord whisper, "Tell her."

Telling her was easier said than done—how do you tell someone, "By the way, I saw your mom watching you from heaven last night?" I wrestled hard with what to say and how to say it, rehearsing various possibilities in my mind, but they all sounded ridiculous to me.

The next day, Elizabeth came to visit me at my apartment, and I did not find a way to tell her. But as we walked back to her hostel, I finally got the courage to haltingly spill out what I had seen and felt. She was more than a little startled. For a short while, we continued walking without speaking. Then she asked me if I thought those in heaven can pray for us and I said yes. I explained that Jesus said we would do even greater things than he had done and if he intercedes for us, then probably our loved ones do, too. I was not sure if that was true, but over the next several days I prayed that the Lord would direct my words and correct me if I was wrong. I did not receive any sense of correction, though I continued to puzzle over the experience itself.

For the next several nights, I slept very little as I continued to process the miracle I had personally witnessed. What did it mean? Among numerous journal entries involving my reaction to what I had encountered that night, I had written:

> <u>May 21, 2011</u>: (4 or 5 a.m.) Another night/early morning of trying to wrestle through/process what happened at the concert. Lord, I think I may have spoken to Elizabeth about it prematurely. Please forgive me & may she forgive me as she processes her response. Use it to grow us both. I'm still really trying to figure out what happened & what it means, how to express it:
>
> • Sometimes, we see heaven & earth touch, ever so briefly—You allowed one of those moments as I sensed her mother's celebration of who Elizabeth is

- I am honored & overwhelmed that You have allowed me to be here in Cameroon to love & encourage Elizabeth
- You are using me for Your purpose. Lord, Lord, keep me obedient to Your purpose!
- Lord, I don't want to mislead Elizabeth in any way—help me to know what to say & when to be quiet. Give me Your wisdom in answering her questions, or the peace to accept that I don't need to know the answers.

Over the next few days, I continued to process the reality of what I had experienced at the concert. During that time, I remained incredibly sensitive to God's Holy Spirit whispering words of wisdom to my soul. Perhaps the unexpected vision had caused me to become a better listener.

And yet, daily life went on as well. One night, I was temporarily distracted from my musings about spiritual matters by a small gathering of Cameroonians who joined my housemate and me for a festive meal at our apartment. I was grateful for a chance to interact with a roomful of friendly Cameroonians, allowing me a brief respite from my intense inner conversations regarding visions and present relational challenges.

However, the respite did not last for long. That same night, I was hit with yet another open rejection from the school. The interim principal told me point-blank that even though I was serving as part of the school staff, I was not welcome at the Spring banquet, which would be attended by all the students and their teachers. The exclusion felt personal and intentionally unkind, but once again, I ran to the Lord with my disappointment. Looking back, I can see now that the enemy was doing all that he could to derail me while the Lord was blessing me with amazing spiritual insights. The Lord was trusting me to keep my focus on Him.

Drama Evangelism

Finally, be strong in the Lord and in his mighty power. Put on the full armor of God, so that you can take your stand against the devil's schemes. For our struggle is not against flesh and blood, but against the rulers, against the authorities, against the powers of this dark world and against the spiritual forces of evil in the heavenly realms.

—Ephesians 6:10–12

Ten days after the concert, I experienced an entirely different type of awakening: this one involved the dark side of the spirit world, the reality of spiritual warfare.

Elizabeth had joined the drama evangelism team for the year. Periodically, they had gone out to surrounding villages to perform short dramas depicting the life of Christ, and then they had moved among the people to visit and evangelize. I was blessed to go with the team for their final presentation.

When we arrived at the village, rain was pouring down and the ground was getting muddy. We found a vacant three-sided shed where we crowded in to stay dry. One of the students suggested that we should ask the Lord to stop the rain, and when we asked, He did stop the rain. Praise God! Then the students went out in pairs to walk through the neighborhoods, inviting each household to come to the village square to watch the drama at 3 p.m.

By the time the students were ready to perform, the ground was barely damp and the square was surrounded by men, women, and children waiting to watch the drama. One of the teachers was fluent in the local language, so she used a portable microphone to narrate the story. The students did a great job of depicting Jesus' ministry, death, and resurrection, but while they performed, one man in the audience kept loudly mocking them as he waved his beer bottle in the air. We had been told that alcoholism and witchcraft were strong in the area, but I had certainly not expected such a visible and audible form of opposition.

The students continued the drama without acknowledging any sense of surprise or confusion whatsoever. When the drama was complete, the audience clapped and the students dispersed into the crowd to personally witness and answer questions. I was touched by their boldness and their expertise in evangelizing.

Meanwhile, I noticed that the drunk man who had tried to disrupt the presentation from the other side of the square was headed straight for the pretty teen girl standing at my side. When he got close, I stepped in front of her and openly confronted the man with verbal prayer, repeatedly commanding him to back off "in the name of Jesus." To my surprise, he did not. I knew that he probably could not understand my words, but I guessed that the demon I saw in his eyes probably could. I spoke the words the Spirit put in my mind, including praying for the man's deliverance from drunkenness, but nothing visibly changed.

I kept praying silently, "Lord, do something!" while praying aloud in the name of Jesus. As he repeatedly tried to get around me, I kept moving to block him from reaching the girl. Each time I did, he railed at me. Then he went after another girl standing next to her, and I sought to protect her as well, still silently praying, "Lord, help me!" Finally, one of the male students standing nearby offered to go get Mr. C, the teacher who had trained the students for evangelism.

When Mr. C arrived, he asked me, "Do you know that you are talking to a demon?" and I replied, "Yes." Then he told me to take the two girls back to the school van while he conversed with the man. The girls and I gladly retreated to safety.

Until Mr. C had arrived, I had felt that I had to protect the two girls by blocking the drunken man's passage, but now that he had joined us, I was seriously relieved to be rescued. When we reached the van, I was still quite shaken, and I was infinitely thankful that someone with more knowledge in spiritual warfare had taken over. At the same time, I was filled with the Holy Spirit and bursting with joy all the way home, silently praising God and rejoicing that He had given me the courage to stand and speak until help arrived.

That experience on top of the concert vision kept me awake for many a night. I sought out a private meeting with Mr. C, who graciously taught me more about spiritual warfare and the specific challenges in that area of Cameroon. I was shocked to learn from him that the school had been built on grounds previously dedicated to evil spirits. A juju tree (home for evil spirits) had been cut down and removed before construction of the school began. Of course, the Christian community had prayerfully walked the grounds to spiritually cleanse them, and then every inch of the property had been dedicated to the Lord. Nonetheless, learning of the previous history of that area made me thankful that the Lord had directed me to pray over the grounds every school day.

During the next several weeks, I continued to pray for the drunken man, often seeing his face and his eyes in my mind. I also prayed for the men, women, and children who lived in that area, that they would be delivered from the evil that entrapped them. A small group of Cameroonian believers had been praying for a long time that a church would be raised up in that immediate area, so I prayed that the students' drama would contribute to that hope becoming a reality.

I also sincerely prayed that the Lord would direct my steps while I absorbed the lessons He was teaching me. I had written in my journal:

May 30, 2011: Lord, Lord, keep me in line! I submit totally to You. May Your Holy Spirit direct my thoughts, words, & deeds. May all that I say & do be to Your glory. Sing alleluia to the King! ... And Father God Almighty, keep me clean in my relationship with Elizabeth. You have me moving from one spiritual awakening to another & she is asking questions—let me share only what is appropriate.

May 31, 2011: Psalm 16: "You have made known to me the path of life." Yes, Lord! You have brought me to Cameroon to teach me so much—open my eyes & ears, my heart, mind & soul to receive Your lessons: Elizabeth's mom watching from heaven, E struggling with righteousness, the demon-possessed man, & the spiritual darkness of the neighborhood. Lord, Lord, bring Your light to this place—& light to my sons! You are showing me that the spiritual realm that imprisons Cameroonians in drunkenness & darkness is the same spiritual realm that imprisons my sons in subtle ways that go unnoticed. O Lord God Almighty, set them free! You are buried in their hearts—O God, may Your Holy Spirit awaken & convict their spirits! May they be drawn back to Your love & purity. May Your Holy Spirit

pierce the darkness, wherever it is. O Lord, I long for
my sons & family to come into the Kingdom.

Every Day a Miracle

*I will pour out my Spirit on all people. Your sons and
daughters will prophesy, your old men will dream dreams,
your young men will see visions.*

—JOEL 2:28

About two weeks after the Spring concert, I had arisen early to spend
time with the Lord, both in prayer and in reading the Word. I knew that
Elizabeth was worried about the Chemistry and Pre-Calculus exams she
would take that day, so I had knelt on the floor to pray for God's peace
to pour over her. As I did, I again sensed her mother's presence! In my
mind's eye, I saw her kneeling next to me, praying the same prayers, but
praying them in the confidence that they were already answered. Again,
I was bowled over by the unexpected vision, and again I asked the Lord,
"What does this mean?"

Later that day, I was assigned to proctor the Chemistry exam, so I
ended up being physically present while Elizabeth took the exam she had
dreaded. The Lord had placed me exactly where He wanted me at that
moment. I spent the next two hours praying for her and the others while
they endured completing the difficult test.

With each new assignment at the school, I recognized more and more
that the Lord had brought me to Cameroon for an intense season of prayer.
I thanked Him for giving me the health, energy, mobility, and stamina to
serve as He chose. With each new day, I realized that the Lord had brought
me back to Africa for so much more than I ever could have imagined!

Elizabeth survived her exams, and as school wrapped up for the year,
she began the painful process of grieving for all that she would leave
behind in Cameroon. On top of that, she had developed a nasty cold and
was not feeling well at all. I did my best to comfort her by helping her to
pack and by listening as she tearfully voiced her heart-felt sadness. But
once again, the Lord was showing me that my greatest gift for her was to
pray for her and with her.

Then graduation night arrived with a moving ceremony followed by a celebration dinner for the seniors. Because Elizabeth's boyfriend was one of the graduates, he invited her and me to attend the dinner, so this time I was included in the festivities. I thanked God for allowing me to participate in a lovely, peaceful evening.

Later, when I returned to our apartment, I discovered that quite coincidentally, there was an all-night party going on somewhere in our neighborhood. I loved hearing the lively Cameroonian music and the sounds of happy laughter! Just like in Tanzania, when I went to bed, I slept soundly in spite of the celebration nearby. For some reason, in Africa I seemed to have an inner mindset that accepted the sounds of community during the day and night to be a natural part of the environment rather than a disruption.

The following day, I returned to the campus for the last time. As a part of my farewell, I walked the perimeter of the school grounds one more time and prayed thanksgiving for all that the Lord had done in the past five weeks. While I walked and prayed, I realized it would be hard for me to say goodbye to Cameroon. My body was weary, but my soul was filled with love for this continent. Yet for the first time, I also realized I was actually looking forward to returning to JAARS, where the Lord had given me a long-term ministry and students I loved.

In God's perfect timing, one of my sons called that night, turning my eyes back toward family. After we had a wonderful conversation, I had written in my journal:

> June 11, 2011: O Lord, I long for my sons to know You as I know You. Draw them unto You, Lord—draw them unto You!
>
> I thank You & praise You for the wonderful work You've been doing in me for a long time—it seemed to intensify during cancer treatment, then again at the home fellowship, & now in Africa. Thanks, Lord—may I drink in the lessons You have for me & be willing to be bold in prayer!
>
> Lord, I'm sensing You're showing me that the battle for my sons' souls is just beginning! Give me

Your strength & fortitude to play my role in the battle, & thank you for the knowledge & confidence that You are the victor & You alone will hold their eternities in Your hands.

The next day, Elizabeth, her boyfriend, and I met for lunch and for several hours of relaxed conversation. Among other topics, they asked me how to maintain purity in a boy-girl relationship. I appreciated that they trusted me to speak into their lives. Toward the end of our time together, the Lord directed me to lay hands on the two of them and pray for their relationship. When I offered to do so, they accepted my invitation.

They remained seated on a picnic bench while I stood behind them, placing one hand on each of them. Then I took a deep breath, silently asking God for the courage to pray aloud whatever He directed. Much of the prayer was in whispered tongues, for only the Holy Spirit knew what they truly needed, but the Lord also gave me a few sentences to speak over them aloud.

The time was rich for all three of us in the presence of the Lord. I again experienced an overwhelming awareness of His presence and guidance. We all three returned to our separate residences quietly subdued by the Holy Spirit's touch upon us.

Banso

The blind and the lame came to him at the temple, and he healed them.

—MATTHEW 21:14

With the school year completed and Elizabeth's bags packed to leave, she and I climbed in to a small four-seater plane to fly to her parents' home in Banso. Even though she was sick, Elizabeth insisted that I sit in the front with the pilot, so once again I was given the adventure of a 180-degree view of the countryside below us. The day was clear and beautiful with minimal winds along the way, so the trip was most enjoyable. We arrived without incident and quickly settled in with her parents, enjoying a relaxing evening with a good meal and simple conversation. Far from the big city, the air was clear and fresh, a welcome respite for my lungs!

The next morning, Elizabeth was running a fever, so her parents plied her with aspirin and juice and tucked her into bed for the day. I spent most of the day just relaxing, reading, and studying the Word, but I also had a long conversation with Elizabeth's stepmom when she asked about my time at the school. When she learned of my relational trials, she was kindly sympathetic and prayed with me that my time with Emma would end well when I returned to the city for my last few days in Cameroon.

My third day in Banso, Elizabeth had recovered well, so the four of us packed up a picnic lunch to go hiking. Elizabeth knew of my foot disability, but over the past weeks I had noticed a growing ability to walk farther and farther. I was excited about trying to hike, and hike we did! We hiked a long distance to reach a waterfall. When the falls were in sight, Elizabeth and I climbed the river rocks while her parents followed the dirt trail. We had a wonderful picnic sitting in the sun on huge boulders by the falls, and then we hiked to a farm. I am guessing we had hiked several miles before we began the long trip back to their car.

Throughout the day, I had periodically shouted, "Look at me, Lord! I'm hiking for the first time in twenty-three years! Thank you!" I think her parents were a little startled by my outbursts, but Elizabeth knew the sincerity of my exuberance. I was amazed that the Lord had miraculously healed my long-term disability. He had answered the earnest prayers said for me one Sunday morning in North Carolina.

Six months earlier, I had had a nasty flu, and some friends had prayed for me at church. One woman who knew of my foot disability and my dance background had placed her hand on my foot and prayed that the Lord would heal the injury so that I could "dance again." At the time that she had prayed, I had thought her prayer was seriously misdirected; after all, I just wanted to break free of the nausea. But within days, I began to feel movement in my toes. I was able to walk with more strength and less pain than I had experienced in a very long time. Until I reached Cameroon, I had not realized the extent of the healing. Thank you, Lord, for Your divine touch!

At some point while we were hiking, I had stooped down in the tall grass and unknowingly picked up a little hitchhiker. Moments later, I had felt a strange shock on my belly several times, but it was not painful enough to cause me any particular concern. I said nothing to the others and continued to thoroughly enjoy the novelty of the day's activity. I would discover later that I had been bitten by a poisonous spider.

When we reached the car, we drove to the local Bible translation center nearby to meet Doris' cousin, who was a Bible translator. When Doris had learned I would be flying to Banso, she had asked me to visit her family. Her cousin ushered us into the building where we briefly observed a team of four men (including him) translating a section of 1 Chronicles. We felt honored that we were allowed to watch them work for a while, and we were fascinated to observe that they took each individual phrase to choose the best wording in their native tongue, a long, painstaking process.

When we were ready to leave, we met Doris' uncle outside and then we drove to Doris' mother's house to visit with her for a while. I took photos of the translation team and of me with her family members to give to Doris later.

On the way home, we drove to a local market to pick up a few groceries. The market itself brought back happy memories of the ones I had frequented in Kenya. Then we went back to the house and took long naps before eating dinner. It had been a perfect day! That evening, Elizabeth and I watched a movie and ate popcorn together, and then we went outside in the pleasant evening and finished our time together with a long conversation and a farewell prayer.

When I changed into my nightgown that night, I discovered the telltale markings of the spider bites. I applied some antibiotic cream and gave the matter little more thought.

The following morning, Elizabeth's father drove me to the airport before she was even awake. I climbed aboard the small plane to enjoy another incredibly scenic journey in the air, and I returned to the city for my final days in Africa.

Sweet and Sour Moments

Praise be to the Lord, to God our Savior,
who daily bears our burdens.

—PSALM 68:19

My days in Cameroon were action-packed from the first day to the last, with new insights and revelations almost daily. In the midst of teaching at the school, supporting my favorite student, and learning new lessons about God's magnificence, I had also been richly blessed by my sweet friendship with Doris.

Several weeks after my arrival, I had invited her and her children to come to lunch at our apartment. I had spent all day cooking and was eagerly looking forward to our time together. When they arrived, I was pleased that her daughter and two sons seemed equally at ease with me as we shared the meal and enjoyed each other's company. I knew it was unusual for a white person to invite an African worker to a social event, but I was pleased that Doris had felt comfortable enough with me to accept my invitation. For Doris and me, the day was all about friendship and sharing the love of the Lord, not about color or status.

After I returned from Banso, I had had the chance to see her again when she came to our apartment to work. I showed her the digital pictures I had taken of her family and promised to send her copies later. While we admired the photos, she invited me to come to her house for a farewell meal together. I was greatly honored that she would welcome me into her home, and I readily accepted her invitation. She gave me the name of the area where she lived and instructed me to take a taxi and to look for her daughter when I arrived.

The next day, I followed her instructions and found her daughter waiting for me on the curb at the entry to a large slum. Her daughter urged me to stay close to her and warned me that it was not safe for a white person to enter their area alone. We walked along crowded pathways surrounded by tiny make-shift homes. There was a narrow stream of sewage along the pathways and only an occasional plank where the stream was wider. At times, I had no choice but to walk right over the foul-smelling stream as we inched our way toward their home. I received a few cold stares from passing neighbors, but no words were exchanged.

We arrived at Doris' home where she, her sons, and her brother welcomed me. We visited for a bit first, and then she presented us with a beautiful meal, including fou fou and jama jama, which I had known in Kenya as Ugali and Sukuma wiki (cornmeal and greens). She had also prepared a very tasty fish dish. We drank bottled water and some kind of a fruity juice. I silently prayed that the foods I ingested would not make me sick. I had no idea what precautions had been taken in the food preparation, and it was probably best that I did not know.

We ended the visit by silently praying together for each other's families, taking a group photo together, hugging one another, and then saying our last goodbyes. Her daughter walked me back out to the curb where I soon caught a taxi back to my neighborhood. Waving goodbye to her daughter, my heart was filled with gratitude for the kindness and hospitality I had been shown by Doris and her family. I would miss them.

Trial by Fire

These (trials) have come so that the proven genuineness of your faith—of greater worth than gold, which perishes even though refined by fire—may result in praise, glory and honor when Jesus Christ is revealed.

—1 Peter 1:7

The final three days in the city were unusually painful as Emma's hostility toward me grew increasingly obvious. Her parents had arrived to visit her while I was gone, so more than ever she resented my being in "her" space. Yet the Lord gave me the grace to remain silent. The night before I left for the States, a fellow teacher took me out to dinner. I was surprised to learn from her that Emma had been undergoing professional counseling all year for "transition stress," a fact which may have accounted for some of her hostility toward me. When I awoke in the middle of the night, I had written in my journal:

> *June 18, 2011*: 2:15 a.m. Lord, I lift Emma to You in the name of Jesus. Help her, Lord, to grow up in You & to adjust to the many changes in her life. Protect her from the enemy & his designs on her weaknesses & help her learn total dependence on You. Give me Your wisdom about every word spoken to her or others involving this situation. May the words of my mouth & the meditations of my heart be acceptable in Your sight, O Lord, my Strength and Redeemer!

With that prayer fresh in my mind, I went back to sleep for a while before arising to pack the last of my items. When I was ready to leave for the airport, I said goodbye to her and her parents, and I recited the Aaronic prayer (Numbers 6:24-26) as I bid her farewell once and for all.

As I headed for the airport, I thanked God for giving me the strength to end on a positive note and the wisdom to avoid saying any words of defense or chastisement. She was His child, and He alone would correct her behavior in His time and way.

I settled in to my seat on the plane to begin the long trek home, content that the Lord had accomplished His purposes in sending me to Cameroon, and that He had showered me with more blessings than I ever could have hoped for.

CHAPTER NINE

BACK TO JAARS
(JUNE 2011-SEPTEMBER 2015)

||||||||||||||||||

I arrived back in Charlotte, North Carolina, in the evening of the following day. Traveling with only my one suitcase had made it considerably easier to board a shuttle for the final one-hour trip back to JAARS. The evening was beautiful, and the first thing I noticed when I arrived at my own little apartment was the amazing silence that surrounded me. I climbed into bed and slept soundly all night.

Spider Bites

Praise the Lord, my soul,
and forget not all his benefits—
who forgives all your sins
and heals all your diseases.

—Psalm 103:2–3

The next morning, I was again impressed by the incredible silence all around me. But before I could give the silence much thought, I became acutely aware of the spider bite on my belly. The bite had become miserably painful and itchy, and when I looked at it, I saw that it was obviously infected. It looked just like the bite I had received in Niger ten years earlier. In both cases, the spider had bitten me multiple times, making a circle of bites that first created the appearance of a target and then became deep red and seriously infected.

I called the JAARS clinic immediately and told the receptionist I had just returned from Africa with an infected spider bite. She told me to come at once; the clinic was only a short walk from my apartment, so I arrived within minutes. When I was seen, I was given antibiotics and was instructed to apply warm compresses several times a day to draw out the infection. The bite healed well, leaving a small matching scar on the opposite side of my belly from the one I had experienced in Niger. Spider bite scars were not exactly the souvenirs I would have chosen, but in both cases the Lord had protected me from becoming seriously ill. Thank you, Lord!

Bloom Where You are Planted

Blessed is the one
who does not walk in step with the wicked
or stand in the way that sinners take
or sit in the company of mockers,
but whose delight is in the law of the Lord,
and who meditates on his law day and night.
That person is like a tree planted by streams of water,
which yields its fruit in season
and whose leaf does not wither—
whatever they do prospers.

—PSALM 1:1A, 2–3

I may have returned to my home in North Carolina, but part of my heart was still planted somewhere in Cameroon. It took time for me to refocus on American life while I was still absorbing the numerous lessons my Father had been graciously teaching me overseas.

After I had settled back in to my apartment, returned to my job, and reconnected with the teens at youth group, I had written in my journal:

June 23, 2011: There's a quietness in me, a quiet thankfulness for the gift of Your taking me back to

Africa—the whole thing seems almost like a dream.
God, You are so gracious. Psalm 37: "Delight in him
& he will give you the desires of your heart." (You did,
Lord! I went back to Africa.) "The Lord helps me &
delivers me because I take refuge in him!" I see how
You sustained me during the pain of Emma's rejection,
& You gave me Diane (my prayer partner) & Elizabeth
to help me hang on. I pray I'll learn every lesson You
had for me in that experience. Sing alleluia to the King!

July 2, 2011: Thank you, Lord! Thank you for every
minute in Cameroon—it was such a rich gift & I loved
it so much. You are the Giver of Good Gifts, the Healer,
Companion, Teacher, Counselor, and Giver of Life.

Two days after I had written that entry, the youth director asked me to leave my position with the business team and join his team at the youth department. So began my transition from the jobs I had filled in obedience to the job that matched my greatest desire, that of actively working with and ministering to teens.

I returned from Cameroon in June, 2011, and served at JAARS until September, 2015, eventually spending most of my time with the teens and the Youth and Family Ministries team. By 2015, my mother was ninety-three years old, and I had recognized that it was time for me to go home to spend my days with her in California. Of course, I also looked forward to finally being near my sons.

I shared my decision with my boss, and with the young woman I was mentoring at that time. When I mentioned that I was researching ways to transport my car from North Carolina to California, she offered to accompany me on a road trip from coast to coast, an idea that definitely sparked my interest. The young woman was in her thirties and perfectly capable of making such a trip. Like me, though she had lived overseas for some years, she had seen little of the United States. Together, we planned our route across the lower states of the nation.

God blessed us with an amazing trip as we both saw parts of our own country that we had never seen before. When we reached California, she spent a day recovering with me at the home of dear friends, and then she flew back to Waxhaw to return to her job. Meanwhile, I began a season of major home repairs to my house and frequent week-long trips to care for my mom.

Welcome Back, Mom!

Being back in my own little house in California, I was thrilled to finally live within driving distance of my sons and mother for the first time in fifteen years. An unexpected bonus was the unplanned arrival of my one and only grandchild, a little boy who has blessed our family with great joy!

I thank God for sending me home in plenty of time to spend three full years ministering and witnessing to my mom. I thank Him, too, for allowing me to see her return to the arms of Jesus Christ on her deathbed. Sing alleluia to the King!

CONCLUSION

Counting the Cost

Anyone who loves their father or mother more than me is not worthy of me; anyone who loves their son or daughter more than me is not worthy of me. Whoever does not take up their cross and follow me is not worthy of me. Whoever finds their life will lose it, and whoever loses their life for my sake will find it.

And everyone who has left houses or brothers or sisters or fields for my sake will receive a hundred times as much and will inherit eternal life.

—Matthew 10:37-39 and 19:29

Niger, Burkina Faso, Kenya, Uganda, Tanzania, Cameroon, and Waxhaw, North Carolina: the Lord had proven His promises to me in a season that was richly filled with His love and constant care. During my years with Wycliffe Bible Translators, I had consistently coped with various medical challenges throughout, including a season of cancer treatment, but He had always faithfully sustained me in ways that only He could do. Looking back, I see how He had reshaped and molded my dream along the way.

I had joined Wycliffe with the sole intention of serving in Africa for ten to fifteen years, but God had had a much greater plan in store for me. He had extended my vision far beyond my own dreams, for not only had He taken me to Africa, but when He brought me home, He had given me students who had lived in nations throughout the world, broadening my worldview and my influence among His children. Truly, His ways are far beyond our own!

241

"My" years of ministry as a Wycliffe missionary did not resemble what I had pictured in my mind, but then it was never <u>my</u> ministry to begin with—it was God's ministry through me.

I turned seventy-five in November, 2021. I am grateful to be in my own home and living near my precious family members. Yet my heart still longs for Africa and the people I have loved through the years. Only in heaven will we have the reunion that brings my two worlds together, and then we are all truly home!

Meanwhile, I am seeking God's next assignment for me here on earth. I am guessing that, once again. it will not be what I would choose but something better. Lord, lead on; Your servant is listening!

AFTERWORD

Unexpected Treasure

And we know that in all things God works for the good of those who love him, who have been called according to his purpose.

—ROMANS 8:28

After my mother adjusted to the idea that I was going to Niger, I presented her with a small email laptop as a gift. Her response was not what I had expected. She flatly refused to let me show her how to use it.

"I've gotten along this far without the internet, and I don't plan on learning how to use it now! You might as well return the machine because I will never open it."

Consequently, I had to come up with another plan to maintain communications with her on a regular basis. Each time I emailed a letter to my family, I asked a relative to print and mail a copy to her. I also periodically mailed her hand-written letters or cards.

This book is partly a result of that practice. Though I kept a daily journal, I did not know that my mother had saved all of our communications in a file in her garage!

When I was visiting my mother in October, 2015, she handed me a large purple folder with all the cards, letters, and emails that we had exchanged during the five years I had served overseas.

What a delightful surprise! Once again, the Lord had proven to me that He truly works all things together for our good. If Mom had not refused to use the internet, I would not have the treasure of such a complete record of those years.

Thanks, Mom! Thanks, Jesus!

Printed in the United States
by Baker & Taylor Publisher Services